Acts of Knowing

Acts of Knowing

Critical Pedagogy In, Against and Beyond the University

EDITED BY

STEPHEN COWDEN AND GURNAM SINGH

WITH

SARAH AMSLER, JOYCE CANAAN AND SARA MOTTA

BLOOMSBURY

NEW DELHI • LONDON • OXFORD • NEW YORK • SYDNEY

Bloomsbury Publishing India Pvt. Ltd
Second Floor, Building No. 4
DDA Complex LSC, Pocket C – 6 & 7
Vasant Kunj, New Delhi 110070
www.bloomsbury.com

BLOOMSBURY, Bloomsbury Academic India and the Diana
logo are trademarks of Bloomsbury Publishing Plc

First published in India 2019
First published 2013

This edition published with permission from Bloomsbury Publishing Plc,
50 Bedford Square, London, WC1B3DP, UK

British Library Cataloguing-in-Publication Data
A catalogue record for this book is available from the British Library.

Library of Congress Cataloging-in-Publication Data
A catalog record for this book is available from the Library of Congress

ISBN: 978-93-88912-16-7

2 4 6 8 10 9 7 5 3 1

Typeset by Newgen Imaging Systems Pvt Ltd, Chennai, India

Printed and bound in India by Replika Press Pvt. Ltd.

On the Critical Attitude

The critical attitude
Strikes many people as unfruitful
That is because they find the state
Impervious to their criticism
But what in this case is an unfruitful attitude
Is merely a feeble attitude. Give criticism arms
And states can be demolished by it.
Canalising a river
Grafting a fruit tree
Educating a person
Transforming a state
These are instances of fruitful criticism
And at the same time instances of art.

BERTOLT BRECHT

We dedicate this book to our children and grandchildren, who like all children represent the hope of the future Jatinder Kaur and Daya Singh, Jude, Keir and Emmet Cowden, Laylah Simone Delkhasteh, Sujey Antoinette and Jaiya Celine Mera-Motta and Katherine Girling-Rogers, Keith Rogers and Lucas Alec Rogers. And to all those teachers and students who are and will go on to fight for an education which is genuinely free

CONTENTS

INTRODUCTION

Critical Pedagogy and the Crisis in the Contemporary University

> It is necessary to clarify what teaching is and what learning is . . . For me teaching is the form or the act of knowing, which the educator exercises; it takes as its witness the student. This act of knowing is given to the student as a testimony, so that the student will not merely act as a learner [rather] teaching is the form that the educator possesses to bear witness to the student on what knowing is, so the student will know instead of simply learn.
>
> PAULO FREIRE, 1990

This book's starting point is a deep and profound concern about the commodification of knowledge within the contemporary university. This is a process which has been going on for some time, but is presently reaching levels which threaten to fundamentally distort the very point and purpose of teaching, learning and 'knowing'. This book aims to provide readers with a means of understanding of these issues from the perspective of Critical Pedagogy; an educational philosophy which believes that 'knowing' must be freed from the constraints of the financial and managerialist logics which dominate the contemporary university. We see Critical Pedagogy as important for three key reasons; first it conceptualizes pedagogy as a process of engagement between the teacher and taught, and secondly that that engagement is based on an underlying humanistic view about human worth and value, and thirdly that the 'knowing' which can come out of this engagement needs to be understood essentially as exchange between people, rather than a financial exchange.

In much of the post-war period universities were criticized for their remoteness from the 'real world'. These struggles culminated in the late 1960s which represented a moment in which students demanded that learning be democratized and that the curriculum be developed to reflect important developments which were taking place in the world; the changing place of women, struggles of workers, the hidden history of the people of former colonies, the visibility of gay and lesbian communities and people excluded from society through disabilities. It was a radical demand for relevance which took as a given the idea that education was a social good, and one which needed to be made as accessible to the many rather than the few. In the contemporary world this language of relevance lives on, but in a radically changed context. The state now demands that the university 'live in the real world' – but what this means now is that universities, like the state itself, become beholden to a financially driven logic in which the demands of 'the market' are paramount. Within this ideological universe, the acquisition of knowledge is presented primarily as commercial transaction, driven only by the benefit to an individual in terms of their position in the labour market. The argument presented in this book is that this commodified logic distorts and impoverishes the fundamental purpose of teaching and learning for students and teachers. In seeking to pose an alternative to this, we argue that it becomes all the more important to re-articulate the demand for a dialogue-based pedagogy, the practice of which itself represents a reclaiming of democratic educational space. In making this argument we take the educational philosophy of Paulo Freire as a vital and radical starting point; radical in that it goes back to this fundamental question of what teaching, learning and 'knowing' really are.

The current economic recession is already having a profound impact across universities in the developed capitalist world, just as it is across the remainder of the public sector. Slavoj Zizek has characterized our present period as one of 'Permanent Economic Emergency', in which 'after decades of the welfare state, when cutbacks were relatively limited with the promise that things would soon return to normal, we are now entering a period in which an economic state of emergency is becoming permanent' (2010:86). In a time like this consent comes to be secured for the continuation and development of neoliberal economic strategies through what Naomi Klein has called the 'shock doctrine' (Klein, 2007). We see therefore, alongside swinging cuts to public services and institutions, an ideological attack on the very purpose of public institutions. This denigration of the achievements and possibilities within public institutions not only facilitates their ongoing handover to corporate capital, but simultaneously undermines those attempts which have been made in recent years to make Higher Education more inclusive and democratic. We are therefore seeing alongside an essentially financially driven agenda by University managers, the return of elitism, and taken together these two elements result in what Charles Thorpe has called 'the complete subordination of intellectual life to instrumental values and, most brutally, to the measure of money' (2008:103). We see this in terms of the ongoing project of neoliberalism, and we use this term to very specifically characterize the nature of the project of social transformation to which elites in the state apparatus and powerful transnational corporations have been and are continuing to impose. In this sense the things which are taking place within Higher Education are not isolated, but are part of a wider imposition and restructuring of the public sector according to the logic of finance. We argue that it is crucial to understand these wider linkages, as well as appreciating that there are at the same time very specific consequences which this doctrine generates in educational institutions. We characterize these as a crisis of thinking, feeling and doing.

Neoliberalism as a crisis of thinking

One of Paulo Freire's most apposite observations was of the inherently and inescapably *political* nature of education:

> Educational practice and its theory can never be neutral. The relationship between practice and theory in an education directed toward emancipation is one thing, but quite another in an education for domestication. (1970:12)

The key insight here lies in the way Freire conceptualizes the relationship between teaching and learning processes in educational institutions and

PAULO FREIRE
Source: http://gseis.ucla.edu/news-events/news-items/10th-anniversary-of-pfi-to-be-celebrated-at-annual-international-forum-sept.-19-22

the wider social and economic structure of society. What this means is that the way in which students and teachers engage in educational settings on a day-to-day basis is a product of a particular *political economy*. In the context of the present moment we see the way the predominance of market-based neoliberal economic models seeks to shape and change the nature of the relationship between student and student and student and teacher by arguing that universities are 'businesses' and students are the 'customers' of those businesses who compete against one another as students and with other graduates in the workplace. This inevitably results in education being constructed purely as an exchangeable commodity and universities in this sense becomes the equivalent of a battery farm growing graduates to fulfil the demands of the market.

The last 15 years has seen large increases in numbers at educational institutions in the developed capitalist economies, with former polytechnics becoming universities. Whereas university places in the past were only available for a small usually privileged elite, the process of 'widening participation' opened Higher Education up to people from more diverse backgrounds, leading to the emergence of what has been called the 'mass university'. This was justified not as something which was socially good in itself, but as part of an overall logic of securing economic advantage in a global 'knowledge economy'. Hence while the traditional elite universities continued to teach small numbers and gain most of their income through research, the new universities emphasized teaching. While we would argue in favour of this expanded sector, the problem here was that the acquisition of knowledge came to be largely seen as analogous to the acquisition of skills: a model of education which resulted in what Henry Giroux has called 'the devaluation of critical intellectual work on the part of teachers and students for the primacy of practical considerations' (1988:123). Instead of the new universities championing the idea that they were producing new intellectuals, their pedagogy was seen as based on technically competent dissemination of information.

With the financial crisis of 2008 and the re-capitalization of the banks as the avenue the state took to resolve this crisis, the mass university is more than ever in crisis. In a moment where state policy is dictated by financial markets the argument is now that large numbers of graduates are no longer required. In the United Kingdom, these tendencies are being demonstrated through the ratcheting up of fees to a level which prohibit large numbers of students from attending university, at the same time as making university funding ever more dependent on league tables of student satisfaction, presented as 'student empowerment'. Defenders of this form of educational consumerism argue that such proposals will drive up standards of teaching and learning. We would argue that it will have the effect of polarizing educational institutions; there will be both a race to the top, as the wealthiest institutions secure their place in an elite market, and a race to the bottom as the less prestigious institutions compete with each other and other new private providers, to try to bring in as many students as they can for the most basic levels of service. These latter institutions, which is where the vast majority of students will be, will find their educational experiences impoverished through increasing standardization of pedagogy, which, combined with cuts to university expenditure, will further undermine critical thinking and creative teaching. The university experience for these students will be understood in individualized and instrumental terms, a view which will be facilitated through students' awareness of the debt they will be accruing for each month they continue to attend.

Where does this leave the idea of education as a social good and a prerequisite of democratic citizenship? We argue there is a huge and dangerous paradox taking place at the moment. We live in a world increasingly beset by crises which require new thinking – an increasing level of ecological catastrophe caused by global climate change, the increasing social problems caused by ever widening class and gender inequalities, the rise of authoritarian religious fundamentalism, and the collapse of dictatorial regimes in various parts of the world. If these crises are to be resolved in ways that are socially just and sustainable, both to societies at large and the earth on which we live, we urgently need new thinking, and universities are unique in their capacity to contribute to this process. Yet university managers are by and large showing themselves to be happily acquiescent with the logic of neoliberal finance, understanding the production of graduates in entirely instrumental terms, just as they rationalize their turn turning to the corporate loan sharks of the money markets as a legitimate alternative to state funding. What we hear less about is the way, in the process handing over control of educational institutions to these people, the financial markets will gain control over institutions which have been built up through decades of public investment. We argue throughout this book that the conception of education as more than a means for securing economic returns for the individual and for the society's positioning in a global marketplace represents a fundamentally impoverished conception of education. As well as literally impoverishing those students and former students who will need to pay back the fees and loans with accrued interest, this change in the focus of universities impoverishes the level of knowledge made available for society as a whole.

Neoliberalism as a crisis of feeling

The global dominance of neoliberalism (Harvey, 2007), and the consequent economic crisis through which we are now living is in similar terms conceptualized as a crisis of the feeling. We focus on feeling because a central issue in pedagogy is not only how we understand, but also how we feel the impact of our increasingly divided and polarized society, both physically and emotionally. The reality is that while the overall level of wealth produced in society has increased, large sections of the community face longer hours of work accompanied by the growth of informal and precarious work. Gregory Albo has noted the way increased inequalities in the labour market have combined with 'sharp cuts in welfare [which] fall especially hard on women and migrants . . . [meaning that] credit is increasingly relied upon for current and future living standards [while] privatization and user fees for public services extend people's dependence on the market in aspects of daily life' (Albo, 2007:359). This is occurring at a time when all of us are encouraged to view our lives as one long process of speculation, from baby bonds, to funding higher education, then a home mortgage through to a pension (Wilby, 2009).

In an increasingly individualized society, in which consumption is encouraged as being at the core of the self, we have lost a sense of the way the damaging and destructive effects of social polarization are played both at the level of damage to the social fabric – the nature of contemporary sociality and connections between individuals, groups and communities – as well as on the way we inhabit our physical and emotional being. The dramatic rise of mental health problems, which studies such as those by Oliver James (2008) have detailed, is directly related to 'selfish' neoliberalized societies, and the individualization of social problems: 'the selfish capitalist toxins that are the most poisonous are the systematic encouragement of ideas that material affluence is the key to fulfilment, that only the affluent are winners, and that access to the top is open to anyone willing to work hard enough . . . [and] if you do not succeed there is only one person to blame' (2008). The aggressively competitive and philistine assumptions which dominate the way social problems are understood by most of the political class and the media are entirely congruent with the economic drive within neoliberalism to articulate all social relations as market relations. It is in this process that other non-market-based forms of connectedness are either sentimentalized or denigrated.

Raymond Williams work on the 'structures of feelings' (1977) is also useful here as a way of exploring what he called the emergent structures of feeling and the relationship of this with the increased neoliberalization of more and more aspects of our lives. This can be usefully linked to the Freirian tradition of critical pedagogy which is distinctive within radical theory for the way it seeks to integrate the emotional impact of oppression, what we might call following Bourdieu 'symbolic violence' (1992:107–8). The overcoming of alienation was for Freire about the way the emotions and the intellect needed to be understood dialectically – in dialogue with each other – rather than separated off from each other, which is how they are presented in dominant discourse. In this sense the alienated marketized conception of human relations prevent people from finding ways to meaningfully connect with other people and to articulate this connectedness – and this issue is crucial for pedagogy.

Neoliberalism as a crisis of doing

Freire, following Fanon, characterized the oppressed as having what he called a 'double consciousness' which is expressed through their being:

> . . . at the same time themselves and the oppressor whose image they have internalized. Accordingly, until they concretely 'discover' themselves and in turn their own consciousness, they nearly always express fatalistic attitudes toward their situation. (Freire, 1970:61)

Freire saw this of 'fatalism' as crucial to the experience of having internalized the dominant logic. This statement expresses the immobility so many people feel faced with the destruction of public institutions, the removal of rights, the privatization of space, all reinforced by an army of neoliberal cheerleaders, gleefully and contemptuously asserting that there is 'no alternative' to the rule of the market over every aspect of social and economic life. Mark Fisher's recent work on Capitalist Realism (2009) has sought to account for the resonance of this notion among the population at large talking about the need to understand what he calls a 'pre-emptive formatting and shaping of desires, aspirations and hopes' to fit 'a "business ontology" in which it is simply obvious that everything in society, including health care and education, should be run as a business' (2009:13–16). Many have commented on the way the present generation of students appear seemingly captured by the logic that underpins this fatalistic web. However it is also important to note the vulnerabilities in this system. Fisher argues for example that capitalist realism can best be de-stabilized by exposing its inconsistency and demonstrating that its 'ostensible realism' and 'apparent naturalness' are themselves imposed fantasies resting on utterly fictitious premises (Fisher, 2009:16–19). We see this fictitiousness residing both in the way neoliberal finance capital appeared to offer a world of unlimited money, which then turns out not to exist, but equally fictitious in the way it obscures to us the high price we are paying – in our bodies our minds and in our relations with each other – for the maintenance of the idea that there is 'no alternative' to dehumanizing relations which increasingly dominate everyday life. We understand the approach of Critical Pedagogy as based on the demystification of this dominant logic, thereby allowing people to question this and in the process to give voice to their real needs; as Freire says, to 'discover themselves'.

It is in this way that Critical Pedagogy links thinking, doing and feeling through the discovery of the power of agency. An analogy for this is the way a very young child discovers how different the world looks when they stand, as opposed to sitting or crawling. Once they acquire the confidence to do this, the world looks different. Recent student protests in Britain, France and Greece, where large numbers have recently taken to the streets, and even more significantly the huge surge of protest across the Middle East, suggests the value of this analogy, and points to the way that, under particular circumstances, fatalism can be radically overturned as people acquire the courage to become involved in mass action. A key theme we would note in all these protests, which are led predominantly by young people, and often young unemployed graduates, is the question of their own futures; in other words, these struggles combine strong idealistic elements alongside directly material questions. These events are a challenge to the crisis of non-doing and fatalism induced by neoliberalism at a global level, and the suddenness and vehemence of their emergence offers crucial insights into the way this internalization of the dominant neoliberal logic can be overturned, an idea which informs a number of chapters in this volume.

The scope and structure of this book

While the book does aim to offer a broad introduction the ideas of Critical Pedagogy, the book is not seeking to offer a detailed overview of the history or different traditions of Critical Pedagogy, such as the recent work of Darder, Baltodano and Torres (2008) and more recently Joe L. Kincheloe (2010). Like these authors we situate our work within a broad tradition of radical literature concerned with developing principles, beliefs, and practices which contribute to an emancipatory ideal of democraticizing schools and Universities, as well as the significance of Critical Pedagogy within Popular Education movements. The contribution of Freire to this tradition is seminal, but in our work we have sought to integrate his work with insights from other traditions, such as the Frankfurt School of critical theory and educational sociologists like Pierre Bourdieu. In this sense our understanding of the tradition of Critical Pedagogy is a broad one.

Part One of this book offers four chapters which discuss these key themes in different ways. Stephen Cowden and Gurnam Singh's first chapter is concerned to capture the economic basis of what they have called the 'new poverty of student life'. Beginning with a discussion of the 1966 Situationist Manifesto 'On the Poverty of Student Life' this chapter moves to a discussion of the way financialization and the power of money is completely changing the face of the life in Universities. Their second chapter on Sat-Nav Education explores the same theme in relation to pedagogical processes in the University, demonstrating another aspect of the way education is being impoverished, but also pointing to the choices which educators and students could make in terms of resisting these. The third chapter by Sarah Amsler looks at the affinity between Critical Pedagogy and Radical Democracy, pointing to the importance of dialogue between these two traditions. The final chapter in Part One is by Sara Motta, who looks at the experience of introducing Critical Pedagogical techniques in her work at Nottingham University. All of these chapters seek to point to the many different ways in which the issue of Pedagogy is inherently political. This discussion is broadened out still further in Part Two of the book, which as well as looking at Critical Pedagogy in classroom settings, also looks at the interface between the universities, schools and the wider community, linking critical pedagogy with action research strategies, activist education and social movements.

Finally this book is written as a collective project motivated by a shared sense of 'critical hope' that in looking at existing strategies in which individuals and groups have sought to transform formal education in the interests of a democratizing imperative, we can begin resisting the process of commodification, and in nurturing critical consciousness, contribute to the process of building an alternative, both within and beyond the institutions of Higher Education. The five of us have met and have produced this and other work out of a desire for communication, recognition and collective action. All of us identified with a practice and a project of critical education, which has become all the more important as we see the increasing closure of democratic space within the university as practices of micro-surveillance, ranking and de-intellectualization become further entrenched. At the same time we have been inspired by the protests and marches that took place in the United Kingdom in opposition to increases in fees and loans, and this book comes out of the process of creating a space through which we have sought to make sense of the nature and experience of neoliberalism, what critical education means and how we might begin to de-colonize spaces within our practices as educators and intellectuals in and outside of the university.

We hope that you the reader find this book useful in your own attempts to make sense of the perplexing times in which we are living, and we conclude with the words of Book Bloc, a creative protest group that came out of the recent student protests:

> Books are our tools – we teach with them, we learn with them, we play with them, we create with them, we make love with them and, sometimes, we must fight with them.

BOOK BLOC 1
Source: http://artsagainstcuts.wordpress.com/2010/12/09/book-bloc-comes-to-london-1/

References

Albo, G. (2007) 'Neo-Liberalism and the Discontented' in Panitch and Leys (eds), *The Socialist Register 2008*. Merlin Press, Monmouth, pp. 354–62.

Bourdieu, P. (1992) 'The Purpose of Reflexive Sociology' in P. Bourdieu and L. Wacquant (eds), *An Invitation to Reflexive Sociology*. Polity Press, Cambridge, pp. 61–215.

Darder, A., Baltodano, M. and Torres R. (2008) *The Critical Pedagogy Reader*. Routledge, London.

Fisher, M. (2009) *Capitalist Realism*. Zero Books, London.

Freire, P. (1970) *Pedagogy of the Oppressed*. Penguin, Harmondsworth.

— (1990) 'Twenty Years Later: Similar Problems, Different Solutions', Interview with Donald Macedo (www.aurora.icaap.org/talks/freire.html) (accessed 23 November 2010.

Giroux, H. (1988) *Teachers As Intellectuals*, Bergin & Harvey, Westport Connecticut and London.

Harvey, D. (2007) *A Brief history of Neoliberalism*. Oxford University Press, London.

James, Oliver (2008) *The Selfish Capitalist: The Origins of Affluenza*. Vermillion, London.

Kincheloe, J. (2010) *Knowledge and Critical Pedagogy: An Introduction*. Springer Press.

Klein, N. (2007) *The Shock Doctrine: The Rise of Disaster Capitalism.* Allen Lane, London.
Thorpe, C. (2008) *Oppenheimer: The Tragic Intellect.* University of Chicago Press, Chicago.
Wilby, P. (2009) 'All of us Live by the Logic of Finance', *New Statesman.* Febrary 5. Available at http://www.newstatesman.com/economy/2009/02/housing-societies-essay. Accessed 6/6/12
Williams, R. (1977) *Marxism and Literature.* Oxford University Press, Oxford.
Zizek, S. (2010) 'A Permanent Economic Emergency', *New Left Review.* July/August 2010, pp. 85–95.

PART ONE

Perspectives on the Crisis in Education

CHAPTER ONE

The New Poverty of Student Life: The Politics of Debt

Stephen Cowden and Gurnam Singh

In this chapter we will:

- Discuss the legacy of the pamphlet *On the Poverty of Student Life* published by the Situationist International in 1966.
- Explain how the current problems within capitalism are a consequence of the vast build up of unpaid debt, looking in particular at Marx's concept of 'fictitious capital'.
- Explain the way the consequence of charging a much higher student fees is part of a whole process through which universities are being 'financialized'; that is, financial power and debt come to structure the whole way in which universities function as institutions, including such fundamental questions as what degree programmes are offered, and who is able to access this.

The modern economic system requires a mass production of uneducated students who have been rendered incapable of thinking.

On the Poverty of Student Life (1966)

Introduction

In 1966, a small radical group known as the Situationist International published a pamphlet entitled *On the Poverty of Student Life*, which caused a minor scandal when it was printed and distributed to new students at the University of Strasbourg. This pamphlet is now regarded as a seminal text of the wave of political protest which occurred in Europe in the late 1960s, and this chapter opens with a discussion of the significance of these writings in the context of the history of radical student literature, but also as a means of considering what this offers in the light of the issues facing students in the current milieu. This leads us on to what we see as the central issue confronting students today and one which will completely change the shape of student life; namely that of debt. We tackle this on two levels. First, we sketch out the role of finance and the significance of debt within this in the context of contemporary capitalism as a whole. We suggest that this is expressed not just as the crisis of financial institutions, initiated by the sub-prime mortgage crisis in the United States in 2007 and which rapidly exported itself across the globe, but in the way finance has become so intensely bound up with the very mechanism of capitalist production. As Christian Marazzi has argued, 'we are in a historical period in which the finances are *co-substantial* with the production of goods and services' (Marazzi, 2010:29). Here we discuss Marx's work on finance as 'fictitious capital' in order to understand the way in which debt and indebtedness are not accidental or aberrant features of contemporary capitalism, as they are sometimes described (e.g. in the phrase 'casino capitalism'). Rather, we suggest they are central to the now financially dominated logic of that system, and not in any sense separate from the production of good and services – indeed, one of the key issues we try to explain here is the way *debts must be understood as both goods and services.*

Having uncovered some of the underlying mechanisms of the symbiotic relationship between dept and capital accumulation, we then focus specifically on the promotion of student indebtedness in the United Kingdom, locating this within the wider logic of 'financialization'. With the exception of some of the private Ivy League institutions in the United States, universities across the globe are now entering the world of private finance for the first time. For this reason it is critical for those concerned with defending the principle of public education as a necessary pillar of democracy to understand the way the construction of mechanisms for student indebtedness works alongside the wider process through which Higher Education is being pushed towards privatization. Henry Giroux exemplifies this when he argues that in the new 'corporatized university' students are 'viewed by university administrators as a major source of revenue for banks and other financial institutions that provide funds for them to meet escalating tuition payments' (2011, para 5). We conclude the chapter with a consideration of how both materially and intellectually these are the new conditions for impoverishment of student life; more importantly, we also consider what mechanisms might be available to resist some of these changes.

The spirit of '68

One of the first developments within the UK government's austerity drive was represented by plans for a massive hike in student fees, and this policy is one which has been and is being pursued by several governments across the globe. The combination of this and the removal of the Education Maintenance Allowance caused a series of major student protests in Britain in 2011 – and this was followed by a series of more determined protests about similar issues in Quebec in Canada. The return of student protests inevitably leads various commentators, as well as some of the protestors themselves, to invoke the spirit of 1968 – the year in which student protests in Paris acted as the trigger for one of the most significant social revolutions of the twentieth century. While at times this invocation can be somewhat clichéd, it also reflects the way this moment has become embedded within the history of student protest.

Although the Paris protests and the strikes which accompanied them have taken on a somewhat legendary aura, the events were not isolated or unique, and were in one sense just one moment within a radical anti-establishment mood characterized by street protests and strikes all over the world – most notably in Italy, former Czechoslovakia, the United States, Mexico, Germany and Algeria. A range of different grievances fuelled this mood. In France large sections of the public, and particularly young people, were disgusted by the brutality of France's colonial war against Algeria; this could be seen to be paralleled with the burgeoning anti-Vietnam movement in the English speaking world, which was driven by the way people were appalled by US government's bombing and invasion of Vietnam. This was also a moment when international events came to mirror struggles against oppression 'at home'; also the period in which the US Civil Rights movement made major advances: Women Liberation and Gay Liberation sprang onto the scene as active movements, and it was a moment of widespread working-class militancy. Kristin Ross gives an example of the way these struggles came to be linked together in the slogan of the striking car workers in Turin, 'Vietnam Is In Our Factories' (Ross, 2002:11). The 1968 Paris protests began with a series of student organized public meetings to express concern about the nature of the curriculum in Nanterre and the Sorbonne Universities. Affronted that students would dare to question their professors, the University administration responded by calling in the police, leading the students to occupy university buildings and take to the streets, building barricades and engaging in street battles with riot police.

These events acted as the triggers for what Kristin Ross has described as 'the largest mass movement in French history, the biggest strike in the history of the French workers movement, and the only "general" insurrection the overdeveloped world has known since World War II. It was the first general strike that extended beyond the traditional centres of industrial production to include workers in the service industries, the communication and culture industries – the whole sphere of social reproduction' (ibid.:4). Many of the workers who went on strike did so in the face of opposition from the 'official' union and party political representatives, while others were involved in completely un-unionized sectors.

The Situationist International and the 'Poverty of Student Life'

While much of the protest in the May events was spontaneous and organized outside of the channels of the official opposition – the Communist Party and trade unions – one group, which exercised hugely disproportionate influence in relation to its size, was an organization known as the Situationist International. Prior to their involvement in the 1968 Parisian protests, members of the group had published a small pamphlet which was distributed to students at the University of Strasbourg. The booklet, whose full title was *On the Poverty of Student Life, considered in its economic, political, psychological, sexual and particularly intellectual aspects with a modest proposal for its remedy* (SI, 1966) has became something of an underground classic, and played a not insignificant role in characterizing and catalysing the basis of student political protest as it took place throughout the late 1960s and 1970s. We want to start our discussion with this and hope that in the process we demonstrate that there is some point in trawling back through what may be seen as a relatively insignificant document written long ago as a means of understanding the present situation of students.

Who were the Situationists?

The Situationists, or Situationist International as they are sometimes known, were a small group of activists, intellectuals and artists who worked together from 1957 to 1972. They were strongly influenced by Marx's writings, though they utterly rejected the dominant forms of this in the form of Communist Parties and the Stalinist regimes in the Soviet Union and Eastern Europe. They were one of the first groupings to understand the significance of the fact that in the post-war period, capitalist societies were becoming 'consumer societies', and their various writings are attempts to understand the impact that this was to have at the level of everyday life. Marx had always argued that the experience of work for the vast majority of people was deeply destructive of people's capacity for personal fulfilment; his theory of 'Alienation' is an expression of this. At the same time, Marx also argued that it would be absolute impoverishment that would drive workers to revolt. In light of this, many of his followers saw socialism primarily as a project for raising working-class people's living standards, a project which was largely successful with the development of welfare states, pensions and improved healthcare in most post-war advanced capitalist societies. The Situationists rejected this exclusive focus on living standards which dominated the official labour and trade union movements, and sought to resuscitate the more radical critique of commodification within Marx's writings, which describes the way everyday life processes and central human needs are made into opportunities for profit. This focus allowed them to speak to the profound dissatisfaction which existed in society at this time in spite of rising affluence. For the Situationists:

> . . . authentic human desires would be always in conflict with alienating capitalist society. Situationist tactics included attempting to create 'situations' where humans would interact together as people, not mediated by commodities. They saw in moments of true community the possibility of a future, joyful and un-alienated society (Libcom, 2009).

While the original Situationist movement was only small, their writings had hugely disproportionate influence for a number of different reasons. First, they were exceptionally prescient in anticipating the political struggles that took place from the late 1960s onwards, and in particular the significance of students within those. Second, they were among the first groups within the Marxist tradition who emphasized the centrality of consumption and of the impact it would have on social relations. In this respect they have been proven absolutely correct as consumption is far more important now than when they first wrote about it; indeed, this concern with the centrality of consumption is now part of almost all mainstream social commentary. A third reason for the extent of their influence concerns the inspirational quality of their work on cultural activity; art, painting and music. This influence was not just among avant-garde art and literature, but also in popular cultural movements like punk rock. The line from the Sex Pistols song 'Anarchy in the UK: *your future dream is a shopping scheme'* is a good example of this.

See the end of this chapter for Further Reading about the Situationists.

In our affluent society, the student is a pauper.

On the Poverty of Student Life (1966)

DON'T CUT OUR FUTURE
Source: http://www.socialistparty.org.uk/articles/11995

On the Poverty of Student Life is centrally concerned with understanding the position of students within contemporary capitalist society, and the pamphlet opens with a stinging critique of the mystification, which they see at the core of what it means to be 'a student'. While students appear to be being offered exclusive access to the portals of Learning and Culture, they argue that in reality, not only are they impoverished – 'in our affluent society the student is a pauper' (1966:4) – but that despite the grandiose visions which society has of the University, the reality is that 'the needs of modern capitalism will oblige most students to become mere *low-level functionaries*, performing jobs comparable to those of most skilled workers in the nineteenth century' (1966:5). For this reason, it is not in the interests of society for students to be genuinely educated, only to be given the illusion that this is taking place. This means there is a gap between students and their families' expectations of and understandings of 'the university', and the often mundane reality of lectures and study, which rather than freeing students to think for themselves are a prelude to and preparation for a life of mundane work:

> . . . the student is a stoical slave . . . He [*sic*] sees himself . . . as the most "independent" of social beings. In fact he is *directly subjected* to the two most powerful systems of social authority: the family and the State. He is their well-behaved and grateful child and, like all *submissive children*, he shares and internalises all the values and mystifications of the system. Illusions that formerly had to be inculcated in white collar workers are now absorbed and passed along by the mass of future minor functionaries. (1966:5)

On the Poverty of Student Life is thus a provocation to students to face up to the reality of what it really means to be a student, rather than 'clinging to the crumbling prestige of the University' and considering themselves 'lucky to be there' (1966:6). But the authors also argue that this illusion serves an important function; by considering themselves special by virtue of having been 'educated', a veil is cast over the reality of the work that most graduates will end up doing. The Situationists saw this role as that of the technicians whose job was to keep the system functioning, and in particular to deflect the dissatisfaction of the population at large and prevent it from becoming a threat to the established order. The title of the first section of the pamphlet is 'To make shame more shameful still by making it public'. This implies that by stripping away the illusions that obscure the reality of university life, students could cease colluding in the grandiose con of university life; instead of shamefully hiding the 'poverty of student life', they should express and articulate their real feelings about this in collective and public situations. In this way, the Situationists exhorted students to stop deluding themselves with a false sense of their own status and instead to grasp the reality of their role within the wider social structure and the nature of their role in reproducing social conformity.

While the Situationists' radical analysis struck a chord in their own period, it is worth asking whether this offers us anything in terms of looking at the situation of today's students. Is going back this period simply an exercise in radical nostalgia? We would argue first that it is hugely important that we learn from history as a means of understanding the present. Secondly, we would make a specific case for *On the Poverty of Student Life* as, like most of the Situationist writings, a remarkably prescient piece of work – in some senses depressingly so, as the things they railed against have become the dominant reality. The appeal of University still rests largely on its 'crumbling prestige', though for institutions which are unable to offer students classes in heritage buildings, the new holy grail is that of 'graduate employability'. The Situationists' discussion of life after graduation is also remarkably accurate, except that the process where graduates compete for jobs as minor functionaries is something which many universities now celebrate rather than try to hide. In a discussion of the legacy of 1968 in relation to the present, Peter Wilby characterizes the work of 'market researchers, media planners, journalists, PRs and personnel officers' (Wilby, 2008) as new graduate castes who play a crucial role in the shaping and manipulating of 'public opinion', much as the Situationists characterized it. One could easily add to this those many companies that organize outsourcing and privatization, which involves actively stripping away the terms and conditions and wages of ordinary workers, as other major employers of graduates. Political office, with its vast entourage of courtiers and advisors, now almost identical among all the major political parties, is almost entirely dominated by the graduates of elite institutions, just as are the many employees of think tanks and private consultancies. The academic Paul Gilroy offers an interesting dimension to this in relation to a discussion of the riots that took place in the United Kingdom in 2011. Gilroy argues that one of the key problems facing young black people today is that many of what used to be community leadership roles have been absorbed into the 'consultariat':

> When you look at the layer of political leaders from our communities, the generation who came of age during that time thirty years ago, many of those people have accepted the logic of privatization. They've privatized that movement, and they've sold their services as consultants and managers and diversity trainers. They've sold their services to the police, they've sold them to the army, they've sold them to the corporate world . . . go to some of their websites and you'll see how proud they are of their clients. And that means that, in many areas, the loss of experience, the loss of the imagination is a massive phenomenon. (Gilroy, 2011)

ALL POWER TO THE IMAGINATION
Source: http://www.flickr.com/photos/rippercut/5149301226/

Gilroy has been one of the few UK academics willing to discuss the relationship between the ways we are all exhorted to 'sell' and 'promote' ourselves by any means necessary on one hand, with the privatization and enclosure of the political imagination on the other. Indeed it is exactly this question of the political imagination, of questioning the limits of the possible, which emerges so powerfully when one reconsiders the legacy of May '68; indeed, one of the most famous slogans from this period was 'all power to the imagination'.

In her work on the legacy of May '68, Kristin Ross has noted that the way these events have been recuperated within the dominant historical and media discourse has been to present them simply as the 'benign transformation of customs and lifestyles that necessarily accompanied France's modernisation from an authoritarian bourgeois state to a new, liberal, modern, financier bourgeoisie' (2002:6). In other words, May '68 threw out old-fashioned statist capitalism and gave us the flexible modern consumer capitalism, which is, we are so repeatedly told, the truest expression of what we all truly desire. What is stripped out of this story is the fact that May '68 represented an assault on capitalism, not just through the demand for an alternative to capitalism, but through the practical experience of people co-operating and learning how to run things themselves at a time when so many people were on strike; the veneer of normal life had cracked, allowing alternatives to surface within everyday life itself.

The erasure of the sense in which May '68 represented an alternative to capitalism is yet another example of what Mark Fisher has characterized as 'Capitalist Realism'. In using this term, Fisher is trying to capture the dominant ethos of our times – the notion that 'realistically' there is no point in worrying ourselves about alternatives to capitalism. The hold that this has in the current period is shown in the way that for the majority of people it is 'easier to imagine the end of the world than the end of capitalism'. Fisher suggests that 'for most people under twenty in Europe and North America, the lack of alternatives to capitalism is not even an issue. Capitalism seamlessly occupies the horizons of the thinkable' (2009:8). On re-reading *the Poverty of Student Life* we were struck by the strength of the connection between belief and action. The attitude of 'Capitalist Realism' regards the ethical commitment on which this position is based as somewhat embarrassing, and responds instead with a chic cynicism:

> Capitalism is what is left when beliefs have collapsed at the level of ritual or symbolic enunciation, and all that is left is the consumer-spectator, trudging through the ruins. Yet this turn from belief to aesthetics, from engagement to spectatorship, is held to be one of the virtues of capitalist realism . . . The attitude of ironic distance proper to postmodern capitalism is supposed to immunise us against the seductions of fanaticism. Lowering our expectations, we are told, is a small price to pay for being protected from terror and fanaticism. (Fisher, 2009:4–5)

What Fisher characterizes throughout this book is the massive price we have had to pay and are continuing to pay for our complacent acceptance of these ideas, central of which is the way Capitalist Realism has 'over the past thirty years . . . successfully installed a "business ontology" in which it is *simply obvious* that everything in society, from healthcare to education, should be run as a business' (2009:17). It is the naturalization of this profoundly ideological position, masquerading as commonsense, which allows the privatization of previously publicly owned and accessible social assets and rights – hospitals, universities, care of older people, etc.

Alongside this goes the enclosure of our political imagination, and nothing demonstrates this more than the way in which in most advanced capitalist societies, all political parties proclaim the impossibility of any alternative to capitalism. Indeed among political parties, opinion formers, think-tanks and media outlets, anyone who challenges the assumptions of capitalist realism is isolated, ridiculed or abused as one either sentimentally living in the past; if not ridiculous then dangerous, a 'terrorist'. These developments have profound implications for the way students are now taught in universities, as a fear of genuine consideration of ideas and thought has taken root in the university itself of a piece with the way those institutions

LONDON RIOTS 2011

"Delinquents are created by every aspect of the current social order; the urbanism of high-rise apartment complexes, the breakdown of values, the spread of increasingly boring consumer leisure, the police control that encroaches on every aspect of daily life, and the economic survival of the family as an economic unit that has lost any meaning. They despise work, but they accept commodities. Whatever they see advertised, they want, and they want it now, but they don't have the means to pay for it . . . To escape this contradiction the delinquent must either resign himself to going to work in order to buy commodities . . . or else he is forced to attack the laws of the commodity, either in a rudimentary way, by stealing it, or in a conscious manner by acquiring a revolutionary critique of the world of the commodity."

On the Poverty of Student Life (1966)

have become subordinate to the power of money, an issue we explore this in the next chapter of the book. We now turn the question of the way money and debt operate within contemporary capitalism, an issue which is crucial if we are to understand how high the price we are all paying for accepting the idea that capitalism is the 'only viable economic system'.

Dysfunctional Debt

The events that were initially called the 'Credit Crunch' began in June 2007, when the hedge fund Bear Stearns, a major investor in sub-prime mortgages in the United States, sought to sell $3.8 billion worth of debt. Within minutes the share price of this once highly rated investment firm dropped from $30 to $2. This was a key moment in which the monumental nature of the chasm between the assets which the banks and finance houses believed they possessed, and the actuality of those assets was materialized. The bubble burst and within a year the contagion represented by this vast build-up of unpaid debt had a domino-like effect on the US banking system, with Washington Mutual, Wachovia, Fannie Mae, Freddie Mac, AIG, Lehman Brothers and Bank of America all revealed to be bankrupt. The international dimensions were demonstrated in the bankruptcy of UK's Northern Rock and Royal Bank of Scotland as well as the Union Bank of Switzerland. It was as though the world financial system had suffered a heart attack, which resulted in the flow of capital literally freezing up. As David Harvey pointed out:

> A world that was awash with surplus liquidity suddenly found itself short on cash and awash with surplus houses, surplus offices and shopping malls, surplus productive capacity and even more surplus labour than before. (2011:5)

What Harvey is alluding to here is the way the crisis was not just about the freezing up of credit, but about the knock-on effects of this, which themselves are an expression of a deeper underlying malaise within capitalism itself; the human dimensions of which were massive job losses accompanied by thousands losing their homes. But the question remains, how can what appears to be such a powerful economic system move from such strength to such weakness in such a short time? Indeed, what are the underlying features of capitalism that makes it vulnerable to what Marx described as 'perennial crisis'? To answer these questions, one needs to go back to Marx's theory of surplus value, which suggests that as a dynamic system, in order to survive the capitalist system needs to grow. It does this by extracting surplus value or profit from the exploitation of human labour (physical and

LEHMAN BROTHERS WHO WILL BE NEXT
Source: http://www.plaincook.com/category/misc/

intellectual) and natural resources (energy and raw materials). However, increased wages and shortage of natural resources reduce surplus value, which in turn reduce the purchasing power of the worker. One way out of this problem is for owners of capital to increase profits through innovation and improving efficiency of the modes of production by, for example, implementing new management techniques, organizational change, automation and exploitation of information technology. However, ultimately this has the effect of reducing the number of jobs available and therefore still reduces consumption levels.

The other option is to inject credit into the system. Here credit fulfils two key functions: it enables producers and consumers to overcome moments where there is a temporary shortage of capital (e.g. purchase of raw materials in the case of producers, or the end of the pay period for consumers). Borrowing for such short-term contingencies is obtained from the banks which in turn borrow from the credit markets at a lower rate than they lend out to consumers and businesses – and it is the difference between these borrowing rates and the lending rate that provides a major source of profit for banks. However, what is distinctive about Marx's understanding of the phenomena of credit is his grasp of the way this allows the market to expand 'beyond its natural limits'; that is beyond the purchasing power of the economy as a whole. In this sense we can understand the events of 2008 as a consequence of this; where debt-based finance produced far more than was able to be consumed, resulting in the drying up of the money supply. Stopgap measures were put in place to inject more credit into the system, but this simply led to a vicious cycle of an increased oversupply of goods that nobody could purchase. A good example of this is the implosion of the 'property bubble' in Spain following a massive building programme fuelled through long-term loans of between 40 and 50 years. A point was reached at which many of these property developers suddenly found themselves unable to rent or sell what had been built, and went out of business. However, as all this production had taken place on the basis of huge amounts of credit, the knock-on effect was massive losses for the banks that had provided the credit. The vast growth of credit in the form of issuing of credit cards and sub-prime mortgages has resulted in a debt-fuelled capitalist orgy that was like a runaway train which eventually crashed when people and companies started to default on their loans and producers could no longer sell their goods at a profit.

In the face of this meltdown of the economy, rather than question the perverse logic of the system described above, most Western governments looked for a solution in the bailing out the investment banks that were complicit in this orgy of 'smash and grab', of which in the United Kingdom alone was undertaken at a cost of around £950 billion in 2008. Simply put, this strategy resulted in the partial or full nationalization of the banks and in a process converting mountains of bad private debt into 'sovereign debt' – meaning that the state, and therefore the taxpayer, took over responsibility for these. The state's vast injection of cash allowed the banks to continue in business, but rather than representing a solution, the massive increase of state borrowing necessitated has itself triggered a new crisis caused by these huge new debt burdens on government. Greece is only the most acute manifestation of this, but it is far from being an isolated case. In Britain, Spain, the United States, Ireland, Portugal and Italy public debt is now above 60 per cent of annual output (or Gross Domestic Product) and rising. As David McNally has noted, this new phase of the crisis is one brought about by investors' 'realisation that governments have borrowed so much, and lost so much potential tax revenue due to job loss, that the public debt in these countries is due to soar to as much as five times the GDP within a generation' (McNally, 2011:3).

Tragically, for ordinary citizens the solution to *this* problem is the unleashing of a wave of austerity across the developed capitalist world. As borrowing is so great, it is now the public who must suffer, in the slashing of state spending where social benefits are cut and publicly owned resources are sold off and privatized. But while the ruling classes act, in time-honoured tradition, by trying to force the working class and the poor to pay the cost of this crisis, this does not solve the underlying problem. In spite of vast amounts of new money poured into the banks coffers from the US Treasury, the UK government and most recently from the European Union's Central

Bank, the underlying systemic crisis simply reappears somewhere else. As the bailing out of even more banks continues, politicians reassure the public that this latest initiative will put everything back on track, restoring profitability and employment. But one has only to turn to the pages of the financial press to see not just how serious a crisis this is, but even that capitalism's best economists really have no idea where it is going to end. As the Economist noted in 2009:

> The scenario at the forefront here is a massive and continuous increase in unemployment on a world scale, and a generalised reduction in incomes and rent. The financial crisis has had devastating effects on manufacturing industry and world commerce with millions of dismissals, closedowns of factories, biblical returns of immigrants to their countries of origin. (Marazzi, 2010:24)

So far, we have outlined some of the characteristics of the contemporary crisis of neoliberal capitalism and in doing so we have drawn attention to contradictions in a system that in its quest for higher profits and new markets will, as Marx and Engels in the Communist Manifesto argued, inevitably sow the seeds of its own destruction. It is the sense of a crisis at the fundamentally economic level that has returned many to a reconsideration of the work of Marx, not least because of all social theorists, it is his work that focuses most fully on the way on the underlying functioning and dynamics of capitalism itself. In his book *Why Marx was Right*, Terry Eagleton suggests that it is precisely because capitalism, despite its apparent capacity to generate massive wealth, it is at once responsible for 'spectacular inequalities of wealth and power, imperial warfare, intensified exploitation, an increasingly repressive state' (2008:8–9) that Marxism is relevant. Specifically, to understand the precise nature of the current crisis, we now turn to the Marxian concept of 'fictitious capital'.

What are use value and exchange value?

In his famous work on modern capitalism, *Capital*, Marx begins the first chapter with a discussion of the Commodity. A commodity is defined as 'the elementary form of wealth under capitalism' (*Capital*, Volume 1); so this could be an apple, a television, a computer microchip, a dress etc. While commodities appear to us simply as inert objects, Marx argues that we can only really understand the significance of a commodity by understanding the *social relationships* which it embodies. In this respect, Marx characterized the commodity as having a dual existence, in which two contradictory elements co-existed. The first element is what Marx called *use value*; by which he meant the usefulness of a commodity to us; so, for example, the 'use value' of an apple is that we can eat it, a computer microchip is that it powers a computer and a dress that we can wear it. The other element within the commodity was its 'exchange value'; this was concerned not with the actual usefulness of something, but focussed solely on the capacity of that commodity to be exchanged for something else, which is of course the medium of money. According to Marx, use value and exchange value are not just different, they are *contradictory*; hence he spoke of the commodity as a 'unity of opposites'. What he means by this is that though the two determinations appear as one thing within a commodity, they are derived from different imperatives; use value derives from things people need, while exchange value is concerned solely with the realization of profit through exchange. This is significant because under capitalism production never takes place *purely and simply* to fulfil human needs. If use value was the only basis on which production was carried out there would never be any need for any person in the world we live in to go without food or shelter or medicines. Instead we live in a world where millions of people lack access to these basic things – they most definitely need them (there's the use value) but the provision of these would not make anyone a profit (so there isn't exchange value). It's in this sense that we can see that use value and exchange value are contradictory. A dramatic example of this was the Great Famine in Ireland, which occurred between 1840 and 1852 when a succession of potato crops failed as a result of potato blight, destroying the livelihoods and the staple food of the Irish peasantry. We usually think of famines as about an absolute lack of food, and during this period 1,000,000 people died and another 1,000,000 were forced to emigrate; but astonishingly throughout the Famine, Ireland continue to export potatoes to Britain! This is a dramatic example of the way exchange value rules over use value. It was the fact that potatoes were commodities with this dual aspect, rather than a lack of food in an absolute sense, that allowed this vast destruction of human life to take place. You may think that this would not happen now, but consider this evidence. In 2007 the global grain harvest was 2.1 billion tonnes. In spite of this fact that in that year around one billion people – mostly in sub-Saharan Africa – teetered on the brink of starvation, while only half of that food was used for human consumption – the rest went on producing biofuels or for animal feed (McNally, 2011:73).

There are two key implications which Marx makes about the fact that a commodity embodies both use value and exchange value. First Marx sees these as reflecting the different needs of workers, as opposed to capital. The perspective of working people is by and large concerned with use value; that is, with the use of commodities to satisfy needs.

The logic of capital is concerned with exchange value, with the realization of surplus value through production, exchange and profit. The one major exception to this is labour, in which these determinations are reversed. Most work has very little use value to the workers who carry it out; that is, it is primarily carried out to obtain money, which allows access to a modicum of social wealth through the wages we earn. On the other hand, the work we do for our employers has use value for them in that workers carry out useful tasks necessary for the realization of exchange value and profit. This is the essence of what Marx sees as the class struggle in that the needs of the working class and capital are fundamentally opposed to each other.

The second implication demonstrates Marx's originality as a thinker in the way he so profoundly points to the irrationality of a system where exchange value rules over use value. In the terms of our previous example, why should so many people in sub-Saharan Africa suffer desperate poverty and starvation, so that people in wealthier western countries can eat enjoy eating meat? Yet Marx insists this is not caused by the greed of people in the West, or even those capitalists who provide these things, but the systemic logic of capitalism itself. Indeed it is the very way in which exchange value rules over use value which has caused the present crisis in banking. The Marxist Philosopher Slavoj Zizek has recently argued that the current crisis of the financialized form of capitalism that we are currently living under concerns the way exchange value becomes autonomous of use value:

> It is transformed into a spectre of self-propelling capital which uses the productive capacities and needs of actual people only as its temporary disposable embodiment. Marx derived his notion of economic crisis from this very gap: a crisis occurs when reality catches up with the illusory self-generating mirage of money begetting more money – this speculative madness cannot go on indefinitely, it has to explode in even more serious crises. The ultimate root of the crisis for Marx is the gap between use and exchange value: the logic of exchange value follows its own path, its own mad dance, irrespective of the real needs of real people. (*Guardian*, 4 July 2012)

What is Fictitious Capital?

We tend to think of the economy as based on what we might call a 'real economy', where actual goods and services are produced, and a financial economy, which developed so as to finance the 'real economy'. Marx was one of the first theorists to understand the way in which the financial economy, once it came to exist as a powerful force within the economy, had the capacity to grow, as it were, autonomously of the production of actual value. Indeed, he argued that periodic financial crises were caused by the tendency of debts to grow exponentially, without corresponding growth in productive powers. Marx called this 'fictitious capital' because these financial gains created must at some point confront the impossibility of the debt claims on which they were based ever being paid off. Marx therefore defined the problem of 'fictitious capital' being that a point must inevitably arrive at which bankers and investors recognize that society's productive capacities can longer support further growth in interest-bearing debt. At this point investors call in their loans and foreclose on the property of debtors, forcing the sale of property under crisis conditions as the financial system collapses in a convulsion of bankruptcy (Marx's *Capital*, Volume 3, chapter 29).

We can understand our present crisis as extension of this essential problematic, except that the level of financialization is so much greater than it was in Marx's day. Many commentators (Harvey, 2007; Marazzi, 2010; McNally, 2011) have noted that the problem of capitalist economies during the 1970s was essentially a problem in declining profit rates. The rise of the Thatcher–Reagan consensus, what we now call neoliberal economics, was based on attacks on trade unions, relocation of industry in areas with low wages, reductions in social welfare and the privatization of state-owned industry. These measures, which have been vastly destructive of communities where the basis of employment of that region has simply disappeared, were undertaken as an attempt to re-establish the profitability of capitalism. Accompanying this is the increasing power of finance over manufacturing within the structure of the economy.

The conventional strategy to deal with the perennial crisis of capitalism from a Keynesian logic would have been to institute a process of guarantees for wages at particular levels alongside public spending or investment to stimulate growth. However, as described above, in a neoliberal scenario this was replaced by a strategy of enabling people to maintain living standards through the perpetual accumulation of debt. Indeed, the logic of neoliberalism was partly based on the ongoing accumulation of debt as a basis for extracting profits. But if profit is what keeps capitalism going, and if profit can only be realized if something is sold, then how does this work in a situation where there is so much debt in the system? Quite simply, *debt itself has been turned into a commodity that can be bought and sold*. In this sense, the crisis of capital was not the responsibility of the workers, students, migrants and welfare recipients and budget deficits, but the money speculators that were operating a system that was built on this contradiction. While this basic mechanism at the heart of the perennial crisis of capitalism is as pointed out by Marx in *Capital*, each historical epoch does have its own specific conditions and conflicts. David Harvey points out that during late medieval times the accumulation of capital was carried out by pirates, priests and merchants who were able to use 'violence, preditation, thievery, fraud and robbery and other "extra-legal" means' (2010:47). He goes on to suggest that perhaps on a much greater scale, both legal and illegal strategies continue to be used today:

> Both legal as well as illegal means – such as violence, criminality, fraud and predatory practices of the sort that have been uncovered in recent times in the subprime mortgage market, or even more significantly in the drug trade – are deployed. The legal means include privatisation of what were once considered common property resources (like water and education), the use of the power of eminent domain to seize assets, widespread practices of takeovers, mergers and the like that result in 'asset stripping', and reneging on, say, pension and health care obligations through bankruptcy proceedings. (Harvey, 2011:49)

The new politics of student debt

If David Harvey is correct, under the logic of neoliberal capitalism, then in some ways it is rather surprising that it has taken so much time for the speculators and asset strippers to get their hands on education systems and universities in particular. But of course, once students become ensnared within the debt culture, these new circumstances will have significant effects at all levels of the education system. We now look at these in the context of the proposed changes in the funding of universities in the United Kingdom and the implications this will have.

At the personal level, just as contemporary capitalism cannot live with and cannot live without debt, we see this very same paradox to be analogous in the way students are exhorted both to aspire to HE, which will force them to incur huge levels of personal debt, at the same time as we are being told by the government to 'learn to live within our means'. As well as forcing out poorer students, the burdening of students with increasing amounts of debt will therefore act as a disciplinary mechanism whereby the debt burden is so great that education is entirely dominated by the need to earn money to pay off those debts. Students' thoughts and behaviour are therefore more likely to be governed by their need to get some kind of 'pay back' and we discuss the implications this will have for the impoverishment of teaching and learning in Chapter Two of this book.

At the institutional level we are likely to see greater turbulence as universities seek to rebrand and reconfigure themselves for the new market realities. Andrew McGettigan's work points to the way the dynamic towards financialization creates a situation where universities themselves begin behaving like financial institutions. This is manifested through leveraging (i.e. borrowing against the value of) their formerly publicly owned assets (McGettigan, 2011a) and financing themselves through the issue of bonds (McGettigan, 2011b, c). Recent developments in this direction have been Cambridge University's setting up of its own bank in 2011 (BBC, June 2011) and Leicester De Montfort University becoming the first post-1992 University to issue bonds, in this case obtaining £110 million from the money markets (THES, 20 July 2012). Developments such as this point to the way that in the context of the removal of direct government subsidies for most courses within the Higher Education sector, the dynamic toward financialization will be accelerated. In many instances it will be this that pushes universities towards full privatization – particularly in instances where, as McGettigan explains regarding Middlesex University, an institution has become so overleveraged it is unable to meet the cost of servicing the loans its managers and directors have taken out (McGettigan, 2011a). According to the THES, Leicester De Montfort will be paying an interest rate of 5 per cent for this money, and for universities which follow this example we will start to see the impact of financialization on public institutions as they become increasingly beholden to the banks and the money markets. It is a mistake to think that this is simply a new model of funding which will allow universities to function as they always have – the impact of this goes right through the entire organization. The most obvious manifestation is the ratcheting up students fees – a crucial income stream when it comes to meeting interest repayments, but this need will also require universities to take additional action to reduce 'costs', in particular redundancy programmes to reduce teaching staff numbers, replacing new staff on lower paying contracts, increasing use of sessional staff with little or no job security. It will also affect the wider functioning of the university through privatization and outsourcing of a range of university functions: admissions, criminal records checking, overseas students, etc. The latter processes not only fragment the functioning of the organization, hugely reducing its overall effectiveness, but at every stage they reduce and undermine the basis of accountability. For these outsourced organizations, their loyalty is purely to their contract and to the profits that flow to their directors and shareholders from that – the question of the overall functioning of the university is not their problem. And indeed, as in the case of Middlesex University where all of the above had still failed to generate enough cash to maintain their interest payments to the banks, the solution to this, according to proposals within the 2011 White Paper, is to allow these institutions to transfer their assets from the public sector into fully private institutions (McGettigan, 2011a:7). The disappearance of public accountability and any sense of a wider public responsibility is without doubt where this process of financialization is taking us.

Even for those institutions that are not entirely privatized, the insidious impact of financialization will be the increasing role of private finance institutions not just on the financing of universities, but on the day-to-day running of the universities. Decisions made by universities on key questions of infrastructure, student fee levels, staff contracts, admissions issues (especially on the issue of home versus the higher-paying overseas students) and even on what courses are offered by universities. We are likely to see both new Higher Education providers and financiers of existing institutions farming data in order to determine what might be the 'best bet', not for society, but for their own extremely short-term gains. The integration of the data streams around University Admissions with those around Student Loan details will allow the profiling of students based on potential future income and debt repayment. In this new arrangement, the rationale for offering a course therefore becomes not the value that course has to the people who want to do it or what it offers to society, but how likely and how quickly that particular student will be able to pay off their debt. The Higher Education Funding Council for England (HEFCE), which will become the industry regulator, will thereby have the capacity to deny access to the funds of the Student Loan Company to any given course or programme if the write down from the loans on that course is too great. This means that it will be financial organizations and the logic of finance which become the central rationale by which education is offered in England.

This will lead not only to an increased divide between rich and poor institutions, but also to a substantially diminished and increasingly segmented higher education system. Historically, as public institutions universities have played a crucial role in creating social mobility and reducing social inequalities. However, this mission will be utterly compromised under a system that is based on the financial profiling of students. It is clear from our argument that this will further hugely cement class divisions within Higher Education; however, the gender impact is not so immediately apparent. The government statistical agency the Higher Education Policy Institute (HEPI) has produced figures that demonstrate the dramatic impact these changes will have on women. The write down on existing debt is highly differentiated on gender grounds; for male students it is currently 5 per cent but for female students 55 per cent (HEPI, 2012). This reflects the way women earn substantially less than men, and often the fact that their earnings are lower after graduation as they work part time due to childcare and family commitments. One can speculate that this will lead to a substantial diminution of the opportunities for female students generally (particularly working-class women), but more specifically it means the courses on which such female students are concentrated become 'liabilities', and may well be reduced or terminated. The new financialized world of education will thus be one which radically turns back the clock on women's access to education. On the basis of the broader evidence of the lower earning capacities of other socially marginalized groups, such as ethnic minorities and people with disabilities, one can reasonably predict similar outcomes of a steady process of exclusion. This illustrates the way this process of financialization will permanently alter the structure of universities as public institutions.

Another key implication is the way this process will herald unprecedented levels of instability for students, both prospective and present, staff and academic disciplines, as the entire focus of university management becomes one of 'economic viability'. One example that demonstrates this is thinking about how important a particular institution is locally or regionally. If it was the case that the level of fee write-down was so high, for example in an area of high unemployment, the decision could be made to close down or relocate an institution, aiding and abetting the existing cycle of disinvestment in poorer regions. McGettigan notes that 'the recent riots in London, overwhelmingly in areas such as Tottenham that have little or no higher education provision' (2011a:8) demonstrate the profound social destructiveness of these new financialized divisions between the haves and the have-nots.

This privatization of material assets that were once publicly owned is accompanied by a privatized sense of the political imaginary, and within this ideology, the value and importance of education as a public good becomes dramatically compromised. As education can only be conceived of as a private benefit, it makes sense to understand the process of going into debt as like a kind of personalized Private Finance Initiative (PFI). Just as in that system, the illusion of gains in the present is mortgaged to a system of repayments the demands of which become so significant that they potentially overtake the original purpose for which the loan was undertaken. In the words of the current UK National Student Union president Liam Byrne 'the bare truth is that students are now in hoc to a loan shark who is himself in hoc to a gangster' (in McGettigan, 2012:4) – it is this bitter truth which characterizes the new poverty of student life.

Conclusion

While the marketization of higher education is likely to strengthen the global standing of a small number of elite universities, for the vast majority of ordinary people the social implications will be disastrous. No doubt the privatization of universities will provide rewards for some relatively well-off individuals and institutions, but tragically it is likely to severely set back the cause for social justice, equality and democracy for society as a whole. It is not that the university per se is in danger, but rather the question of the place and role that universities will have in social, cultural and economic life. What is planned in order to accommodate the financialization of public institutions is a return to a much more overtly segmented system of HE, whereby, with a few exceptions, working and lower middle-class students will be increasingly locked out of the more prestigious institutions, which move towards much greater independence and self reliance. Just as the sub-prime mortgage fiasco was a disaster when it came to addressing the housing needs of the vast majority of who took up these 'new opportunities' to participate in property-owning democracy in the long term, so will the new financialization of universities lead to similar outcomes for the many. The dramatic haemorrhaging of public funding on the one hand, and the rapid privatization on the other have created a perfect storm that is likely to compromise what Edward Said suggests is the 'one public space available to real alternative intellectual practices; no other institution like it on such a scale exists anywhere else in the world today' (2004:72).

It is in such a situation that the egalitarian and moral imperatives for higher learning become increasingly compromised by narrow personal financial priorities. The egalitarian ideal that one goes to university to become a better citizen and critical thinker in order to contribute to building a fairer and more just society is rapidly diminishing. In this new system 'exchange-value' comes to rule every aspect of the student experience. Far from extolling the virtues of learning as an end for itself, today's neoliberalized universities stress the exchange value over the use value, captured in the mantra 'get a degree and get a well-paid job'. But in reality, as the current crisis of the banking sector has revealed, given that the system's success is largely based on 'fictitious' capital, students taking out huge loans to fund their privatized education are likely get trapped into a vicious cycle of debt where to avoid paying back increasingly expensive loans they choose to remain on low-paid work. Moreover, the exchange-value of a qualification will be increasingly set, not by the content of learning or attainment per say, but on a financial calculation of the future earning potential of a given graduate.

While the present economic order faces a massive crisis, one needs to note Lenin's often-quoted warning that there is no such thing as a 'final crisis for capitalism'. The ruling elites have historically found ways out of such crises, but always at the expense of others. While our primary focus in this chapter has been to highlight the contradictions that are unfolding within Higher Education, we also see this as reflective of a broader crisis of neoliberal capitalism itself, so dramatically highlighted in the collapse of the investment banking sector in 2008, and the ongoing crisis of state finances globally. We therefore suggest that opposition and resistance to this must be necessarily political, in the sense that it seeks to articulate the pedagogical project as one not only concerned with what goes on in a classroom, that is the act of teaching, but more importantly the relationship between the students and teachers, universities and the wider public.

Hence, like the Situationists did several decades earlier, we argue that a response to the financialization and privatization of universities must go beyond demands of rejecting tuition fees and break with 'capitalist realism' itself, arguing for an egalitarian project, socialist and feminist in nature, where the rationale of education, as well as other social goods and services is fundamentally in terms of their use-value. Moreover, in terms of the academics and resistance to these policies, we will need to develop a different kind of 'applied' scholarship to the one envisaged by neoliberal administrators. This is one that Pierre Bourdieu characterizes as a 'committed scholarship' which requires 'academics to enter into sustained and vigorous exchange with the outside world, especially with unions, grassroots organizations, and issue-orientated activist groups' (2000:44).

In the book that is often called a handbook for revolutionary education, Paulo Freire's *Pedagogy of the Oppressed* (1970), Freire reminds us that there is no middle ground when it comes to the question of education; consciously and unconsciously, one either sees education as a transformatory act or one which is used to maintain and reinforce the existing patterns of power and privilege. Although Freire is drawing from a particular political and educational context in Brazil in the 1970s, he is at pains to point out that in seeking to bring literacy to the masses, that is create the conditions for a massive expansion of intellectuality, he was creating and envisaging the conditions for the Brazilian masses to uprise against an oppressive system (Elias, 1994). Subsequent chapters will explore what kinds of possibilities that critical pedagogy offers in seeking to confront this new financially driven poverty of student and academic life. In short, we argue that this will require a new revolutionary praxis where, in addition to defending, physically and with ideas of the public university, we can also develop alternative forms of free popular education exploring the possibilities offered by new technologies in access knowledge. It is in this way that we seek to foster the development of a new revolutionary consciousness and movements for free public education where as the Situationists argued, 'humans would interact together as people not mediated by commodities' (Libcom, 2009).

Suggestions for further reading

On May '68 and the Situationists

The original document of *On the Poverty of Student Life* (1966) is available online at: http://cddc.vt.edu/sionline/si/poverty.html and is well worth reading.

There is much written on the Situationists, but one of the best recent histories is McKenzie Wark's (2011) *The Beach Beneath the Street: The Everyday Life and Glorious Times of the Situationist International*. Verso, London.

There is also much written on May '68 but Kristin Ross's 2002 book *May '68 and its Afterlives* is one of the best among these.

On Marxist understandings of the economic crisis
David McNally's 2011 book *Global Slump: The Economics and Politics of Crisis and Resistance* (PM Press/Merlin Press) is very clear and accessible, and gives an excellent account of the issues.
David Harvey's *The Enigma of Capital* (2010) is also very good, though it may require a little more background in Marx's work.

For a recent introduction to Marx for those unfamiliar with his work we recommend Terry Eagelton's *Why Marx Was Right* (2011, Yale University Press).

On the financialization of the universities in United Kingdom:
Andrew McGettigan's pioneering research has demonstrated the devastating impact which financialization will have and is having on English Universities. His article 'Privatisation: The Truth about Middlesex' in *Research Fortnight*, 7 September 2011 is a good place to start. He offers an overview of some of the more detailed research in 'Who let the dogs out? The privatization of Higher Education'. *Radical Philosophy 174* (July/August 2012).

References

BBC Business News (11 June 2012) 'Cambridge University launches new bank with Council', http://bbc.co.uk/news/business-18397064 (accessed 13 July 2012).

Bourdieu, P. (2000) 'For a Scholarship with Commitment', *Profession*, 40–5. Modern Language Association, http://jstor.org/stable/25595701 (accessed 10 July 2012).

Eagleton, T. (2011) *Why Marx Was Right*. Yale University Press, New Haven and London.

Elias, J. (1994) *Paulo Freire: Pedagogue of Liberation*. Kreiger, Florida.

Fisher, M. (2009) *Capitalist Realism: Is there No Alternative*? Zero Books, London.

Giroux, H. (2011) Beyond the Swindle of the Corporate University: Higher Education in the Service of Democracy, Tuesday, 18 January 2011, Truthout | Op-Ed. http://truth-out.org/index.php?option=com_k2&view=item&id=69:beyond-the-swindle-of-the-corporate-university-higher-education-in-the-service-of-democracy (accessed 10 July 2012).

Gilroy, P. (2011) 'Paul Gilroy speaks on the riots, August 2011, Tottenham, North London', http://dreamofsafety.blogspot.co.uk/2011/08/paul-gilroy-speaks-on-riots-august-2011.html (accessed 26 June 2012).

Harvey, D. (2011) *The Enigma of Capital and the Crisis of Capitalism*. Profile Books, London.

Libcom (2009) 'The Situationists: An Introduction', http://libcom.org/thought/ideas/situationists/ (accessed 25 June 2012).

Marazzi, C. (2010) *The Violence of Financial Capitalism*. Semiotexte, Los Angeles.

Marx, K. (1990) *Capital, Volume 1*. Penguin Classics, London.

— (1992) *Capital, Volume 3*. Penguin Classics, London.

McGettigan, A. (2011a) '1. Privatisation: The Truth About Middlesex', *Research Fortnight*, 7 September 2011 (supplement to issue no. 374).

— (2011b) '2. Bonds: the market', *Research Fortnight*, 21 September 2011 (supplement to issue no. 375).

— (2011c) '3. Bonds: Californian Future', *Research Fortnight*, 7 September 2011 (supplement to issue no. 374).

— (2012) *False Accounting: Why the Government's Higher Education Reforms Don't Add Up*. Intergenerational Foundation, www.if.org.uk.

McNally, D. (2011) *Global Slump*. Merlin Press, London.

Ross, K. (2002) *May '68 and its Afterlives*. University of Chicago Press, Chicago & London.

Said, E. (2004) *Humanism and Democratic Criticism*. Columbia University Press, New York.

Situationist International and Students of Strasbourg (1966) *On the Poverty of Student Life, Considered in its Economic, Political, Psychological, Sexual and Particularly Intellectual Aspects, and a Modest Proposal for its Remedy*. http://www.cddc.vt.edu/sionline/si/poverty.html (accessed 9 December 2012).

Times Higher Education Supplement (20 July 2012) 'De Montfort takes plunge into bond market', http://timeshighereducation.co.uk/story.asp?sectioncode=26&storycode=420638&c=1 (accessed 24 July 2012).

Wilby, P. (2008) 'Humanity's Last Rage', *New Statesman*, 8 May.

CHAPTER TWO

Sat-Nav Education: A Means to an End or an End to Meaning?

Stephen Cowden and Gurnam Singh

In this chapter we will:

- Outline and discuss the problems with new forms of pedagogy used in contemporary universities, which we see as impoverished through being based on the assumption that the fundamental purpose of attending university is to obtain a 'good job'. We argue that this is creating what we call 'Sat-Nav' education; that is that students are being taught how to operate the equivalent of a Sat-Nav, rather than to how to discover the terrain for themselves.
- We discuss the distorting consequences of seeing education as a form of 'service provision' in which teachers are 'service providers' and students 'consumers'.
- We conclude by outlining the ideas of Paulo Freire as an alternative to this, looking at his underlying philosophy of education, as well as his practical alternatives at the level of teaching and learning.

Pedagogy is never innocent. But if it is to be understood and made problematic as a moral and political practice, educators must not only critically question and register their own subjective involvement in how and what they teach, they must also resist calls to transform pedagogy into the mere application of standardized practical methods and techniques. Otherwise, teachers become indifferent to the ethical and political dimensions of their own authority and practice.

Henry Giroux (2010)

Introduction

The significant expansion of higher education across the world, coupled with the prevailing technological consumer-driven culture has had a significant impact on the role and identity of academics, but arguably the impact on students has been even more profound. In the previous chapter, we argued that the macro-economics of neoliberalism are not only undermining universities as public institutions, but that this wider process of privatization is, as Macrine (2009) argues, precipitating a crisis of democracy itself. However, within the logic of 'capitalist realism' (Fisher, 2009), policy makers argue that the maintenance of an expanded higher education system in a climate of huge public sector debt means that students must pay for the career advantages of attending university. Further, they argue that due to massive governmental budget deficits and austerity measures state funding for universities is no longer viable, hence the only place for universities to go for additional funding is to the money markets. For the ideologists of neoliberalism, far from representing a cliff edge over which large sections of the university sector could so easily plunge, this will release these institutions from the shackles of state bureaucracies into an open market in which universities are much better placed to respond to the increasingly discerning student as customer, offering a new world of choice and flexibility. In confronting what they see as a 'romantic' notion of higher education, advocates of marketization suggest that the hopes, aspiration and make-up of today's student is radically different to previous generations for whom university was an opportunity to 'discover themselves', a rite of passage marking their initiation into an exclusive community of graduates. Within this argument the apparent freedom that students once enjoyed is looked upon as an indulgent nostalgia, and it is seen to be only right that this has now been displaced with an appropriately hardnosed utilitarian approach to education where the student's first and foremost priority is to get a job in an increasingly ruthless employment market.

In the previous chapter we explored the way that while the carrot of the good job and career is the one dangled before students and their families, it is cycles of debt which will define the reality of going to university, both in the way the university itself functions and certainly afterwards when debts must be paid. This chapter looks at the same process from a different angle with a focus on the impoverishing impact which the neoliberalization of education is having on pedagogy, and by implication on the identities of teachers and students. Our central concern is with the way teaching and learning in the contemporary university have been utterly reduced to a narrow utilitarian concern with producing graduates who are 'employable'. The assumption that this forms the fundamental purpose of education has led to the rise of an instrumentalized pedagogy based on a prescriptive competency-based curriculum (Barnett, 1994; Fanghanel, 2012), which is used as a means of disciplining both staff and students. Michael Burawoy (2011) has argued that through the twin barrels of 'commodification' and 'regulation', 'the university is being turned into a means for someone else's end' (Para 8). Giroux is even more unequivocal in his assertion that the present debates around pedagogy in the university represent 'one of the most important spheres in which the battle for democracy is currently being waged' (2007:6).

While these new pedagogical approaches are presented as benign, ideologically neutral and indeed essential in order to facilitate participation in university education, particularly of 'non-traditional' students, what they demonstrate is a process where the encounter with ideas and what Meyer and Land (2005) term *'troublesome knowledge'* as an end in itself is no longer seen as part of a university education. There is a profound anti-intellectualism involved in the notion that ideas are 'too difficult' to teach to today's students and in any case not particularly 'relevant'. For us, the reductionism of these approaches represents yet another dimension of the new poverty of student life; which is not just about the being materially poor, but about the poverty of a pedagogy which fails to give students the opportunity to be intellectually provoked and challenged. It is in this sense that we argue that a university educational experience has become synonymous to a Sat-Nav system whereby in a commoditized system of exchange – student as consumer, university as provider – undergraduates are increasingly guided through their studies in ways which fundamentally erode intellectual integrity.

The expansion of Higher Education: Does more mean worse?

In order to enter a debate about pedagogy within the contemporary university, it is first necessary to set out the context in which debates on Higher Education have unfolded. In the United Kingdom in recent years, both the broadsheet and tabloid news media have regularly carried reports associating the inclusion of 'non-traditional' students and/or 'non-traditional academic subjects such as 'media studies' with so-called dumbing down. This is exemplified by the headline in the *Daily Mail* newspaper on 13 January

2012 – '"*Dumbed-down*" *degrees: University standards under fire as 50% more students awarded a first*'. These views draw on a long tradition of conservative argument concerned with the positive value of educational elitism. The High Tory T. S. Eliot argued in his 1948 essay *Notes towards the Definition of Culture* that:

> There is no doubt that in our headlong rush to educate everybody, we are lowering our standards . . . destroying ancient edifices to make ready the ground upon which the barbarian nomads of the future will encamp in their mechanised caravans. (Eliot, 1948:111)

While the language here might come across as a bit stiff for today's conservatives, the same essential ideas resonate in the utterances of the former Chief Inspector of Schools in the United Kingdom, Chris Woodhead, regarding the policy of 'Widening Participation':

> A university ought to be an institution in which those young people who have the intellectual ability to benefit engage with the best that has been thought and written. The government's . . . bleakly utilitarian view of higher education is unlikely to deliver the knowledge and skill the economy needs; its commitment to social inclusion is calculated, through the manipulation of admissions procedures and the dumbing down of academic standards, to destroy the prize it wants all to enjoy (Woodhead, 2002).

These quotes characterize the idea that tertiary education should essentially be the province of the select few and that in Kingsley Amis' infamous adage 'more will mean worse'. However, we would also note that this position is no longer confined to traditional conservatives. In his 2004 book *Where Have All the Intellectuals Gone?* sociologist Frank Furedi attacks this issue of inclusivity with a remarkably similar line of argument to Chris Woodhead. The desire to be inclusive is for him also chief culprit when it comes to the declining standards of today's university, which he characterizes as a place where:

> . . . there are desperate attempts made to ensure that people achieve some kind of qualification. As a result standards are continuously reconfigured to ensure that students succeed. (2004:17)

While Furedi denies that he is writing a 'lament for a golden age' (2004:22), these debates about the purpose of pedagogy are, as Henry Giroux notes earlier, 'never innocent'. All of the above arguments appeal to the authority of the past, which is compared to the present moment of declining 'standards' and the loss of 'intellectual authority'. While Furedi's argument incorporates a critique of the kind of instrumentalization we are similarly criticizing, we disagree with the way he locates the source of this not in terms of the inadequate funding of education or the way universities are expected to bow before the often myopic demands of employers, but excessive concern with inclusivity – 'widening participation' – that is, greater numbers of working-class students entering tertiary education. As well as sharing a deeply unpleasant social elitism, these arguments set up an entirely false dichotomy between inclusivity versus standards. One might well ask those who have promoted this line of argument whether they believe the current rise in student fees, which will exclude large numbers of working class potential applicants, is therefore likely to raise standards. Unfortunately, apart from those in the small world of elite universities, tomorrow's students will get the worst of both worlds – increased fees and debt *as well as* an ever more instrumentalized pedagogy. It is precisely for this reason that we emphasize the danger of basing a critique of these new pedagogies upon nostalgia for 'the good old days'. The way in which this line of argument is being used to attack state education across the board was illustrated in a recent statement by Michael Gove, UK Secretary of State for Education, in an appeal to 'restore elitism to our schools' when he argued that parents were:

> '. . . yearning for their children to learn "rigorous" intellectual subjects, for ordered classrooms with strict discipline, and for teachers who are guardians of knowledge and figures of authority'. (Chapman, 2011)

The irony of this paean to the educational conservatism of the past is that Gove's vehicle for delivering these objectives are profit-based academy schools whose entire business model is based on cutting running costs to the bone and taking the instumentalization of knowledge even further than it has already gone. An indication of how they will be achieving their objectives was demonstrated with Gove's recent proposal to give these schools permission to hire unqualified teaching staff (*Guardian* 28 July 2012). The rhetoric of restoring past glories here acts as a bridgehead to the wholesale privatization of secondary education. So while there were many valuable things about public universities in the post-war years, this was a time also characterized by extremely limited participation across the social spectrum. We would also argue that the widening participation agenda in the United Kingdom has been a hugely successful initiative, and that it should be defended not simply on an economic rationale, but for its wider social benefits.

Consumerist pedagogy

There can be little doubt that the commodification and instrumentalization of education as a whole has resulted in many students having different expectations of university life. For the privileged few that may end up in an 'elite' institution, expectations may still remain relatively located in what to the majority is a bygone age. However, for the vast majority of students, their expectations of university life in general, how they learn and engage with academic work, such as reading, research and critical thinking, and how they perceive the role of tutors, are very different to the Humboldian notion that the primary purpose of going to university is to 'read' and discourse with a community of scholars.

One of the key assumptions underpinning the changes that have been introduced within the consumerist model of education that is being heavily promoted by government and some educationalists – and something that is encouraged by such things as the National Student Survey and league tables in general – is the assumption that the 'customer knows best'. Within HE, this is characterized most overtly in the ritualistic course evaluations, where students are 'empowered' to provide feedback, usually in the form of Lickert scale ratings on things as lecturer performance and curriculum content. This data is then collated and increasingly utilized by managers to discipline lecturers who are seen in students' assessment to fall short of the mark (Titus, 2008).

There is a growing body of evidence that highlights flaws in student (as consumer) based teaching evaluation surveys. In eliciting students' feelings they do not achieve what they proclaim to, namely, evaluate teaching and learning, which are complex processes (Light et al., 2009; Hand and Rowe, 2001). Such consumerist instruments, where feelings about learning take precedence over learning outcomes per say (analogous to enjoying food as opposed to its nutritional value) can have damaging effects on pedagogy and professional integrity and ultimately end up distorting the university's mission to educate. As Titus notes:

> . . . students' enjoyment gains a distorted level of importance in SETs. Because their sense of enjoyment is so widely used by students as the sole criterion by which they rate every item on the form, their level of pleasure becomes conflated with teaching quality. The ratings these students give are not considerations of specific teaching behaviors; instead, their ratings represent their general opinion of the instructor's acceptability. (Titus 2008: 403)

This requirement to be 'liked' can result in the most insidious effect of consumerist student feedback, namely its impact on teacher autonomy, creativity and confidence. The point here is not that students should be silenced, but rather the valorization of a particularly myopic form of consumerism into which students are co-opted. As well as constructing antagonistic relations between students and lecturers, this also gives students an entirely false sense of 'empowerment' which usually only results in cosmetic changes. More worrying is the way this can act to undermine the creativity and confidence of teaching staff, as well as strengthen the regulatory hand of managers whose role is of course purely to ensure the high quality of the 'student experience'. Indeed, the approach can encourage risk averseness among teachers and managers, who end up conspiring to offer up things that are recognizable and likable to students (Kember and Wong, 2000).

As well as discouraging creativity, like fast food the consumerist approach tends to encourage instant and simplistic feedback. Putting aside the potential distortions that can result from general 'evaluation' overload (Porter et al., 2004), if we know anything about learning it is that this is a continuing process and not units of 'experience' to be given scores like performances on a television talent show. Rowley (2003) argues that more effective evaluation is likely to be achieved during a period of consolidation after the teaching in focus has been completed, examined and students' achievements reported on.

The hegemony of consumerism, of which these changes are an expression, reflects a wider social and cultural shift concerning the relationship between the state and the citizenry. One key manifestation of this is the fact that we are now seen as a much less 'trusting' society. In her Reith Lecture series, the moral philosopher Onora O'Neill has characterized this as one in which:

> Mistrust and suspicion have spread across all areas of life, and supposedly with good reason. Citizens, it is said, no longer trust governments, or politicians, or ministers, or the police, or the courts, or the prison service. Consumers, it is said, no longer trust business, especially big business, or their products. None of us, it is said, trusts banks, or insurers, or pension providers. Patients, it is said, no longer trust doctors (think of Dr Shipman!), and in particular no longer trust hospitals or hospital consultants. 'Loss of trust' is in short, a cliché of our times. (Onora, 2004)

Alongside this apparent decline in trust is also a distrust of professional and/or expert knowledge. The historian Dominic Sandbrook in his work on the United Kingdom in the 1970s (Sandbrook, 2012) has noted how pervasive the culture of deference to professional and expert knowledge was during this period. Universities, like schools, social services departments and hospitals as they developed in the United Kingdom in the post-war period, were based on a culture in which 'professionals knew best'. It was through the radical and counter-cultural movements of the 1970s that this began to change. We have written elsewhere (Singh and Cowden, 2007) about the impact of this in Health and Social Care through the rise of the concept of 'service-user involvement' in services. In particular, we suggest in this piece that while the demands of the social movements were hugely important as an expression of shifts in the relationship between the state and citizenry in Britain, they have entered social policy, ideologically speaking, through the lens of neoliberal dominance in the political and economic sphere. Margaret Thatcher, the then British Prime Minister articulated a powerful new common-sense discourse when she appeared to speak for the 'ordinary person' *against* the state, by which she meant public services. Contemporary neoliberal social policy thus gives us a strange kind of reverse panoptican where professionals are always under the microscope, though it has to be said that the new consumerism offers only the mirage of control, rather like the way a Sat-Nav gives you the illusion that you will never be lost.

The dominance of consumerism also reflects Fisher's concept of 'capitalist realism'; just as a business ontology becomes naturalized throughout all social institutions (2009:17), so we are all now either 'consumers' or 'service-providers'. While this notion of the student as expert in education may be superficially appealing to some as a critique of old-style elitism, this model distorts the relationship between students and teachers by denying the actual expertise that educators possess. In effacing this, the new consumerist pedagogy deprives students of the opportunity to genuinely experience learning through the encounter with a historically developed body of knowledge. As Fanghanel notes:

> . . . a narrow consumerist model potentially leads to restricting the possibility to engage students fully with the meaning of the educational enterprise, and of its relation of the wider world. These broader conceptions allow for different imaginings of learning, and of the relation between students and academics. (2012:65)

The consumerist model epitomizes the idea of Sat-Nav education, where the potential experience to be gained in attempting to navigate between two points is reduced to a mechanical act of inputting some codes into a machine that then does the thinking for you. While one may manage to get to one's destination much of the time, this is achieved without any sense of *how* this process took place. This is akin to students being offered no real sense of where the course of study they are embarked upon comes from, or being unable to see why this matters. The quote from Paulo Freire which gave us the title for this book expresses this idea; that it is this encounter and engagement with new, difficult and often 'troublesome' knowledge (Meyer and Land), which allows a student to move beyond 'learning' to 'knowing'. It is through such experiences that genuine educational processes are embodied. The anti-intellectualism inherent in these new forms of instrumentalized pedagogy works alongside the commodification of university life, discussed in the previous chapter, in the sense that their fundamental purpose is to standardize and commodify knowledge. Ursula Huws has noted that this process is always what has to happen for public services to be rendered capable of being taken over by profit-making outsourcing operations, where 'services are standardised and [thereby] capable of being delivered by a compliant and interchangeable workforce' (Huws, 2011:65). Despite the glossy leaflets of smiling carers and happy grateful recipients, these outsourcing organizations are all about cutting costs to the absolute minimum and eliminating the human relational element which is so central to any relationship of 'care'. This standardization of knowledge in the contemporary university follows the same logic – it is not concerned with the embodied processes of learning and knowing. Instead we see these equated with the fulfilling of assessment requirements configured around prescribed and packaged learning objectives. In other words, students are being taught how to operate a 'Sat-Nav' system instead of how to navigate a real terrain, and in the process to really discover that terrain for themselves.

TICK BOXES
Source: http://www.sociology.org/pedagogy/giving-grade/

The academic's experience

So far, we have discussed the impact that consumerism is having on student identities. We now turn to focus on universities as institutions and specifically the roles and identities of academics. In thinking about identity and pedagogy, it is important to reflect upon how one might conceptualize the university. What we see are institutions with multiple functions (political, ideological, economic), with much diversity within and between institutions (size, age, range of subjects, geographical appeal, funding etc.) and which serve many different thought-related functions (research, instruction, innovation, etc.). As we noted in the previous chapter, the really huge change that is going to take place involves the shift of the burden of funding education from the state and the transformation of universities from essentially public institutions to private corporate entities. How are these changes impacting on educators? For some, it has meant constant restructuring, reorganization, more pressure, and for some loss of jobs and departments, such as many recent closures for university departments for no other reason that they were not bringing in enough money; the closures of the philosophy departments at Middlesex University and at Kings College in 2010 were examples of this in the United Kingdom. The consequence for academics are profound in many ways, and this has forced them to make choices; a relatively new thing for this group of professionals who historically have been insulated from neoliberal labour market reforms (see Fanganel, 2012 for a wider discussion of this). For those who respond 'pragmatically' to these changes, discomfort can be tempered by the new career opportunities which have emerged within the framework of corporatized academia. The price often paid is in the abandoning of original career aspirations as teachers and/or scholars, often accompanied by complete reskilling as managers of departments and courses. For those that choose to resist, the most basic practices of critical, ethical and politically conscious pedagogy become political acts, and many once-straightforward matters of professional/academic discretion, have become matters of political principle. This is true in other fields as well: health professionals, artists, social workers, journalists, civil servants, etc. all suggest that it is increasingly difficult to work within existing social institutions with any kind of personal or professional integrity, so alienated have these institutions become from the basic principles of public service and individual autonomy that even the mainstream professions have been built around.

In a similarly utilitarian vein, the recent Research Excellence Framework in the United Kingdom contains within it a need to demonstrate the 'impact' of research. This does not concern the value or impact of work among particular fields of study where it could be highly significant – this has been substituted by a populist market-driven notion of impact. Anthony Grafton has highlighted the dangers of an approach to research and teaching that devalues academics and which is simply driven by populist market trends. Using the metaphor of food and cooking, he talks about the need to avoid the culture of targets and the kinds of student assessment that elevate instant gratification over slow realization or form over substance:

> Accept the short term as your standard – support only what students want to study right now and outside agencies want to fund right now – and you lose the future. The subjects and methods that will matter most in twenty years are often the ones that nobody values very much right now. Slow scholarship – like Slow Food – is deeper and richer and more

> nourishing than the fast stuff. But it takes longer to make, and to do it properly, you have to employ eccentric people who insist on doing things their way. (Grafton, 2010)

This quote highlights the relationship between neoliberalism and the standardization of pedagogies. What makes these 'eccentric people' Grafton is referring to such good teachers is that they have high levels of tacit knowledge that it is difficult to standardize and commodify. It takes less than two weeks to train someone to work in McDonalds – a business that epitomizes the 'interchangeable workforce' which we discussed earlier. To teach someone to really cook takes years, but it is the fast food ethos which is exercising such influence on teaching, on the funding of courses and on research. As Joyce Canaan and Wesley Shumar have noted in their work on the 'Neoliberal University', the same processes which have been used in high schools have been similarly deployed in HE, where under a populist rhetoric of participation, consumer choice and flexibility, and a market-driven form of managerialism dominates. The process of marketization is essentially deployed as an instrument to extract 'more for less', that is, a 'disciplinary apparatus to create greater efficiencies' (2009:4). This process of commodification thus changes the nature of interpersonal relationships on which teaching is based; in being commodified the process is instrumentalized and dehumanized, and this is the hidden implication of the characterization of students as 'customers' and staff as 'service providers' and 'income generators'.

The student experience

If these reforms create confusion for academics, then equally they throw up contradictions for students. The glossy brochures, elaborate complaints mechanisms, online resources, course packs, detailed coursework guidance and endless student surveys discussed earlier may give them a sense of power and influence. While the professed rationale for these measures may be about improving the quality of the learning experience, this often simply masks an insidious and often invisible process where resources are redistributed away from teaching and towards servicing the new business-facing structures that universities these days are all so keen on. The Higher Education Policy Unit's report on UK universities in 2009 demonstrated exactly this point – and it showed that despite the fact that students were paying £3,000 and upwards in fees to study at university, there was no evidence of even the slightest increase in the amount of contact time students had with lecturers. (HEPI, 2009; UCU News, May 2009). In spite of the rhetoric about quality, standards and 'the student experience', the reality is that much of this extra income was used to develop the business and marketing arms of universities; developments which were no doubt seen as much more important by university managers than spending money on teaching.

Students and their families these days are bombarded with information about how the quality of teaching in this or that institution is improving or declining. From a student's point of view, there is nothing wrong with wanting to attend the best institution available to you, or from an academic's point of view of wanting students to have appreciated their teaching. The problem lies in the way these ratings act as distorting mechanisms. Marketing departments of universities these days spend considerable sums of money collecting student feedback, not simply because they want their institution to be good, but primarily because positive ratings will improve that institution's position in league tables. One consequence for students, as has been happening in schools for many years, is that parents and students come to see this as the most important measure of the quality of an educational experience. University managers therefore direct teachers to focus their work on things that will lead to increases in positive student rating, such as focussing purely on results and nothing else. Again, this focus on measurable outcomes instrumentalizes teaching, and as Canaan and Shumar argue, leads to a limiting of creative and critical capacitates and encouraging their 'dulling down' (2009:7).

An example of this is the modular system, which has been thrust upon Higher Education ironically in order to create flexibility with and between institutions. Maggie Savin-Baden has noted that the main effect of this is to 'fragment and striate learning' (2007:23). She goes on to lament the emphasis on a performative curriculum design driven by the culture of learning objectives that tend to emphasize behavioural and measurable traits. This places the attention on what students are expected to learn and likewise what lecturers are expected to assess. These devices so easily become like Sat-Nav systems, providing an easy formula for teaching and learning which closes down the possibility of creative curriculum design, structures and

BORED STUDENTS
Source: http://brewright.blogspot.co.uk/2011/02/attribution-error-in-teaching.html

spaces. In an approach where certainty becomes paramount, there appears to be little space for what Savin-Baden (2007) terms 'transitional spaces' which are characterized by ambivalence, critical reflexivity, liminality, as well as the idea of education as 'troublesome knowledge'.

By managerializing pedagogic practices, the sense of teaching as a craft is undermined and replaced by a series of standardized and ritualized pedagogic practices. And one manifestation, as Henry Giroux (1988) has noted, is the way that a profound anti-intellectualism turns the classroom into a place where students are passively trained for rote-learned information – the sense that ideas could be interesting, exciting or transformative is entirely lost. Hence the language of skills and competencies in the contemporary university is, far from the ideological neutrality it claims, about a process where creative independent thinking is severely discouraged, as crucial ideas and concepts are replaced with formulas. This is yet another dimension of the new poverty of student life, as the inestimable value of encountering new ideas and concepts is stripped out of university life.

Critical Pedagogy

In order to challenge these processes, we argue that there needs to be a multi-pronged strategy which begins with developing a critique and understanding that far from being benign and/or inevitable, the changes taking place in higher education are ideologically driven, undemocratic, anti-intellectual and antithetical to the principles of education itself. The most important steps toward resistance are those that begins within our own minds and those of our students; through a realization that teaching in Higher Education at its best is about being creative, taking risks, having passion, celebrating intellectual pursuits and the transformative power of education. While recognizing there will always be a need for 'technical education', it is crucial that we reject the kinds of abstracted and packaged forms of commodified learning, be it in the form online learning or didactic instructional learning.

Most important of all, we believe that teachers and students need to see each other as jointly collaborating to 'build networks and communities of learning' that transcends boundaries of 'race', class and gender. In the previous chapter we noted how important it was for academics not to collude with financially driven understandings of 'applied research' and instead 'to enter into sustained and vigorous exchange with the outside world, especially with unions, grassroots organizations, and issue-orientated activist groups' (Bourdieu, 2000:44). Some of these alliances will be funded and others will not be. Some will be within and between subject disciplines, departments and universities; some will be outside (examples in the United Kingdom have been things such as the Nottingham Free School, University in the Park and Lincoln Social Science Centre) while others will transcend the two spheres. While we need to see the limitations of work within existing institutions, we also see it as important to work 'in and against' those institutions. For example at an organizational level, many universities have remits for internationalization, public engagement and promoting diversity. Instead of remaining at the rhetorical level, staff can use these as bases for developing alternative progressive interpretations.

Our previous chapter made extensive use of Marx's work, and as well as regarding it as being one of the most important attempts to understand the basis of capitalism's economic crisis, we have sought to develop Marx's legacy as an attempt to challenge the profound lack of confidence among progressive and critical academics in challenging the hegemony of neoliberalism. There is an urgent need for academics to regain confidence in the relevance of radical critiques of capitalism, of which Marxism is still the most powerful. In relation to pedagogical strategies, we see the task of building an alternative pedagogy as beginning with an understanding of the contradictory function of education in modern capitalist societies like ours. A crucial starting point within this for us has been our engagement with the work of the Brazilian radical educationalist Paulo Freire. While the context in which Freire developed his ideas was radically different from our own, we see the insights of his seminal 1970 text *Pedagogy of the Oppressed* as incredibly relevant to our situation today. Freire is particularly important for the way he emphasizes the fundamentally *political* nature of pedagogical processes. He argues that it is only through recognizing this that we can begin to, in his phrase, 'humanise the curriculum'. A key issue in which we have sought to use Freire in our own pedagogical work has been to recognize the way today's students are ontologically caught between a desire for predictable and bite size learning (Sat-Nav learning) alongside an innate human desire to experience something that is new and aesthetically challenging. Freire is distinctive for the way he saw this paradox as not just about human ambivalence in the broadest sense, but as particularly concerned with questions of power and powerlessness, which frame his discussion. He expressed this as follows:

> The oppressed suffer from a duality, which has established itself in their innermost being. They discover that without freedom they cannot exist authentically. Yet although they desire authentic existence, they fear it. They are one and the same time themselves and the oppressor whose consciousness they have internalised. The conflict lies in the choice between . . . following prescription or having choices, between being spectators or actors . . . between speaking or remaining silent. (1996:30)

For Freire, pedagogy was the basis by which education produced silent domesticated students for whom 'learning' remained entirely separate to their consciousness and subjectivity, as opposed to students who were given licence to speak in their own voices and in that process discover and develop insights into both themselves as well as the world they lived in. His central distinction is between what he calls 'banking education' and 'problem-posing education'. Within banking education, students are conceived of as:

> . . . 'recepticles' to be 'filled' by the teacher. The more completely she fills the recepticles, the better teacher she is. The more meekly the recepticles permit themselves to be filled, the better students they are. Education thus becomes an act of depositing, in which the students are the depositories and the teacher is the depositor . . . In the banking concept of education, knowledge is a gift bestowed by those who consider themselves knowledgeable upon those who consider they know nothing . . . The students, alienated like the slave in the Hegelian dialectic, accept their ignorance as justifying the teacher's existence – but unlike the slave, they never discover that they educate the teacher. (1970:53)

Problem-posing education sees the fundamental purpose of education as concerned with:

> . . . posing the problems of human beings in their relations with the world . . . [It] consists of acts of cognition, not transferrals of information . . . The teacher is no longer the one-who-teaches, but one who is himself taught in dialogue with the students, who in turn while being taught also teach. (1970:60–1)

This idea of education where the teacher and the student are both engaged in teaching each other and learning from each other reflects the deep egalitarianism and democratic impulse in Freire's philosophy. The teacher's knowledge is not a private accumulation, but rather something that becomes efficacious through engagement with students. In this sense we see the Freirian idea of 'dialogue' not just as about the inherent value of people talking with each other, but rather as a mutual engagement based on a dialectical interchange of theory and experience.

We see this model of banking as one which has been massively revived in the contexts of new instrumental pedagogies. While we noted earlier the paradox of student wants and needs, we think it is very important to note the significance of recent research in this area. The good news is that given the choice of an instrumental or emancipatory learning experience, most students will choose the latter most of the time. In a study of over 1000 undergraduate students from both so-called Russell group and Non-Russell group, HEI's Ainley and Weyers (2009) revealed that the most important priorities identified by across the sector tended to be intrinsic factors associated with interest in their subject, the desire to develop as a person, whereas extrinsic motivators, namely to compete with others and getting a qualification to obtain a good job, were ranked lowest. In terms of student approaches to studying, there was consensus across the groups of a preference for deep learning over surface learning (Biggs, 1999) while valuing equally instructive teaching and teaching that encouraged autonomy.

Conclusion

Just as neoliberal finance has created a mirage of ever-increasing wealth which turned out to be non-existent, the managerial formulas of neoliberal education are, we believe, equally empty. The instrumentalization of universities through the conflation of education and training, commodification of knowledge and standardization of curriculum has, we suggest, not only undermined students' capacities to think critically for themselves and to see the intrinsic value in education, but it has also radically altered the roles and identities of academics. From the Humboldian conception of a scholar exercizing high levels of academic and institutional freedom, as Fanghanel describes, we now have the 'managed academic' characterized as a member of a 'compliant tribe' who is only able to 'operate within the parameters of instructions and regulations' (2012:29). It is as though the academic has morphed from an explorer in his/her own right to an embodied Sat-Nav system whose purpose is reduced to help students navigate their way through university and into a job by the shortest possible route.

The paradox within all this is that we are living in extremely turbulent times. As the BBC journalist Paul Mason has noted, in the last few years we have seen not only the overthrow of western-backed dictators in Tunisia and Egypt, but also 'in Ireland [we have seen] young techno-savvy professionals . . . agitating for a "Second Republic"; in France the youth from banlieues battled police on the streets to defend the retirement rights of 60-year olds; in Greece striking and rioting have become a national pastime. And in Britain we've had riots and student occupations that changed the political mood'. He goes on to argue that the key wider social dynamic in this as 'at the heart if it all is a new sociological type: the graduate with no future' (Mason, 2011). It is precisely because of the nature of the economic crisis, as characterized in the previous chapter, that the central rationale of instrumentalized pedagogy – getting a job – cannot be guaranteed. This is the inherent problem of a strategy based on the simultaneous promotion of indebtedness and austerity. In a situation where there is such a chasm between the neoliberal image of society and the reality of people's real lives, it becomes so important that we as educators recover and reinvent the

YOUNG PROTESTORS
Source: http://www.guardian.co.uk/education/blog/2010/nov/30/student-protests-live-coverage

tradition of critical pedagogy, and particularly the concept of education as the capacity for nurturing critically engaged citizenship.

As academics marking students, work we may at times lament the absence of critical thinking and the much remarked-upon apathetic attitudes among the young. But it is crucial to realize that this deficit of imagination is precisely that which is encouraged by a commoditized Sat-Nav education system. As academics we can either behave as technicians and instructors assisting students to learn how to input data into the Sat-Nav system, or we can help them to read maps, to go off the beaten track of certainty and to orientate them to find their way through what is often an unpredictable, uncertain but ultimately extremely fulfilling terrain of learning. The very instability of the times in which we are living will itself create opportunities to open a debate, not only about what education is for but also what education could be for, and this debate needs to be informed not just by academics, but by students and young people themselves. If we are to create genuine alternatives, we will need to build new kinds of alliances between teachers and students, which will themselves give rise to new conceptions of both education and democracy.

References

Ainley, P. and Weyers, M. (2009) *Twenty Years of Schooling: Student Reflections on Their Educational Journeys*. SRHE, London.

Barnett, R. (1994) *The Limits of Competence. Knowledge, Higher Education and Society.* Open University Press, Buckingham.

Biggs, J. (1999) 'Teaching for Quality Learning at University' *The Society for Research into Higher Education. Research and Development* 8(1): 7–25.

Burawoy, M. (2011) 'Redefining the Public University: Developing an Analytical Framework'. Institute of Public Knowledge, http://publicsphere.ssrc.org/burawoy-redefining-the-public-university/ (accessed 12 June 2012).

Canaan, J. E. and Shumar, W. (2009) *Structure and Agency in the Neoliberal University.* Routledge, New York and London.

Chapman, J. (2011) 'Restore Elitism to Our Schools: Gove Takes on Education Establishment in Passionate Rallying Cry for a Return to Traditional Teaching Values', *Mail Online* 25 November, http://dailymail.co.uk/news/article-2065907/Michael-Goves-rallying-return-traditional-teaching-values.html (accessed 18 July 2012).

Fisher, M. (2009) *Capitalist Realism: Is there No Alternative?* Zero Books, Winchester.

Freire, P. (1970) *Pedagogy of the Oppressed.* Herder and Herder, New York.

Giroux, H. (1988) *Teachers as Intellectuals: Toward a Critical Pedagogy of Learning.* Granby, Bergin and Garvey, MA.

— (2007) *The University in Chains: Confronting the Military-Industrial-Academic Complex.* Paradigm, London.

— (2010) 'Dumbing Down Teachers: Attacking Colleges of Education in the Name of Reform (Part I)' – truthout Tuesday 25 May, http://truth-out.org/dumbing-down-teachers-attacking-colleges-education-name-reform59820. (accesssed 1 June 2012).

Grafton, A. (2010) 'Britain: The Disgrace of the Universities', *New York Review of Books* (9 March), http://nybooks.com/blogs/nyrblog/2010/mar/09/britain-the-disgrace-of-the-universities/ (accessed 20 June 2010).

Guardian 28 July 2012 'Gove Tells Academies They Can Hire Unqualified Teaching Staff'.

Hand, L. and Rowe, M. (2001) 'Evaluation of Student Feedback', *Accounting Education* 10(2): 147–60.

Higher Education Policy Unit. (2009) *The Academic Experience of Students in English Universities (2009 report)*, http://hepi.ac.uk/466–1393/The-Academic-Experience-of-Students-in-English-Universities-(2009-report).html (accessed 18 July 2012).

Huws, U. (2011) 'Crisis as Capitalist Opportunity: New Accumulation through Public Service Commodification' in Panitch, Albo and Chibber (eds), *The Socialist Register 2012.* Merlin Press, London.

Kember, D. and Wong, A. (2000) 'Implications for Evaluation from a Study of Students' Perceptions of Good and Poor Teaching', *Higher Education* 40: 69–97.

Light, G., Calkins, S. and Cox, R. (2009) *Learning and Teaching in Higher Education: The Reflective Professional.* Sage, London.

Macrine, S. (ed.) (2009) *Critical Pedagogy in Uncertain Times: Hope and Possibilitites.* Palgrave MacMillan, New York.

Mason, P. (2011) 'Twenty reasons why it's kicking off everywhere', BBC, http://bbc.co.uk/blogs/newsnight/paulmason/2011/02/twenty_reasons_why_its_kicking.html (accessed 15 July 2012).
Meyer, J. and Land, R. (2005). 'Threshold Concepts and Troublesome Knowledge (2): Epistemological Considerations and a Conceptual Framework for Teaching and Learning' *Higher Education* 49(3): 373–88.
O'Neill, O. (2004) A Question of Trust: The BBC Reith Lectures, 'Lecture 1: Spreading Suspicion', http://bbc.co.uk/radio4/reith2002/lectures.shtml (accessed 29 May 2012).
Porter, S. R., Whitcomb, M. E. and Weitzer, W. H. (2004) 'Multiple Surveys of Students and Survey Fatigue', *New Directions for Institutional Research* 121: 63–73.
Rowley, J. (2003) 'Designing Student Feedback Questionnaires', *Quality Assurance in Education* 11 (3): 142–9.
Sandbrook, D. (2012) *Seasons in the Sun: The Battle for Britain 1974–1979.* Allen Lane, London.
Savin-Baden, M. Learning Spaces. (2007) *Creating Opportunities for Knowledge Creation in Academic Life.* McGraw Hill, Maidenhead.
Singh, G. and Cowden, S. (2007) 'The "User": Friend, Foe or Fetish? A Critical Exploration of User Involvement in Health and Social Care', *Critical Social Policy* issue 27(5): 5–23.
Titus, J. J. (2008) 'Student Ratings in a Consumerist Academy: Leveraging Pedagogical Control and Authority', *Sociological Perspectives* 51(2): 397–422.
UCU News. 7 May 2009 'Higher fees have not created an improvement in student contact time, says report', http://ucu.org.uk/index.cfm?articleid=3873 (accessed 18 July 2012).
Woodhead, C. (2002) 'Trouble in the Trades', THES 29 March, http://timeshighereducation.co.uk/story.asp?storyCode=168114&sectioncode=26 (accessed 28 May 2012).

CHAPTER THREE

Criticality, Pedagogy and the Promises of Radical Democratic Education

Sarah Amsler

Chapter Summary

In this chapter, I:

- ask what, if anything, critical education can contribute to the defence and creation of democracy in 'post-democratic' societies;
- argue that the traditions of critical pedagogy have much to offer this project, but also that those seeking to engage with them need to do so creatively;
- introduce a range of work in the critical-pedagogical tradition, showing that each one offers a different definition of 'criticality'; and
- illustrate how these are relevant for students and teachers who want to create deeper and more radically democratic forms of life.

Introduction

'What is it to offer a critique? This is something that, I would wager, most of us understand in some ordinary sense. But matters become more vexing if we attempt to distinguish between a critique of this or that position and critique as a more generalized practice, one that might be described without

reference to its specific objects. Can we even ask such a question about the generalized character of critique without gesturing toward an essence of critique?

(BUTLER, 2002)

'Critique has been at the forefront of projects for radical social change from their earliest incarnations. [. . .] And yet today it appears that critique has come to dominate radical pedagogies without the accoutrement of an alternative vision'.

(VANHEERTUM, 2009)

'I can't help but dream about a kind of criticism that would try not to judge but to bring a work, a book, a sentence, and idea to life; it would light fires, watch the grass grow, listen to the wind, and catch the sea foam in the breeze and scatter it. It would multiply not judgments but signs of existence; it would summon them, drag them from their sleep. Perhaps it would invent them sometimes – all the better. Criticism that hands down sentences send me to sleep; I'd like a criticism of scintillating leaps of the imagination. It would not be sovereign or dressed in red. It would bear the lightning of possible storms'.

(FOUCAULT, 1997A)

We are living in very perplexing times. We are faced, on the one hand, with a crisis of liberal democracy. Some have described the condition as a 'dictatorship of no alternatives' to neoliberal capitalism, a logic of social order believed to be so dehumanizing that it has defeated democratic energies and become rooted in the very making of our selves (Fielding and Moss, 2011). The general social milieu seems to be not only hostile to and 'fatigued' by critique, but impervious to its logic (Kompridis, 2005). On the other hand, we are presented with evidence that the system is cracking through its own contradictions, with news of everyday resistances to its power, and with knowledge that a 'new political imaginary' has matured from a diverse field of social struggles during the 1990s to more coherent movements for radical democracy (Day, 2005; Holloway, 2009). In this conjuncture, the undesirability – or for some, the impossibility – of living in familiar ways and making sense of the world with familiar concepts is creating space to imagine, experiment with and practice alternatives. It is for this reason that social theorists have begun to attend more watchfully to developments in the 'politics of possibility' (Gibson–Graham, 2006:xxvii; Dinerstein and Deneulin, 2012) and to explore cultural practices that can 'reopen the future and unclose the past, [and] regenerate hope and confidence in the face of conditions that threaten to make even their regeneration meaningless' (Kompridis 2006, p. 277). The question exercising many minds now is how, in this age, are we to imagine and create an alternative post-capitalist politics?[1]

In this chapter, I consider what contributions education – particularly higher forms of learning – can make to this new political imaginary. I am especially concerned with the possibilities of critical pedagogy, a historical project that I consider myself to be part of. While the term is often used synonymously with 'emancipatory' or 'transformative' education, it also represents a paradigm of criticality which is itself in crisis. There is a concern that some of our most familiar definitions of critical pedagogy do adequately illuminate our present conditions or facilitate the emergence of more desirable paths into the future. There is a need to rearticulate the critical-pedagogical project in ways that undermine, sap and challenge dehumanizing practices of power in the one hand, and to build, strengthen and breathe life into humanizing practices of a liberating and flourishing social life, on the other.[2] Critical pedagogy, defined in its narrowest sense, is a necessary but not sufficient foundation for developing forms of education that can deepen such a politics of possibility in contemporary post-democratic circumstances.[3] In what follows, I will attempt to illustrate how different paradigms of criticality can be brought into constructive conversation, in a way that allows us to bridge classical critical pedagogical work with emerging theories and practices of radical democracy.

---

[1]'Post-capitalism' is the name given to forms of politics, both actually existing and envisioned, that are neither dominated by nor limited to the logic of capitalism. A post-capitalist 'political imaginary' is a vision of a world where political life embraces a diversity of non-capitalistic forms of economic relations and ways of being human, and that is not, in the words of J. K. Gibson–Graham, 'capitalocentric' (2006, p. xxxiv). The significance of the book in which they map out this new imaginary is that it is not simply a figment of imagination, but the product of decades of transnational activist research which illustrates the extent to which we already live in the midst of post-capitalist economies and polities, and the relative ease with which we may break away from the ideological enchantments that seduce us into believing otherwise.

[2]In a conversation with Giles Deleuze, Michel Foucault once argued that the role of the theorist is to, in the service of the humanist project, 'not to "awaken consciousness" . . . but to sap power, to take power', or rather, to take the power of power through its deconstruction; see Foucault and Deleuze (1972).

[3]The term 'post-democracy' refers to a situation in which formal institutions of democracy exist, but 'simply do not function to represent or to enact effectively the collective will of the citizenry' (Gilbert, 2009). It refers more specifically to the legitimacy crisis of liberal democracy in the age of advanced finance capitalism (Crouch, 2004).

The term 'radical democracy' may mean a number of different things. Most generally, it refers to a way of organizing everyday life and political relationships that is independent from organized institutions of power, egalitarian, and collective and participatory. There is an additional emphasis in most cases on the process of self-governance and organization, and on continually struggling to overcome the institutional, material, cultural, cognitive, symbolic and emotional obstacles to democratic relationships which are encountered in this process. Radical democracy is sometimes used as another term for 'deep' democracy, which Jason Vick characterized as having six elements: 'a strongly egalitarian sensibility, an emphasis on citizen participation, a concern for individual development, an expansive notion of the political, a critique of existing democratic institutions and practices, and a critique of capitalism as it currently operates' (2012:1). He distinguishes truly radical democracy, however, by three additional dimensions: receptivity to 'agonism and concern for difference', a belief that real politics is an 'often sporadic and rare' activity, and an attention to 'the surplus time, resources and localism that is necessary to partake in politics' (Vick, 2012:1). For John Dewey (1937), democracy was always-already 'radical' because it is such a highly demanding form of political organization, which requires significant change not only at the level of institutions but at the level of everyday life. 'The fundamental principle of democracy', he wrote, 'is that the ends of freedom and individuality for all can be attained only by the means that accord with those ends'. The end of democracy, he continued, 'is a radical end, for it is an end that has not been adequately realized in any country at any time'.

'Critical pedagogy' as a discipline, project and way of life

In order to construct this conversation, it may be useful to conceptualize critical pedagogy as a historical project, and in the broadest sense a way of life, rather than simply as an academic discipline or methodology for teaching and learning. Projects of radical, democratic and progressive education extend back centuries, though our knowledge of many remains obscured in the undocumented shadows of social history (McManus, 2004; Waugh, 2009). The emergence of critical pedagogy as a distinctive field of academic knowledge and practice, however, is a more recent phenomenon. While there are some references to critical pedagogy in German educational literature from the 1970s, the term was more formally coined and popularized by Henry Giroux during the following decade (Darder et al., 2003:2; McLaren, 2003). Key works such as *Theory and Resistance in Education* (Giroux, 1983) and *Schooling for Democracy* (Giroux, 1989) articulated what had until then been a diffuse landscape of critical-theoretical arguments, historical and geographical experiments, and normative philosophies of education into a body of knowledge that offered a theoretical foundation for articulating 'pedagogical challenges to oppressive social formations' (Ellsworth, 1994:300).[4]

Since then, there have been numerous attempts to map the contours of critical pedagogy across time and space, explore the impacts of particular intellectual traditions on the field, and redefine it in response to theoretical challenges, the voicing of excluded subjectivities, or the emergence of new collective social needs (Giroux, 2003; McLaren, 2003; Coté et al., 2007). The development of the field has thus incorporated, almost from its inception, vigorous debates about the meaning of critique, the relationship between pedagogy and politics, the uses and abuses of conceptual abstraction, and the durable dominance of patriarchal and Eurocentric prejudices within critical theory. More recently, however, it has been argued that the institutionalization of critical pedagogy within the academy has not only domesticated the radical potential of the traditions from which it grew, but in theoretical terms created a situation in which 'critique has come to dominate radical pedagogies without the accoutrement of an alternative vision' (van Heertum, 2009:103). For, while there are many gains in clarifying a constellation of guiding principles and establishing a sense of historical location, there are also risks that a perpetually emergent terrain of thought and practice may become reified into a fixed discipline that can be known, applied and 'developed'. If we believe that critical pedagogical work in all of its variety is rooted in a theory of knowledge as being produced through 'invention and reinvention; through the restless, impatient, continuing, hopeful inquiry human beings pursue in the world, with the world and with each other', then to speak about the practice as if its meaning is determined does not honour its critical traditions, but transmogrifies it into a disciplinary 'ism' (Freire, 2000:72).

Today, however, more a two-decades deep into a period of far-reaching reforms to higher education and the growth of academic capitalism, the idea of critical pedagogy seems to have acquired an aura as the obvious 'alternative' to all forms of commodified and marketized education. At the

[4]The field of 'critical pedagogy' was constructed through the recombination of a wide range of educational and critical-theoretical work – certain Frankfurt School critical theorists; Antonio Gramsci's Analysis of intellectual power, education, hegemony and public pedagogy; the American pragmatist and democratic educational theory of John Dewey; neo Marxist critiques of educational curricula and institutions; British cultural theorists' research into reproduction and resistance in education; the post-structuralist theories of power, knowledge and subjectivity of Michel Foucault and subsequent Foucauldians; and the dialogical philosophy and popular education methods of Paulo Freire (Coté et al. 2007, Darder et al. 2003; Gur-Ze'ev 1998).

JOHN DEWEY (1859–1952)
Source: http://ece205.wikispaces.com/John+Dewey

same time, depoliticized forms of 'critical thinking' have been integrated into the curricula of university programmes oriented towards shaping the 'entrepreneurial' student–subject. And yet, what it means to think, teach or 'be' critically, in theory and in practice is rarely articulated in practice among university students or teachers. It is time, once again, to take stock.

To do so, I will take a cue from John Dewey. In 1938, after a decade of experimental work in the 'progressive' educational movement within the United States, Dewey argued that teachers should talk less about their 'progressiveness' and more about the work of education itself. The defence of any practice worthy of the progressive name, he said, should begin from 'a comprehensive, constructive survey of actual needs, problems and possibilities' within a particular society, rather than from an attachment to particular methodologies or from reacting to the traditional forms of authority that the early progressives sought to overthrow.

> '. . . Those who are looking ahead to a new movement in education, adapted to the existing need for a new social order, should think in terms of Education itself rather than in terms of some 'ism about education, even such an 'ism as 'progressivism'. For in spite of itself any movement that thinks and acts in terms of an 'ism becomes so involved in reaction against other 'isms that it is unwittingly controlled by them. For, it then forms its principles by reaction against them instead of by a comprehensive, constructive survey of actual needs, problems and possibilities'. (Dewey, 1938:6)

For Dewey, the moral and political value of pedagogical work was not lodged in their reactive opposition to 'traditional' forms of education, but rather articulated around theories of learning, experience and human flourishing in concrete circumstances. Educators' and students' decisions about what, how, why and where to teach can thus never be based on purely technical skill or theoretical knowledge. Instead, they emerge from theorizing conditions for a particular form of democratic life, articulating the practical role that certain forms of education play in this life, and attempting to create conditions for such work to be effective. This reflexive process was an integral dimension of the radically democratic transformation of the person and society itself. But when the experimental attitude of 'progressive education' ossified into a discipline to be mastered, transmitted and policed, as well as one that assumed an aura of moral and pedagogical superiority, Dewey decided that it had stopped 'progressing' as an normatively defined way of life and begun to regress into an 'ism'. I would suggest that, in a similar way, the institutionalization of critical pedagogy as a legitimate field of knowledge and practice sometimes makes the tradition appear as an authoritative source of answers for contemporary problems of education. It might more usefully be understood as a rich archive of collective problem-posing, theorization and experience that we can draw on and contribute to through our own intellectual and political projects.

Critical reason as liberation: The classical promise of critical pedagogy

Critical pedagogy is a grand tradition, which makes many promises: the development of social wisdom and a deeper understanding of one's possibilities for being and becoming in the world, liberation from all forms of self- and other-imposed repression, emancipation from states of domination, expanded social and intellectual freedoms, intellectual and political equality, the possibility of building authentic forms of community, positive experiences of personal and social transformation, mental and affective autonomy, de-alienation and human fulfilment, cultural and material empowerment, the cultivation of revolutionary subjectivities and the nurturing of sensual and erotic joy. And, in many ways, this grand tradition honours its promises over and over again, in both ordinary and extraordinary ways.

What is thus remarkable about the promise of critical pedagogy is not that so much social hope is invested in education itself (although the relationship between critical pedagogy and other forms of critical practice is an important matter of concern). What does matter is that these promises are made on the basis of a multitude of paradigms of 'criticality' – all of which assume somewhat different relationships between theoretical criticism, the production of critical knowledge, acts of liberation, practices of freedom and experiences of radical transformation in both individual subjectivity and social relationships – and one of which tends to prevail. I would like to suggest that the reliance of critical-pedagogical work on this narrow conception of criticality is what we need to better understand and, perhaps, to transgress.

To illustrate the spirit of this notion of criticality, I turn attention briefly towards another, now renowned, treatise on critical theory and social research. In 1959, C. Wright Mills wrote that the 'task and promise' of a 'quality of mind' which he called the 'sociological imagination' was that it 'enables us to grasp history and biography and the relations between the two in the society'. Through cultivating this particular form of critical reason, he argued, ordinary people cultivate their own freedom. They become less mystified by social forces and complex historical transformations, can see a 'big picture' in which to make sense of their lives, are able to question commonsense beliefs about the world, and gain the confidence to produce new narratives of their problems that reveal opportunities for acting upon them. In Mills' eyes, all of these capabilities were imperative for anyone wanting to 'make history' in societies that had gradually become dominated by bureaucracy, technocracy and scientific rationalization, and by corresponding sensibilities of confusion, fatalism and anxiety. However, for Mills, practicing the sociological imagination neither required nor justified a revolutionary politics, although it also did not exclude one. Its ambition as a force for 'rearranging human affairs in accordance with the ideals

Source: http://christopherscottsarno.blogspot.co.uk/2012/06/videos-worth-seeing-ol-man-river-by.html

of human freedom and reason' was instead tempered by Mills' more modest assertion that 'the educational and the political role of social science in a democracy is to help cultivate and sustain publics and individuals that are able to develop, to live with, and to act upon adequate definitions of personal and social realities' (Mills, 1959:192).

Mills wrote the *Sociological Imagination* in the midst of a neoconservative reformation of academic social science in US universities, in the years just following the decline of fascisms and just prior to the social and cultural revolutions of the 1960s, and as both the European welfare state and the Soviet technocratic dictatorship were briefly in ascendance. Perhaps not surprisingly, his most radical conceptions of freedom and of the role that critical reason played in defending and expanding it still resembled the brightest promises of both the Enlightenment and liberal democracy. The ontological bases for this promise were that critical reason is the quintessential capability of the free human being; that intellectually autonomous and politically emancipated individuals are the foundations of both democratic life and social transformation; and finally that the dominant social logics of capitalism, technocracy and authoritarianism not only repress this critical capacity in human beings, but more disturbingly negate the conditions of its emergence in the first place (Marcuse, 1964; Amsler, 2011). Mills, like other of his critical-theoretical contemporaries, thus argued that the 'decline of reason in human affairs' was an urgent problem, and that any vision for an alternative society must include the education of a political subject 'whose independent reasoning would have structural consequences for their societies, its history, and thus for their own life fates' (1959:174).

It followed from this that the main purpose of progressive education is to enable people to understand how 'given social structures, especially power structures, increase or decrease the ability of self-determination, what kind of conditions they establish for the self-understanding of individuals, and under what conditions they support positive self-esteem through social esteem' (Scherr, 2008:147). The classical image of the critically educated subject is that of an individual who is *discerning* – capable of confident, independent judgement about her own experiences, not easily dominated through deception, manipulation or ideology; *autonomous* – capable and desirous of questioning, challenging and transcending the status quo; sceptical of authority in both its legitimate and illegitimate forms; *critically oppositional* to power for reasons justified by the rigorous study of its mechanisms; and *reflexive* – willing and able to turn these arts of critical reason back onto her own knowledge claims, actions and relationships in order to rationally minimize her own role in reproducing power relations.

Versions of this rational–critical subject appear throughout the critical-pedagogical imagination. We can see her in the person who is challenged through learning 'to recognize, engage, and critique (so as to transform) any existing undemocratic social practices and institutional structures that produce and sustain inequalities and oppressive social identities and relations' (Leistyna and Woodrum, 1999). She is the 'other' of the person that Paulo Freire feared was produced through authoritarian forms of education – 'not a conscious being (*corpoconsciente*) [but] rather the possessor of a consciousness: an empty "mind" passively open to the reception of deposits of reality from the world outside' (Freire, 2000:75); a dominated person who is 'crushed, diminished, converted into a spectator, manoeuvred by myths which powerful social forces have created' (Freire, 1974:5). We can see her in Peter McLaren's argument that emancipatory knowledge 'helps us understand how social relationships are distorted and manipulated by relations of power and privilege', and can help us to create 'the conditions under which irrationality, domination and oppression can be overcome and transformed through deliberative, collective action', and that it constitutes 'the foundation for social justice, equality and empowerment' (2003:73).

This rational–critical subject figures most prominently in work shaped by the theoretical concerns of the Frankfurt School around 'education in the subjects of knowledge, autonomy, reflectivity and agency, transformation/production/reproduction, and representation of reality' (GurZe-ev, 1998), and thus by themes of political economy and the critique of capitalism; the politics and culture of knowledge, ideology, hegemony and instrumental reason; and acts of resistance, praxis, and counter-hegemony (Darder et al., 2003; Giroux, 2003). However, she also features more widely in all work which maintains that there is an inherent relationship between individual consciousness, the collective recognition and understanding of power, the production of critical knowledge, the transformation of the knowing subject, and social liberation.

Despite the persuasive – and not altogether ungrounded – power of this narrative, it has rarely been accepted at face value. It is understood, for example, that for this type of critical practice to effectively disrupt power in everyday life, the social structures and institutions in question must be at least democratically accountable enough that knowledge *could* play a serious role in their transformation. Indeed, as Michel Foucault (1997b) argued in one of his later interviews, this particular type of 'critical attitude' must be understood as a historical formation that developed in response to a very particular form of governance, rather than as a universal human capability that can be liberated or repressed in any situation ('What is Critique?'). Nevertheless, this rationalist paradigm of criticality, although heavily qualified and transformed, continues to exert considerable influence on our commonsense understandings of the relationship between knowledge, learning, transformative politics and human freedom in critical pedagogical work. It also often does so in the absence of systematic reflection about whether this paradigm is most appropriate for guiding our educational work in the

BAR CODE EDUCATION
Source: http://www.blackyouthproject.com/2012/03/bull-sht-youth/

present moment. The question is, how do we renew the cultural traditions of critical pedagogy for the needs of our own time and place in such a way that is critically discerning about what we would like to renew in this tradition, and what we desire to transform?[5]

In response to this question, I will suggest that we begin with an analysis of our current struggles, needs and desires, and a map of desired and possible future paths, and that we work from these to identify the particular kinds of knowledge, relationship, skills, spaces and times, and sensibilities that could facilitate a journey from here to there. Before doing this, however, I would like to introduce traditions of work in feminist and indigenous pedagogies, public pedagogy and some untapped pedagogical insights from critical philosophy that offer different paradigms of criticality, and that emphasize the constructive and creative practices which critique-centric pedagogy seeks more implicitly to defend and proliferate. I am principally interested in the practices which are generally regarded as essential within

[5] Here again, I take inspiration from both the critical project of Nikolas Kompridis (2005, 2006) and Mills' *Sociological Imagination*. For, although the latter has become sociological common sense, it emerged in its time as a radical rethinking of the role of critical reason in defending and advancing human freedom. He argued that the theoretical paradigms which had emerged dominant from the Enlightenment – liberalism and socialism – had 'virtually collapsed as adequate explanations of the world and of ourselves' because they had become 'guidelines to reflection about types of society which do not now exist' (Mills, 1959, pp. 166, 167).

critical theory, but simultaneously not seen as being directly related to critique: non-alienating relationships with self, others and the environment; affirmation and respect; respect for difference and alterity in encounters with others; the emotional and affective conditions for and experiences of critique, experimentation, dialogue and understanding; individual and collective courage; creativity and imagination; and the construction of community, friendship and solidarity.

Beyond and before critique: Critical pedagogy's silenced selves and quiet others

Critical pedagogy is most commonly identified with themes of political economy, the politics of knowledge, dialectical processes, ideology, hegemony, resistance, praxis, dialogue and conscientization (Darder et al., 2003). However, the term may just as easily be identified with themes of formation and transformation, creativity, plurality and multiplicity, imagination, affective experience, and the creation of friendships, communities and solidarities. I would here like to call attention to work that privileges the latter concepts, which resonate with key principles of radical democracy, including the epistemology of ambiguity; a generous faith in human possibility; respect for a plurality of knowledges, including the affective and embodied; and an embracing of practices of experiment and encounter.

Some of the most exciting paradigms of criticality in higher education today are those that question the epistemological and ethical privilege of

KARIN TURNER – FAME FORTUNE AND ROMANCE
Source: "Fame, Fortune and Romance" by Karin Turner
http://legacy.library.ucsb.edu/subjects/blackfeminism/ed_phil.html

conceptual critique itself. Decades of work by feminist scholars and activists, for example, has demonstrated how claims to some sort of generalized 'empowerment' can obscure how even the most 'critical' pedagogy can reproduce androcentric, ethnocentric, logocentric, colonialist and heteronormative knowledge and relationships within educational spaces (Darder et al., 2003:17; Gore, 2003:332–3), and how the apparent inability of many theorists to descend from conceptual abstractions such as 'critical democracy, individual freedom, social justice and social change' inhibits understandings of people's everyday lives (Ellsworth, 1994:302). Much of this work has not begun from the assumption that critical pedagogy constitutes an inherently radical challenge to dominant regimes of power. On the contrary, it has often emerged from situations in which women have experienced critical-pedagogical work as being alienating, oppressive or exclusionary in its own right (hooks, 1994; Delgado Bernal, 2006; Villenas et al., 2006; Elenes, 2010). This is beautifully illustrated in the work of feminist and indigenous scholar Sandy Grande, whose particular vision of 'red pedagogy' for American Indian children eschews abstract principles of empowerment or generalized critiques of capitalism, which she argues are themselves imbued with colonial power, and is instead grounded in a form of pedagogy that 'cultivates a sense of collective agency, both to curb the excesses of dominant power and to revitalize indigenous communities' and local knowledge and traditions (Grande, 2004).

A few other examples may suffice to indicate the decentring significance of this experience. We may look to Elizabeth Ellsworth's (1994) exposition on how abstract concepts such as 'empowerment', 'voice', 'dialogue' and 'criticality' worked in her US university classroom as 'repressive myths' that perpetuated dynamics of racism, sexism and classism. She and her students had underestimated the extent to which pre-existing power relations shaped their own 'critical' activities in ways that were not illuminated by the conceptual orthodoxies of critical pedagogy. She also illustrated how teachers who assume that 'rationality [is] a self-evident political act against relations of domination' may unwittingly silence students who, rather than mastering the arts of polite theoretical discourse, might be better served by finding ways to 'talk back' to epistemologies of power and privileged languages. In other contexts, feminist educators have illustrated how the general will to 'empowerment' in critical pedagogy can be compromised by the assumption that power is a capacity which can be revoked and bestowed, and that any human being can 'exercise . . . power in an attempt to help others exercise power' without also being integrated into the exercise of power itself (Gore, 2003). The complexities of such power have been drawn out by writers such as Diane Gillespie, Leslie Ashbaugh and JoAnn DeFeiore (2002), a group of scholars teaching 'white women about white privilege, race cognizance and social action'. For many of their students, the conceptual criticism of racial systems also required acts of radical self-critique and uncomfortable encounters with others, and the discomforting encounter with these in turn demanded attention to emotional as well as intellectual pedagogies. Far from being regarded as distractions, however, conceptualizing critique as an intrinsically affective practice allows us to see such moments as vital for the cultivation of critical sensibilities; as 'border crossings' into new territories of difference and possibility (Giroux, 2005:20). It also allows us to understand that genuinely transformative learning often evokes collective feelings of anger, fear and loss, and to see that these feelings that under ordinary circumstances play a powerful role in preserving power relations even when they are intellectually dismantled (Boler, 1999; Boler and Zembylas, 2003; Do Mar Pereira, 2012). One of the most important insights of this work is therefore that the theoretical critique of systems of power cannot be separated from critical pedagogies of the self. We have learned from these redefinitions of criticality that the attributes of the classically defined 'critical subject' – discernment, autonomy, independence and reflexivity – are themselves products of pedagogical work which is often unconscious, invisible, and not necessarily critical. Here, while the epistemological privilege of critique is not revoked, it is repositioned as being partial and contingent on other cognitive, affective and social practices, including the 'somatic, felt, "noncognitive, nonrepresentational processes and events such as movement, sensation, intensity, rhythm, passage" and experiences that are not typically emphasized in traditional sites of education' (Ellsworth, 1994:352).

There are, in addition, other conceptions of critical pedagogy which expand the notion beyond a conscious, specialized activity that is performed in formal educational settings in relation to predefined theoretical or political concerns, to include the embodied, situated, everyday processes of learning and becoming. In traditions of public pedagogy, the practice of

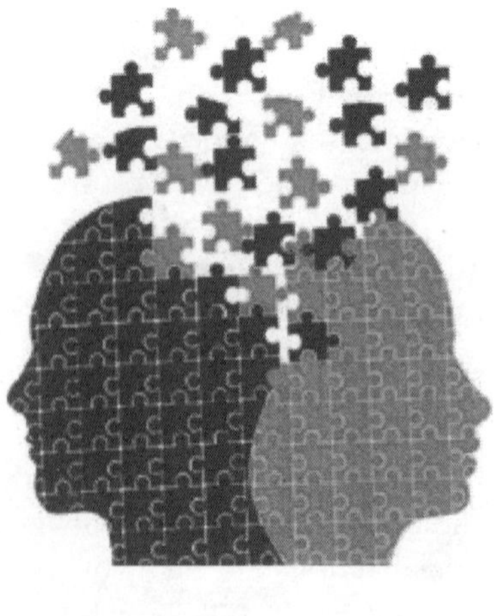

JIGSAW HEADS
Source: http://www.letswowyou.com/go.php?subsection=33

pedagogy is widely conceived as processes subject-formation that permeate everyday life through film, television and other visual media, advertising, social networking, sites of consumption, spaces of social activism and cultural spaces and institutions, as well as through the 'pervasive, undergirding neoliberal ideologies' and discourses of resistance that circulate in all of the above (Burdick and Sandlin, 2010:350; Sandlin et al., 2011). Related concepts, such as 'education-in-its-broadest-sense', also define pedagogy as a holistic and not necessarily institutionalized activity concerned with 'fostering and supporting the general well-being and development of children and young people, and their ability to interact effectively with their environment and to live a good life' (Fielding and Moss, 2010:46). Within this paradigm, critique does lose some of its politico-intellectual aura, being defined less as a specialized type of analysis or formally educated capability and more as an ordinary survival skill – what Antonio Gramsci called having 'good sense' about 'common sense'. Pedagogy here is not a set of methods which are used to teach techniques of critical analysis, but is 'a mode of cultural production and a type of cultural criticism that is essential for questioning the conditions under which knowledge is produced, values affirmed, affective investments engaged, and subject positions put in place, negotiated, taken up or refused' (Giroux, 2004:64).

In addition to the ordinary critical potential of public pedagogy, I would like to call attention to dimensions of critical philosophy that are not commonly identified as contributing to 'critical pedagogy' but that deal as much, or sometimes in more detail, with problems of learning, experience, knowledge, power, subject-formation and social formation and transformation. Some are already implicit in the critical-pedagogical canon, but not often remarked upon in the more critico-centric literature. For example, Paulo Freire's theories about the power of 'problem-posing pedagogy' and dialogue were grounded not only in his practical experiences of culture circles, but also in his philosophical analysis of the phenomenological complexities of perception, intersubjective understanding, and the limits or horizons of human intelligibility (Jurema et al., 2006; Irwin, 2012). Dismissed by materialist interpreters as an idealist distraction from political critique, Freire's insights into the phenomenon of transformative knowledge have been more seriously engaged by philosophers and theologians than by critical educators (Rivera and Arias, 2004). And yet, in circumstances where the articulation of future possibilities requires an 'ontological reframing' of reality rather than its oblique critique, a phenomenological accounting of how and why we produce knowledge with one another becomes critically important.[6] When Freire writes that 'the correct posture of one who does not consider him or herself to be the sole possessor of the truth or the

[6] For a discussion of the technique of 'ontological reframing', see Gibson–Graham (2006).

passive object of ideology or gossip is the attitude of permanent openness', and thus that 'openness to approaching and being approached, to questioning and being questioned, to agreeing and disagreeing [is] an openness to life itself and to its vicissitudes', he is offering more than a straightforward description of dialogical learning. He is also offering a theory of knowledge that is conducive to the practice of radical democratic politics – one that he urged was inconsistent with the fetishization of critical pedagogy as either a methodology or a discipline.

Finally, from a different angle, educators are being increasingly called upon to make serious replies to pedagogical questions that are being thrown open, but left unanswered, by theorists of radical democracy. There is, at least within the critical social sciences and movements, a general sense that education is a central dimension of struggles for economic and political justice, and that it 'has an important contribution to make to survival, flourishing and democracy' (Coté et al., 2007; Fielding and Moss, 2011:34). There is no shortage of theories about the types of subjects, practices, ways of knowing, institutions and relationships that make democratic life possible. However, many of these do not directly address questions of *how* these forms are to be cultivated, created, defended and contested in everyday life.[7] In their otherwise meticulously detailed book on *Postcapitalist Politics*, for example, J. K. Gibson–Graham allude to the pedagogical processes of 'self-cultivation that might equip [them] to become ethical subjects of a postcapitalist order', and to the material and social conditions of their possibility (2006:x). However, it was beyond the scope of the book to focus explicitly on these processes. Similarly, C. Douglas Lummis has argued from a different perspective that democracy is neither a system nor a set of institutions, but a 'state of being', and that democratization is thus not a process of institutional change or discernible revolution but an almost ineffable 'change of state' (1996:159). However, if this is so, what is the democratic status of our existing educational institutions, and what work might we undertake in order to make them more appropriate? In another example, Nikolas Kompridis claims that our present system of politics is a 'form of politics that drains our energies, drains our hopes and confidence in democracy, and worst of all, our very capacity for hope and confidence' (2011:256). He also argues that we need to create 'cultural practices that can reopen the future and unclose the past, cultural practices that can regenerate hope and confidence in the face of conditions that threaten to make even their regeneration meaningless' (2006:277). Much of his work to date therefore has questions of social learning at its core, and yet again, there is little scope within it to deal seriously with the futures of critical education.

[7] One very notable exception to this is Michael Fielding and Peter Moss's *Radical Education and the Common School* (2011).

What we need, therefore, is another dimension to the sociological imagination; a third arm that means we are not only developing a quality of mind that allows us to link history and biography, but also learning practices that enable us to connect these to the creation of the future. But what are these practices? They clearly cannot be confined to the operations of rational critique that have dominated critical-theoretical and critical-pedagogical orthodoxies in recent decades, any more than they can afford to abandon them. The post-democratic, neoliberal societies we presently inhabit have not become less mystifying or more accountable to reason. What we require, in the effort to cultivate radically democratic, post-capitalist forms of life in this milieu, are more theoretically and philosophically worked-out and practically embedded projects of critical education. One way forward towards this end may be to continue developing the rich and diverse traditions of progressive education that comprise contemporary critical pedagogy, and to bringing these into more intimate conversation with parallel bodies of work in critical philosophy, radical democracy and the politics of possibility. It is to the relationship between these last two practices and the future of critical pedagogy that I finally turn.

Education as a practice of freedom and becoming: Pedagogy, prefiguration, politics

As someone who is 'looking ahead to a new movement in education, adapted to the existing need for a new social order', I will heed Dewey's advice to undertake a 'comprehensive, constructive survey of actual needs, problems and possibilities' to frame my argument about the possible purpose of critical education in everyday life today (1938:6). A number of needs seem immediately pressing: the need to find effective ways of challenging deterministic and fatalistic ontologies, of responding to (or working autonomously from) democratic institutions that are neither accountable nor reformable, of challenging forms of power that operate through as well as on the self, and of producing knowledge which has an efficacy in social affairs. The problems – or, at least, some of the problems facing teachers in higher education today – are that the dominant forms of education work to reinforce one-dimensional determinism, and that we are plagued by non-democratic ways of life, repressive forms of governmentality and empty notions of criticality both in our educational institutions and in our everyday lives. And some of the most promising possibilities for resolving these problems, I would argue, are emerging from the new political imaginaries that are being crafted through the 'hope movements' and local projects in radical democracy – all of which offer forms of radical critique whose strength draws not from opposing power, but more simply from existing as evidence of its contingency and limitations.

To imagine the pedagogical practices that could contribute to advancing this work, we may consider first some of the social and political practices that characterize radical-democratic formations in both educational and other social spaces:

- a conception of democracy as an historical project, ethical way of life and/or state of being, rather than a system of institutions or an institutionalized response to them (Lummis, 1996:22, 112; Fielding and Moss, 2011:42);
- a conception of democratic practices as necessarily here and now, rather than elsewhere in the future following education or revolution (i.e., a privileging of 'prefigurative practice') (Gibson–Graham, 2006; Fielding and Moss, 2011:147);
- a commitment to social, political and economic justice in both the concrete struggles of everyday life and issues of global scale (Fielding and Moss, 2011);
- faith in human potentiality and the 'insistent affirmation of possibility', or hope (Dewey, 1939; Fielding and Moss, 2011:82);
- social relationships based on mutual trust, aid and solidarity, with the possibility for 'positional restlessness' (Fielding and Moss, 2011:154);
- an ethos of and passion for intellectual and social experimentation, particularly 'democratic experimentalism' (Dewey, 1938, 1939);
- a dedicated ethics of care and attentiveness to others (Lummis, 1996:88; Gibson–Graham, 2006); and an ethics of care for the self (e.g. 'revolutionary self-cultivation'; see Gibson–Graham 2006:xxxv);
- a politics of open-hearted, open-minded and open-ended encounters with difference, otherness and 'the new'; and
- a recognition that the self, our relationships and our histories are all 'becoming', or unfinished and not finishable (Dewey, 1937, 1938, 1939; Lummis, 1996:42; Fielding and Moss, 2011:161).

What is striking about this list is that definitions of the desired society and political subjectivities are explicitly articulated, while the theoretical critique of that which represses and oppresses them is more implicit. What is even more striking is the extent to which the project of critical pedagogy maps on to these broader principles and ideals, particularly as it has been articulated in its minoritarian lines in pedagogies of *discomfort* and *dissensus* (Boler, 1999, Boler and Zembylas, 2003; Do Mar Pereira 2012); *autonomy* and *emergence* (Dewey, 2005); and *sociality* and *community* (hooks, 2003); as well as in the *education of desire* (Levitas, 2005) and of *hope* (Bloch, 1991; Freire, 2005; Giroux, 2002). Reasoned criticism is a necessary but not sufficient condition of possibility for each of the above. It is decentred but not diminished, and comprises part of a more holistic constellation of critical and affirmative practices through which a transformative politics can be created. From within this paradigm, we no longer need presume that critique dominates radical pedagogies without hope of alternative (see van Heertum, 2009). If a major concern for some critical theorists today is 'not simply whether one can inject some optimism into the critical analysis, but whether it is still possible to formulate a critique of capitalism that points to the possibility of a different organization of social life', we can say with confidence that critical pedagogy has many things to contribute (Postone, 2012). The bringing of any of these principles into practice within the context of post-democratic social institutions constitutes a radical kind of immanent critique that, as Foucault once wrote, works 'not to judge but to bring a work, a book, a sentence and idea to life', and in doing so demonstrates the futility of regarding its alternatives as inevitable (1997a:323).

Developing new philosophies and practices of higher education around such principles allows us to move beyond forms of learning that prioritize critique of the existing order of things and towards practices that incorporate such critical work into a process of creating something new – a piece of work, a relationship, a sense of self, a feeling, a space, an imaginary, a possibility. It is here that the notion of pedagogy is rescued from the 'methods fetish' (Bartolomé, 1994) and regarded as the 'education force of our whole social and cultural experience' (Raymond Williams in Giroux, 1994). The question for those working as teachers in institutions of formal and informal education, however, is – what *do* our environments teach, and what *shall* we, or indeed, shall we, teach? What can be taught, and learned, of criticality?

I have not yet articulated adequate answers to these questions in the contexts of my own work in either formal or popular universities in England. However, I think there is much to be learned from Michel Fielding and Peter Moss's 'inventory' of the characteristics of radical-democratic education at the level of the school. These dimensions are:

- 'a proclaimed democratic vitality;
- radical structures and spaces;
- radical roles;

- radical relationships;
- personal and communal narrative;
- radical curriculum,[8] critical pedagogy and enabling assessment;
- insistent affirmation of possibility;
- engaging the local;
- accountability as shared responsibility; and
- regional, national and global solidarities'. (Fielding and Moss, 2011:73)

We might use this inventory as a framework for asking what would be required of us intellectually, affectively, politically and socially – what we would need to learn to think, feel and do – to make genuinely critical pedagogies possible and meaningful at the level of the university. In addition, I would suggest that we must continue to educate ourselves and others in the craft of an expanded sociological imagination, linking our histories and biographies to activities in the practical politics of possibility as well. This may require a tempering of certain grand promises of critical pedagogy – or at least of the narratives in which transformative experiences of emancipation, liberation and non-alienated existence are produced, as if by magic, through operations of theoretical critique. But this does not mean abandoning the radical promises of critical pedagogy or critical theory in a moment where they are so obviously required. The pedagogies of possibility that are alluded to in this chapter, which combine operations of rational critique, an ethic of care and attention to affective politics, a philosophy of contingent subjectivity and a commitment to defending social, economic and political justice in the here and now – are necessary for the defence and vitalization of real democracy. They are more radical, not less, than critical-pedagogical orthodoxies which proclaim radicality from within the systems of power they work to undermine. Again following Dewey (1939), the task of cultivating 'creative democracy' – a task renewed in each generation and for each collectivity in its own way – is still before us, and we have a wealth of theoretical and practical experience from a multitude of critical-pedagogical traditions to challenge and inspire us as we undertake it in these times.

---

[8]Fielding and Moss denote four features of a 'radical curriculum', which are 'a focus on the purposes of education', working to make sure that those studying have 'the desire and capacity to critically interrogate what is given and co-construct a knowledge that assists us in leading good and joyful lives together', a commitment to acting in one's own sphere of action, and some attention to holism in relationships and knowledge (2011:81).

References

Amsler, S. (2011) 'From "Therapeutic" to Political Education: The Centrality of Affective Sensibility in Critical Pedagogy', *Critical Studies in Education* 52(1): 47–63.

Bartolomé, L. (1994) 'Beyond the Methods Fetish: Toward a Humanizing Pedagogy', *Harvard Educational Review* 64(2): 173–95.

Bloch, E. (1991) *The Principle of Hope*. MIT Press, Cambridge, MA.

Boler, M. (1999) *Feeling Power: Emotions and Education*. Routledge, London.

Boler, M. and Zembylas, M. (2003) 'Discomforting Truths: The Emotional Terrain of Understanding Difference', in P. Trifonas (ed.), *Pedagogies of Difference: Rethinking Education for Social Change*. Routledge, London and New York, pp. 110–136.

Burdick, J. and Sandlin, J. (2010) 'Inquiry as Answerability: Toward a Methodology of Discomfort in Researching Critical Public Pedagogies', *Qualitative Inquiry* 16: 349.

Butler, J. (2002) 'What is Critique? An Essay on Foucault's Virtue', in D. Ingram (ed.), *The Political: Readings in Continental Philosophy*. Basil Blackwell, London, http://tedrutland.org./wp-content/uploads/2008/02/butler-2002.pdf (accessed 15 November 2012).

Coté, M., Day, R. and de Peuter, G. (eds) (2007) *Utopian Pedagogy: Radical Experiments against Neoliberal Globalization*. University of Toronto Press, Toronto.

Crouch, C. (2004) *Post-Democracy*. Polity Press, Cambridge.

Darder, A., Baltodano, M. and Torres, R.(eds) (2003) *The Critical Pedagogy Reader*. Routledge Falmer, NY.

Day, R. (2005) *Gramsci is Dead: Anarchist Currents in the Newest Social Movements*. Pluto Press, NY.

Delgado Bernal, D., Elenes, C., Godinez, F. and Villenas, S. (eds) (2006) *Chicana/Latina Education in Everyday Life*. SUNY Press, NY.

Dewey, J. (1937) 'Democracy is Radical', in *John Dewey, The Later Works, 1925–1953, Vol. 11*. Southern Illinois University Press, Illinois.

– (1938) *Experience and Education*. Touchstone, NY.

– (1939) 'Creative Democracy: The Task Before Us', in *John Dewey, The Later Works, 1925–1953, Vol. 14*. Southern Illinois University Press, Illinois.

– (2005) *Art as Experience*. Perigree Books, NY.

Dinerstein, A. and Deneulin, X. (2012) 'Hope Movements: Naming Mobilization in A Post-development World', *Development and Change* 43(2): 585–602.

Do Mar Pereira, M. (2012) 'Uncomfortable Classrooms: Rethinking The Role of Student Discomfort in Feminist Teaching', *European Journal of Women's Studies* 19(1): 128–35.

Elenes, C. (2010) *Transforming Borders: Chicana/o Popular Culture and Pedagogy*. Lexington Books, Plymouth.

Ellsworth, E. (1994) 'Why Doesn't This Feel Empowering? Working through the Repressive Myths of Critical Pedagogy' in L. Stone (ed.), *The Education Feminism Reader*. Routledge, NY, pp. 300–27.

Fielding, M. and Moss, P. (2011) *Radical Education and the Common School: A Democratic Alternative.* Routledge, Oxon.
Foucault, M. (1997a) 'The Masked Philosopher' in P. Rabinow (ed.), *Michel Foucault: Ethics, Subjectivity and Truth – the Essential Works of Michel Foucault.* The Free Press, NY, pp. 321–28.
– (1997b) 'What is Critique' in S. Lotringer and L. Hochroth (eds), *The Politics of Truth.* Semiotext(e), NY, pp. 23–82.
Foucault, M. and Deleuze, G. (1972) 'Intellectuals and Power', http://libcom.org/library/intellectuals-power-a-conversation-between-michel-foucault-and-gille s-deleuze (accessed 15 November 2012).
Freire, P. (1974) *Education for Critical Consciousness.* Continuum, NY.
– (2000) *Pedagogy of the Oppressed.* Continuum, NY.
– (2005) *Pedagogy of Hope: Reliving Pedagogy of the Oppressed.* Continuum, NY.
Gibson–Graham, J. K. (2006) *A Postcapitalist Politics.* University of Minnesota Press, Minnesota.
Gilbert, J. (2009) 'Postmodernity and the Crisis of Democracy', Open Democracy, 28 May, http://www.opendemocracy.net/article/opendemocracy-theme/postmodernity-and-the-crisis-of-democracy (accessed 15 November 2012).
Gillespie, D., Ashbaugh, L. and De Feiore, J. (2002) 'White Women Teaching White Women about White Privilege, Race Cognizance and Social Action: Toward a Pedagogical Pragmatics', *Race, Ethnicity and Education* 5(3): 237–53.
Giroux, H. (1983) *Theory and Resistance in Education: Towards a Pedagogy for the Opposition.* Greenwood Press, CT.
– (1989) *Schooling for Democracy: Critical Pedagogy in the Modern Age.* Routledge, NY.
– (1994) 'Doing Cultural Studies: Youth and the Challenge of Pedagogy', *Harvard Educational Review* 64(3): 278–308.
– (2002) 'Educated Hope in an Age of Privatized Visions', *Cultural Studies – Critical Methodologies* 2(1): 193–212.
– (2003) 'Critical Theory and Educational Practice' in A. Darder, M. Baltodano and R. Torres (eds), *The Critical Pedagogy Reader.* Routledge Falmer, NY, pp. 27–56.
– (2004) 'Cultural Studies, Public Pedagogy and the Responsibility of Intellectuals', *Communication and Critical/Cultural Studies* 1(1): 59–79.
– (2005) *Border Crossings: Cultural Workers and the Politics of Education*, 2nd ed. Routledge, NY.
Gore, J. (2003) 'What We Can Do for You! What *Can* 'We' Do for 'You'? Struggling over Empowerment in Critical and Feminist Pedagogy', in A. Darder, R. Torres and M. Baltodano (eds),*The Critical Pedagogy Reader.* Routledge Falmer, London and New York, pp. 331–50.
Grande, S. (2004) *Red Pedagogy: Native American Social and Political Thought.* Rowman and Littlefield, NY.
Gur-Ze'ev, X. (1998) 'Toward a Nonrepressive Critical Pedagogy', *Educational Theory* 48(4): 463–86.

Holloway, J. (2009) *Crack Capitalism*, Pluto Press, NY.
hooks, b. (2003)*Teaching Community: A Pedagogy of Hope*. Routledge, New York.
– (1994) *Teaching to Transgress. Education as the Practice of Freedom.* Routledge, London.
Irwin, J. (2012) *Paulo Freire's Philosophy of Education Origins, Developments, Impacts and Legacies*. Continuum, New York.
Jurema, A., Pimentel, M., Cordeiro, T. and Austregésilo, A. (2006). Disclosing the Making of Phenomenological Research: Setting Free the Meanings of Discourse [33 paragraphs]. *Forum Qualitative Sozialforschung / Forum: Qualitative Social Research* 7(4), Art. 7, http://nbn-resolving.de/urn:nbn:de:0114-fqs060473.
Kompridis, N. (2005) 'Disclosing Possibility: The Past and Future of Critical Theory ', *International Journal of Philosophical Studies* 13(3): 325–51.
– (2006) *Critique and Disclosure: Critical Theory between Past and Future* MIT Press, Cambridge, MA.
– (2011) 'Receptivity, Possibility and Democratic Politics', *Ethics & Global Politics* 4(4): 255–72.
Leistyna, P. and Woodrum, A. (1999) 'Context and Culture: What is Critical Pedagogy?' in P. Leistyna, A. Woodrum, and S. A. Sherblom (eds), *Breaking Free: The Transformative Power of Critical Pedagogy*. Harvard Education Press, Cambridge, MA, Harvard Educational Review. 1–11.
Levitas, R. (2005) 'The Imaginary Reconstitution of Society, Or, Why Sociologists and Others Should Take Utopia More Seriously', Inaugural Lecture, University of Bristol, 24 October, www.bristol.ac.uk/sociology/staff/pubs/Levitasinaugural (accessed 15 November 2012).
Marcuse, H. (1964) *One-dimensional Man: Studies in the Ideology of Advanced Industrial Society*, Beacon Press, Boston.
McLaren, P. (2003) 'Critical Pedagogy: A Look at the Major Concepts' in A. Darder, R. Torres and M. Baltodano (eds),*The Critical Pedagogy Reader*. Routledge Falmer, London and New York, pp. 69–96.
McManus, A. (2004) *The Irish Hedge School and Its Books, 1695–1831*. Fourcourts Press, Dublin.
Mills, C. W. (1959) *The Sociological Imagination*. Free Press, NY.
Postone, M. (2012) 'Thinking the Global Crisis', *South Atlantic Quarterly* 11(2): 227–49.
Rivera, R. and Arias, A. (2004) *A Study of Liberation Discourse: The Semantics of Opposition in Freire and Gutierrez*. Peter Lang, Oxon.
Sandlin, J., O'Malley, M. and Burdick, J. (2011) 'Mapping the Complexity of Public Pedagogy Scholarship: 1894–2010', *Review of Educational Research* 81: 338.
Scherr, A. (2008) 'Social Subjectivity and Mutual Recognition as Basic Terms of a Critical Theory of Education' in G. Fischmann (ed.),*Critical Theories, Radical Pedagogies and Global Conflicts*. Rowman and Littlefield, NY, pp. 245–a54.
vanHeertum, R. (2009) 'Moving from Critique to Hope: Critical Interventions from Marcuse to Freire' in D. Kellner (ed.), *Marcuse's Challenge to Education*. Rowman and Littlefield, NY, pp. 103–16.

Vick, J. (2012) 'Participatory Democracy, Radical Democracy, and the Future of Democratic Theory', paper presented at the Western Political Science Association, Portland, Oregon, 20–22 March, http://wpsa.research.pdx.edu/meet/2012/vick.pdf (accessed 15 November 2012).

Waugh, C. (2009) '"Plebs": The Lost Legacy of Independent Working-class Education', a *Post-16 Educator occasional publication*, London, http://ifyoucan.org.uk/PSE/Home_files/PSE%20Plebs%20pamphlet.pdf. (accessed 15 November 2012).

CHAPTER FOUR

Pedagogies of Possibility: In, against and beyond the Imperial Patriarchal Subjectivities of Higher Education

Sara C. Motta[1]

In this chapter:

- I discuss my experience of introducing critical pedagogy into an MA course in an elite University.
- I critically interrogate the assumed resonances and compatibilities between critical pedagogy and institutionally recognized (and produced) 'critical' subjectivities.
- I conceptualize and analyse the relative openness and closure in student subjectivities to a critical pedagogy committed to multiplicity, horizontalism and 'otherness'.
- I develop a pedagogical pragmatics (Gillespie et al., 2002) in light of my reflections.
- Talk about what this has taught me in thinking about what critical pedagogy as political project actually represents.
- I conclude with a discussion and analysis of student experiences of this teaching.

---

[1]Sara Motta completed this work while working at the University of Nottingham. She is currently Senior Lecturer in Politics at the University of Newcastle, NSW, Australia. Her research focus continues to be concerned with the politics of subaltern resistance, with particular reference to Latin America and the reinvention of new forms of popular politics, political subjectivities and ways of life that seek to transcend neoliberal capitalism.

> *'It is not enough to change the content of the conversation, it is of the* ***essence*** *to change the terms of the conversation. Changing the terms of the conversation implies going beyond disciplinary or interdisciplinary controversies and the conflict of interpretations. As far as controversies and interpretations remain within the same rules of the game (terms of the conversation) the control of knowledge is not called into question. And in order to call into question the modern/colonial foundations of the control of knowledge it is necessary to focus on the knower rather than the known'.*
>
> (MIGNOLO, 2009:4)

This chapter seeks to theorize the possibilities and limitations of introducing critical pedagogy into an elite HE university setting with a majority of students and staff *not* desiring social and political transformation. Reflecting upon my practice as part of the Nottingham Critical Pedagogy Group, this chapter builds on previous research (Motta, 2012a) where I theorized neoliberalism as not merely a set of institutional procedures, standards and dictates but rather as a process that is embedded in, and reproduced through, the construction of particular forms of disciplined and (self)-disciplining subjects. Within this setting, and from this theoretical framework, the possibilities of critical pedagogy became not the construction of collective struggle, the development of *a* political strategy or the formation of activists but rather the creation of emotional, embodied, and intellectual pedagogies of possibility. Such pedagogies of possibility aim to foster openings in students and teachers/researchers to other ways of doing, being and thinking which, however momentarily, transgress the reproduction of the competitive, individualized and disembodied academic labourer and the docile, depoliticized consumer student.

In this research and that of other critical pedagogy scholars Megan Bolen (1999), Elizabeth Ellsworth (1989) and Diane Gillespie et al. (2002), resistances to critical pedagogy in the classroom have been most visible and palpable at the interface of our classroom interactions with students. The experience of introducing critical pedagogy into the classroom to challenge 'race', class, gender and epistemological privilege through de-centering and deconstructing dominant frames of knowing can result not in opening but rather closure, derision, anger and rejection. For others being asked to bring mind, body and self into the classroom when the norms of student subjectivity involve instrumental and disassociated learning can be reacted to by disassociation from the class, teacher and course. As Gillespie et al. comment: 'We walk a fine line in challenging and engaging our students while not losing them altogether' (2002:245).

Our initial experience of introducing critical pedagogy onto an MA module, not explicitly identified with social justice or critical pedagogy but embedded in a critical pedagogy philosophy of education, seemed to confirm that student resistances were the result of having dominant frames of knowing, being and producing the world actively decentred and destabilized (Motta, 2012a). However, in the subsequent development of our critical pedagogy project, particularly the design and implementation of a core MA module, Social and Global Justice in Action, which is explicitly organized around a critical pedagogy model of student-based learning, we found that resistances came from subjects that not only identified with dominant subjectivities but also those who identified as 'revolutionary' and 'critical'. The latter, were subjects whom we had assumed would identify with the objectives, methods and pedagogies of the course.

This raised a series of questions:

- Is there of necessity a symbiotic and mutually reinforcing relationship between critical pedagogy and all critical subjectivities?
- What are the limitations of the critical subjectivities that are fostered and 'allowed' within the commodified and elitist knowledge-producing space of the neoliberal university?
- How might we conceptualize with greater depth, nuance and sensitivity the relative openness and closure to critical thought and practice in the subjectivities of students?
- How might we use this process as a means to collectively deepen our understanding of the possibilities and limitation of our critical pedagogy praxis and develop that pedagogical practice?

In this chapter I aim to contribute to the work of beginning to answer these questions by mapping them around three areas, the nature of knowledge, the subject of knowledge and the practice of learning. This is based on my participation as a convenor of the MA module and a series of interviews with seven students from its first cohort. I conceptualize these resistances, tensions, closures through post-colonial, and subaltern and black feminist writings. The 'critical' subjectivity fostered, encouraged and recognized in the university setting in many ways mirrors the liberal humanist subject of the enlightenment, a subject integral to the (re)production of the power/knowledge nexus of patriarchal colonial capitalism premised upon alienated separations and hierarchies between mind/body, intellect/emotion, theory/practice and education/life. Both subjectivities reproduce these hierarchical separations which allow them to be easily imbricated into the current contours of neoliberal subjectivity. My critical reflection on the possibilities and limitations of our praxis of introducing critical pedagogy into an elite HE setting aims to disrupt any reading of the problematics of the neoliberal university through its comparison with the heyday of liberal humanist higher education system. I rather pull out the continuities in both systems and therefore foreground the need to disrupt and decentre enlightenment epistemological politics and subjectivities, both liberal humanist and revolutionary/critical.

The estrangements of patriarchal colonial capitalism

I develop a theoretical framing which draws on the theorizations of subaltern feminist Gloria Anzaldúa (2007) and black feminists Audre Lorde (2000) and bell hooks (2000), particularly their insights about the relationships between power, knowledge and the production of the alienated, gendered subject of patriarchal capitalism, and post-colonial theorist Walter Mignolo (2009) who compliments this with his focus on the representational and epistemological aspects of alienation within the politics of colonial capitalism.

For subaltern and black feminists patriarchal capitalism is built upon alienations and separations embedded within a world view of individualism and materialism. This produces an instrumental and indifferent relationship to nature, the denial of other worldviews, the devaluing of the emotional and embodied and its manifestation in relationships of power-over, hierarchy and competition in the subjective and social realms (Anzaldúa, 2007; bell hooks, 2000, particularly Chapters one and two).

Such alienated subjectivities and social relationships are also gendered. Emotionality while feminized is also associated with the irrational, the unruly and the shameful, something to be controlled to avoid disruption to the normal and rational social and physic order (Anzaldúa, 2007:38–40; Lorde, 2000:1–4). Alienation thus becomes embedded in our bodies, impoverishing our bodily relationships with each other and ourselves, and distorts our emotions resulting in toxic blockages and repressions (Lorde, 1984). The pinnacle of the knowing subject within such a structuring of social relationships is symbolically represented by Rodin's statue, 'The Thinker', who is the detached, rational (masculinized) subject, able to control their unruly and irrational emotions and bodily desires (Lorde, 1984; hooks, 2000).

For post-colonial thinkers the legitimization and naturalization of the unequal power relationships of global capitalism is also produced through a particular way of thinking/approach to knowing which situates 'the West', the individual rational subject, theory as conceptual abstraction and

RODIN'S THINKER
Source: http://i.materialise.com/blog/entry/3d-printing-rodins-thinker

a project of homogenizing universalism as/at the pinnacle of development and progress (2009:2–3). In this the letter and word become the anchor of knowledge which entails a divorcing of the word from the world. The result is to situate the European epistemological bourgeois monological and individualized subject as the centre through which all other contents and forms of epistemological practice would be judged and devalued.

Therefore for subaltern and black feminists and post-colonial thinkers there is a clear politics of knowledge which is based on a monological closure and silencing of all 'others'. Emotional, embodied, oral, popular and spiritual knowledges are delegitimized, invisibilized and denied (Mignolo, 2009:2). Such a conceptualization creates relationships of 'power-over' between the knower and the known subject. A particular form of knowing, knowledge-generation and knowledge has thus become transformed into the universal epistemology (Mignolo, 2009:3–4).

The enlightenment liberal knowing subject was, and is therefore an alienated subject enacting power-over 'others'. Such alienation and separations also mark twentieth-century hegemonic understandings of critical social theories such as Marxism and anarchism. In different ways, each posited and reinforced an essentialized humanist subject of transformation and a conceptualization of the role of theorists/intellectuals as guides of the political activities of movements. Within both, power was often viewed as object manifested in structures of state and capital, humanity understood as having an essentialized nature that was oppressed by such power; and *a* utopia and strategy were proposed in which true knowledge was to be found in the realm of rational thought (Motta, 2012b:394–95). Such ontological and epistemological assumptions and resultant political praxis mirror and reproduce the separations between mind/body, intellect/emotion and practice/theory embedded in the epistemological politics of the liberal subject of patriarchal colonial capitalism (Mignolo, 2009:15–19).

Thus, theory was assumed to take the form of conceptual and theoretical knowledges, invisibilizing other forms of knowledge. Theory was conceptualized as a practice occurring through a process of abstraction perfected by individual thinkers who analysed the nature of power and of resistance, inevitably speaking for the oppressed. Such a paradigm of theoretical production reproduced a representational praxis of epistemology (and politics) in which there was a division labour between doers and thinkers, intellectual labour and practical labour and an invisibilization and de-legitimization of 'other' forms of knowing and creating knowledge (Motta, 2012b:394–95). The logics of the political became a performance of the knower who sought to disprove and eradicate his political opponents and convince others of the rationality and truth of his arguments and analysis.

Neoliberal marketization in Higher Education marks an intensification, not a break, with the epistemological logics of patriarchal colonial capitalism. It is embedded in the intensification of the separations and unsustainable logics of estrangements between mind and body, intellect and emotion, knower and known, and education and life. Distinct from the liberal humanist period of Higher Education is the attempted erasure of the possibility of thinking otherwise in the realm of theoretical abstraction.

This monological conceptual closure is constituted through multiple micro-practices of bureaucratization and professionalization. Through these practices, university educators are produced as particular disciplined subjects enacting particular performances of self with emotional repertoires and embodied enactments. The ideal type neoliberal subject is grounded in individualization, infinite flexibility, precarious commitments, orientated toward survivalist competition and personally profitable exchanges. This produces a space of hierarchy, competition and individualism through the eradication of spaces of solidarity, care and community. Some subjects and forms of behaving, feeling and embodying space are empowered and legitimized. While others are delimited, disciplined and subjected to the dominant logics, allowing some to judge and others to be judged. Imposed standards of excellence and quality are those to which the ideal subject is produced against and through (see Motta, 2012c, for a more systematic development of this analysis).

These logics are intensely embodied through the production of self-disciplining subjects articulated through abrasive dynamics of power against self and other. As Michalinos Zembylas has observed we must 'regulate and control not only our overt habits and morals, but [our] inner emotions, wishes and anxieties' (2003:120). Within this the rational, disembodied competitive and output-oriented aspects of intellectual production (present in the liberal humanist and dominant critical theorizations of knowledge production and the knowing subject) are intensified. Marketized HE reinforces and teaches the embodied, intellectual and emotional rule regimes of self-subjectification that maintain the hegemonic raced, classed and gendered subjectivities and separations constitutive of the epistemological logics of patriarchal colonial capitalism.

Pedagogies of possibility in, against and beyond the epistemological logics of colonial, patriarchal capitalism

One of the key problematic that educators committed to transgressing these epistemological logics face is how to create a pedagogical practice of non-hierarchical differences. Central elements of this are an ethics of love; love as an ethic of affirmation of power with and within, love as openness to multiplicity (both ontologically and epistemologically). As Peter Mclaren suggests, 'authentic love opens up the self to the Other'. (2000:171). The characteristics of the educator imbued with an ethics of love are to question and dare with courage yet not as an anesthetized self-denying love but as an intensely embodied practice in the present and processes of embodied spaces and relationships. Pedagogical commitments must be attentive to the concrete and the rootedness of everyday life. This sets the grounds for difference in intimacy in which life unfolds through openness to multiplicity and difference (in self and other). As Paolo Freire argued, 'As individuals or as peoples, by fighting for the restoration of [our] humanity [we] will be attempting the restoration of true generosity. And this fight, because of the purpose given it, will actually constitute an act of love'. (2000:45).

Actualizing in a meaningful way such an ethics of love involves commitment to a politics of care. Such a politics of care implies an affective and intellectual recognition of the 'other' which forms the basis from which to forge commitment, responsibility and sociability which can contribute to the building of the pedagogies of possibility that can create openings to being, thinking, and acting otherwise. Our ethical commitments therefore suggest that the pedagogical spaces we create need to be mindful to creating trusting and safe spaces and for this we need our own space which transgresses the logics of being of neoliberal patriarchal capitalism. Only through creating such spaces can we weave together conditions for openness, courage and transgression. These ethical commitments mean that our pedagogies are not about transmitting a particular knowledge, conceptualizing knowledge as theory, and imagining the role of the pedagogue as giving the gift on knowledge to those who 'lack'. Rather as critical educators our role is to create spaces imbued in an ethics of love and care embodied in the concrete realities of everyday life in which multiple knowledges can be shared and students (and facilitators) can collectively develop their self-understanding for transformation (with no pre-determined end of self/other or political orientation).

This commitment therefore involves opening up conceptual, affective and embodied pedagogical possibilities to transgress the dualisms between thought/practice, life/education, mind/body and intellect/emotion. This involves an orientation towards the other (both in self and other), an act of bridging which as Anzaldúa (2002:3) suggests means, 'loosening our borders, not closing off to others. Bridging is the work of opening the gate to the stranger, within and without. To step across the threshold is to be stripped of the illusion of safety because it moves us into unfamiliar territory and does not grant safe passage'.

To embrace the stranger within and without involves a deconstructive embrace and a constructive affirmation which does not seek to envelop all in a singular one but enables multiplicity to flourish. Pedagogically this involves deconstructing the dominant frame of knowledge and dethroning the imperial subject of knowing from his epistemic privilege (see Motta, 2012a for a fuller discussion of this pedagogical practice). It also involves fostering pedagogical processes of collective construction of knowledges and an embrace of multiple knowledges as a means of creating prefigurative moments beyond the epistemological logics of patriarchal capitalist coloniality.

Nottingham Critical Pedagogy Project

This epistemological and pedagogical orientation has shaped and been shaped by my participation in the Nottingham Critical Pedagogy Project. This project has its origins from discussion among a number of staff and postgraduates based in the Centre for the Study of Social and Global Justice (CSSGJ), University of Nottingham, begun in the summer of 2008. We

"THE ARRIVAL" by Shaun Tan
Source: From "The Arrival" by Shaun Tan http://www.shauntan.net/

agreed to develop a project that would focus on the systematization of our experience and knowledge of critical pedagogy and develop this as a core strand of our praxis as researchers, teachers and intellectuals. An underlying orientation of the project was the idea that we were opening spaces of possibility for thinking, acting and being otherwise against the logic of a commodification of social relationships and subjectivities in the neoliberal university (see http://nottinghamcriticalpedagogy.wordpress.com/ and Motta, 2012a for further details).

In the Critical Pedagogy working-group with MA students on our Social and Global Justice MA from the 2008/9 cohort and the three co-organizers of the Critical Pedagogy Project, we agreed that a new MA module embedded in a student led methodology of critical pedagogy would be an ideal way to further the practical implementation of critical pedagogy. Importantly in our theorizations and curriculum development we were explicitly **not** attempting to homogenize the praxis of critical pedagogy in our centre or with our colleagues, but rather open up spaces for experimentation and a 'reaching beyond' ourselves. Out of this process of critical reflection we mapped out the basic contours and underlying philosophy of education for a new core MA module Social and Global Justice in Action.

The course has run for 2 years. It lasts one semester (10 weeks) with each week organized around a key question in social and global justice. The nature of the questions chosen has varied immensely from discussion over food sovereignty and security, to the contemporary relevance of Hegel's thought for social justice, to the role of art in social and political change. Weekly classes run for three consecutive hours in which two members of the teaching team are present (See Annex A for an example of the module guide). The first two hours explore the problematic/question of the week and is run and facilitated by students. In the final hour a member of the teaching team introduces the topic of the following week and supports students in the mapping out of key issues related to the topic and the selection of two or three questions they would like to explore in the seminar. The teacher-facilitator of that theme then meets on at least one other occasion to discuss the student-facilitators' class plan and rationale.

In the first year of its implementation particular resistances, tensions and closures became visible, not merely from students with attachments to neoliberal student subjectivities but from those who self-identified as revolutionary and critical. Below I map out and reflect upon three areas along which these tensions manifested, offering reflections of their origins and implications for the possibilities and limitations of introducing CP into our elite HE setting.

On expertise and truth

From the beginnings of the course it was palpably clear that some students were sceptical of a course in which they did the majority of the 'visible' labour of teaching, and in which there was no lecturing. This scepticism manifested in silently spoken comments, which were not obviously antagonistic, but which had an energy of derision and doubt. It also manifested in discontent outside of the classroom, in mutterings and comments during the break and in what Scott (1987) would call foot-dragging which when asked to break into groups and undertake certain tasks these would be done with obvious reluctance. These were everyday forms of resistance. The subjects who were the most discontented with this way of teaching the course fell into two groups: the majority subject in our setting – white middle class, confident and academically successful; and the revolutionary middle class and highly academically successful. When interviewed individuals that feel into these groups felt that there were true and right knowledges and that those with expertise in those knowledges needed to take the lead in teaching them to students. As Student A, representative of the profile of the majority of our students reflected:

> It was an interesting and fun approach . . . but overall in the class I didn't get the same benefit as if an expert and a teacher had led it.

Or as Student E, representative of the revolutionary, critical and highly successful student expressed:

> If you are learning something new for the first time, I would want to have an expert, a teacher, who can lecture me. After that I can do my readings and come up with arguments . . . after that but first I want to know the established positions by someone who knows that . . . maybe because we were expected to do all this some sessions didn't work as the students facilitating didn't know about these subjects.

The everyday resistances expressed by these students had their origins in feelings of disappointment and a belief that they were not getting the same quality of learning as in 'traditional' teaching formats. This understanding is embedded in a sense of epistemological lack which needs to be filled by the expert-teacher. It mirrors the banking understanding of knowledge in which knowledge is an object/a set of ideas and facts that need to be deposited by the knower-teacher into the student. In some sense it represents a level of doubt about one's ability to know and learn autonomously. The flip side of this is an embrace of the need for the passivity of the student and a belief that some forms of belief and understanding are irrational and non-scientific. As Student A reflected:

> I don't agree that all knowledges are equal . . . some are preconceived ideas, traditions, religious views . . . I don't see how these are equal to scientific knowledge that comes about through scientific research . . . the readings took this too far . . . I couldn't follow or identify with this . . . just because something is popular doesn't make it scientific.

An outcome of this perspective is that there are also some who know and those who don't know in the class, positioning these students in the position of knower within the student-group and either feeling or enacting a position of power over others. As Student A continues:

> I wasn't confused, unconfident or uncertain in any of the topics . . . others might be uncomfortable depending on social background or knowledge of a topic, or with discussing with someone with much more experience.

Or as Student E expresses:

> Some of us dominated the space . . . I might be one of them . . . Some people had great problems just understanding basic concepts . . . The week on Marxism there was a girl who hadn't studied any Marx who said to me a number of times 'please can you do the talking' and obviously you can't say no . . . So this theoretical broadness made it very challenging for some people.

Such understandings of the true and better nature of some theoretical knowledges over others, of knowledge as a set of arguments that can be transmitted from expert teacher to lacking student, and the concurrent conceptualization that some students lack more than others, reinforces (despite by Student E's, for example, explicit opposition to) the epistemological hierarchies (or as Mignolo would argue 'remains within the terms of the conversation') that the neoliberal university reproduces (albeit with a different content).

Conversely we found that students who came from non-traditional backgrounds or came to the university via a non-traditional route – those who in our elite context are clearly marked as 'other' – were sceptical about the objective nature of academically produced theoretical knowledge. As Student B, a white lower middle-class student, reflects on his initial feelings about the course:

> I sort of always had an interest in questions of social and global justice . . . I felt in a lot of these cases I wanted to learn how groups bring themselves into action rather than ideas passed on to them . . . I liked therefore the idea that teachers and ideas can be used in a proactive way by just normal people.

Or Student D a mature working-class student explains:

> I had struggled to do the MA course because of financial reasons this affects my opinions and outlook . . . I work heavily and borrowed to scrape together enough for the course . . . I thought it was fantastic . . . anything getting away from hierarchy in teaching and knowledge.

As Student C, a mature working class local student, discusses:

> I've always liked other perspectives . . . African and feminist . . . It feels quite different here from where I last studied. There I was taught by black and feminist lecturers. Here I've realized that there is racism and sexism and academia isn't free of this like I'd assumed from my experiences.

Students from these non-traditional backgrounds who were 'other' in our setting came with a level of openness that stemmed from their life and educational experiences. This openness enabled significant transformations. As Student B continues:

> I feel more empowered . . . the idea that as students you can be part of the process of creating knowledge makes me feel confident to be part of academia not just produced passively. My theoretical perspective has changed. I do feel that there are other knowledges . . . you don't just have to rely on academic work or official politicians to understand politics.

Or as Student C, explains:

> By the end I felt different. I felt we'd been part of something quite special . . . a radical way of being taught . . . this is rare . . . I now notice who makes theory and that the majority is dominated by rich white men but in the course we looked at knowledges created by women, communities from the Global South, working class people which made me aware of this.

Such 'other' student subjectivities which are immediately marked as different in our elite setting and who self-identified as concerned with questions of social and global justice were open to challenge the epistemological hierarchies of the imperial all-knowing subject. This confirms the experiences of black feminist bell hooks (2000:108–16) from her work with black and working-class women who when they found themselves in pedagogical situations that actively de-centred and critiqued epistemological privilege and engaged with their own experiences (not without difficulty) began to feel seen, heard and valued for the first time in the University setting. The reactions from our students can also be fruitfully conceptualized through Mignolo's (2009) and bell hooks' (2000) conceptualization that it is the 'other' and 'marginal' through their experiences and positionalities who have epistemic privilege for constructing social and political transformation. As bell hooks argues in relation to black feminist struggle but is relevant to all 'others': 'Black women with no institutionalized 'other' that we may discriminate against . . . or oppress often have a lived experience that directly challenges the prevailing . . . social structure . . . It is essential for continued feminist struggle that black women recognize the special vantage point our marginality gives us and make use of this perspective to criticize the dominant racist, classist, sexist hegemony'. (2000:16). When this positionality is actively engaged in the classroom, particularly an elite context, then there is a potential epistemological and subjective openness to move beyond the borders of certainty and truth as constituted by the powerful. However, this openness remained at the level of ideas and emotions fostering emotional commitments and ease with such critical reflection about knowledge. It did not lead to self-reflection about internal estrangements, complicities in reproducing power-over relationships nor did it result in embodied transformation.

On the nature of knowledge

For students who either identified with a hegemonic subjectivity or with a revolutionary subjectivity this had implications for how they engaged with the assumption of multiple knowledges and knowledge as a process that underlay the course. The use of art, music, voices of movement participants and for example of shanty-town women's reflections next to established critical theorists ranging from Hegel to David Harvey combined with the emphasis that every student had knowledge and that we collectively could develop critical praxis in a multiplicity of ways not merely textual and conceptual proved challenging and at times unsettling. Student A for example chose to remain closed to these epistemological dynamics as he explained he could not 'identify with this'. Thus as he reflects:

> As a teaching tool it is nice to try something different. It was fun . . . I think the main focus of the course was to get people involved in class and I personally have never had that problem. I'm not sure it helped me personally . . . for others it helped them stand up more in class.

From a situation of normally being at the centre of the class, both in terms of content (an intelligent and successful student able to understand theories) and form (an able discussant of ideas) this student's reaction to having this dominant positionality decentred was to retreat and remove himself emotionally and intellectually from the space. It became a space of otherness to him, a space that went too far in letting the students take control and in valuing all types of knowledges. Thus he was closed to the realities of affective, oral and historical knowledges that were included in the class materials. As I have previously argued (Motta, 2012a), this can be seen as a form of active resistance and not just a reinforcement of the student as passive consumer, even if it can be uncomfortable for the facilitator. By challenging the philosophy of education of the convenors, this student was enacting his own intellectual and epistemological agency and becoming conscious of what he was comfortable with and what not. As Anzaldúa explains, the first step of any critical awakening and process of transformation is the coming to consciousness of one's positionality (2007:89–90). In this case, however, this coming to consciousness could also be a form of closure to reflexivity and rather an intellectual and emotional way to remain more tightly wedded to a hegemonic subjectivity. As Gillespie et al. (citing Frankenberg, 2002:239) reflect in relation to teaching white women about white privilege, but which is relevant to this case of epistemic and class privilege 'White people's conscious racialization of others does not necessarily lead to a conscious racialization of the white self . . . Indeed, . . . whiteness makes itself invisible precisely by asserting it normalcy, its transparency, in contrast with the marking of others on which its transparency depends'.

Student E, unlike Student A, did not close off to the multiple knowledges or the idea of the collective construction of knowledges. However, he did maintain an orientation to the course in which different methods were fun and not experienced or understood as involving an epistemological process of facilitating the co-construction of knowledge. As he explains:

> I enjoyed the course . . . having four lecturers and getting their opinions and knowledge of subjects was great . . . it was more diverse like this and fun . . . Their effect (facilitators) was to do with the content not them or how they taught . . . so the last weeks were much more concrete in the world . . . you could get more involved . . . but we'd have had similar discussions whoever had run the session.

He understood his participation in the course as a process of learning about academic theories to be able to develop his arguments (to dispute' other's and win the debate). As he explains:

> In discussion you would know what position they'd take and it would make it easy to come up with something to dispute that position . . . The only time I was uncomfortable was when I didn't do my readings properly . . . but other than that I never felt uncomfortable discussing anything.

His critical and revolutionary subjectivity meant that he explicitly and naturally identified with a critical pedagogy course and with the idea of multiple knowledges and the co-construction of knowledge. However, the construction of this critical subjectivity within the contours of a traditional intellectualism created closures towards embracing this epistemologically and emotionally as a means to reach to the borders of the self and decentre the epistemic privilege and exclusions enacted through a critical subjectivity based on Rodin's model of 'the thinker'. In many ways his embrace of the course at the level of language but not the level of practice mirrors Gillespie et al.'s reflections in relation to white students being confronted with their race privilege in which 'white students will attempt to reinterpret any pedagogical strategy that disrupts their sense of entitlement and comfort' (2002:240).

For 'other' subjects who initially identified with multiple knowledges and questioned the epistemic privilege of theoretical knowledge and experts then the embrace of multiple knowledges and processes of co-construction of knowledge was more easily enacted and embodied. As Student C describes:

> I've looked at Freire before. I didn't how it would work in an elite university as opposed to South American peasant communities in the 1970s. In the first week when they said we'd be taking seminars I wasn't expecting that . . . I knew it was all about all speaking and reversing power relations between teacher and student but at first I thought oh my god! But it was through facilitating group interaction and experimentation that I found it wasn't actually so hard.

As Student D describes:

> It was great to move away from hierarchy in teaching and knowledge . . . and to try to produce group and collective knowledge . . . I liked the more experimental stuff, listening to music, drawing when we pushed the boundaries of the classroom . . . with more traditional stuff . . . I felt here we shouldn't be doing this as these spaces are hard to find . . . you need to defend them . . . this is our space and time to be experimental.

As Student B also explains:

> It's helped me understand things more deeply . . . I've become more confident in my own views and more willing to accept others . . . it really helped me to understand that there are so many different perspectives in politics beyond traditional understandings and theories . . . for some of us in other courses we've gone back to discussion from this course to bring in ideas of multiple perspectives and others forms of knowledge.

Their identification with other knowledges and ways of creating knowledge meant that when the focus was on more traditional theoretical texts they felt disappointment as opposed to excitement, particularly the case for Student D who describes, 'when we were more traditional I felt disappointment . . . we could have done more'. This deconstructive embrace of the other and affirmative engagement with multiplicity facilitated processes of embracing 'the stranger within and without', particularly enabling critical self-reflection and fostering recognition of other's perspectives, experiences and positions. These subjective orientations and openings are key elements in the process of creating pedagogical spaces that are embedded in an ethics of love and care for self and other and therefore create possibilities for transgressions beyond the borders of self. They enable student-led critical pedagogy to foster in students courage to dare to critique dominant epistemological logics and knowledges, to believe in their own experiences and the multiple knowledges of others. As bell hooks argues (2000:92), 'One of the most significant forms of power held by the weak is the refusal to accept the definition of oneself that is put forward by the powerful . . . the exercise of this basis personal power is an act of resistance and strength'. For some this also led to epistemological experimentation in their everyday lives. For Student D, already politically engaged, this resulted in focusing his political practice on worker education. As he explains:

> I have begun to run a course in worker education implementing some of the methods that we used in this course. Mostly I have tried to take the idea of the co-construction of knowledge further, not having a fixed course contents or particular people to run a particular week. Rather the ideas for the week are developed by the group and I try to help them all be involved in preparing, planning and developing a topic.

Practices of learning

For those students with a dominant conceptualization of the nature of knowledge their practice in the classroom tended to be one of polemical discussion with the aim of winning the debate by proving the inaccuracies and lack of rigour of others. As Student A describes:

> I don't want to generalise but from the leftist side there was a group heavily involved in political activism who definitely expressed their opinions. I was on the other side, worked in politics. I've done internships . . . Yes, personal politics was at play. My role was I saw the same problems as the more left-wing but very different source and solutions, so I defended this.

Student E mirrors this understanding of the practices of learning:

> In discussions you would know what position they'd take and it would make it easy to come up with something to dispute that position . . . after a certain point I was able to predict what each person would say in a discussion.

Such an understanding of the practice of learning fostered a performance in the classroom space that mirrored dominant forms of masculinized power-over of liberal and neoliberal subjectivities in the academy. These practices created and reinforced a competitive space in which the knower is able to display their knowledge and disprove those of others. The unconscious reproduction of this practice of learning and occupying the learning space created exclusions and self-censure in other students, particularly those who did not have epistemological, class or gender privilege. This resulted in a space that was often dominated by a few students. This was noticed and problematized in interviews with students with 'other' subjectivities. As Anzaldúa describes, those who have experienced exclusions, oppressions or inequalities often develop *la facultad* – an emotional awareness to others, or what we might more commonly call empathy' (2007:60) As Student B reflects in relation to his fellow students:

> Outside, before the session, there was often a feeling there were people who would talk all the time and so it was definitely something consciously noted by people.

Or as Student C describes:

> I noticed, particularly early on, the men speaking more than the women. I thought 'ooh I don't like this' but as time went along there was more diversity in voices. In our session we split people up purposely. We grouped people to make sure people who hadn't spoken would be with those who would help them to speak.

Important to Student C's reflections are that students, not only the teacher, can play a pivotal pedagogical role in creating safe and inclusive spaces that encourage the expression of multiples voices and decentre dominant practices of learning. As the course explicitly involved students taking on the role of facilitator, then as in Student C's case, they could consciously and actively think about the dynamics of inclusion using material from the course and their reflections with the tutors to fine-tune their emotional and intellectual discomfort with exclusions and gendered silence. We can usefully conceptualize this like Gillespie et al. (2002:247) as the role of the proactive student. As they describe, 'JoAnn's story stimulated us to think systematically about the role proactive white women could potentially play in our efforts to remain connected with more resistant student'.

Student D was fascinating in that over the duration of the course he went through a politically transformative process (linked also to his involvement in the student occupation at the University and the student movement). Student D was an 'other' in our elite context, coming from a Northern working-class background. He was politically active in a revolutionary left group whose epistemological logics mirrored those in which there is a true knowledge, the practice of political learning is to win arguments and disprove those of others, and knowledge is conceptual and theoretical. He came therefore with an emotional commitment to the oppressed and already questioning the knowledges of the powerful but not the dominant epistemological logics of what knowledge is and how it is produced. This emotional openness to others and logic of questioning was in tension with a polemical practise that reinforced closure. Yet for Student D this dissonance created openness to critical reflection. As he explains referring to this tension:

My positionality in discussion, well I can be quite confrontational . . . I would say that it (the course) did allow me to think through some of the problematics of that type of discussion . . . to give people space to talk. I'm quite loud, I can talk over people but I think it helped me with some of the issues around that . . . how it can silence and alienate people. It made me realize the contradictions and problematics.

This gendered dynamic of voice and silence which marked the seminar space was also shifted by the active identification and intervention by the teacher-facilitator. When I worked with a group of two women who were to facilitate the session entitled, 'Whose knowledge for social and political change?' I explained to them that critical pedagogy was not about creating a space without boundaries or limits. Rather the critical teacher uses their authority to foster anti-authoritarian logics, practices and relationships. We thus discussed the possibility of them setting ground-rules in their session as a means of bringing to consciousness to the group the problematic of voice and inclusion. They decided that they liked the idea of ground rules and went ahead with this. This caused active resistance by those male students who had been dominant up until then. I used this moment of resistance as an opportunity to explain the difference between authority and authoritarianism and that often critical pedagogy spaces had ground rules. Two students remember this as a pivotal moment that changed seminar dynamics. As Student C recounts:

People would talk over each other . . . one set of students had a set of ground rules, to respect and not talk over each other. This set a precedent but at the time there was an argument with some saying there should be no rules as CP is not about rules. I remember Sara said at the time well actually often there are rules at the start so people respect each other.

Or as Student F remembers:

Some were very dominant and some felt their opinions wouldn't be valued and then week four I think, was one about knowledge and importance of all knowledges. That was the week that it broke down the barriers. They began with rules and one was all opinions should be respected and that sparked off massive debate with some people saying 'how can all be valued' and then some arguing that they can and should be . . . Then people thought 'you know what I can speak'. That week turned things around.

Difference in practices of learning created tensions and discomfort among the group. However, when consciously problematized with students as issues of power, voice and inclusion they could become a pedagogical moment of opening and transformation for the class. Here discomfort was

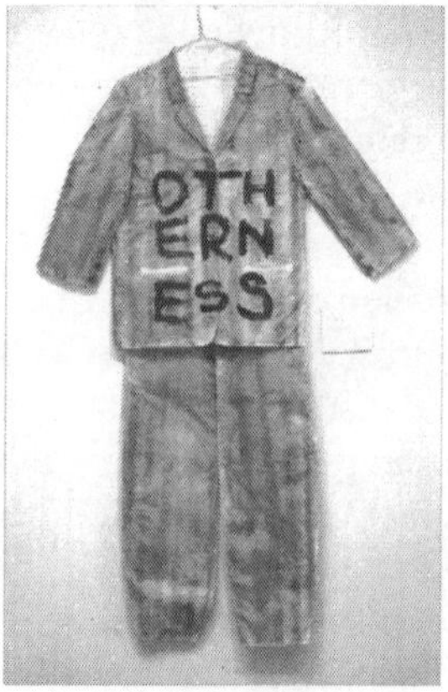

OTHERNESS (SUIT). 2011 by Mike Saijo
Source: http://msaijo.com/

pivotal in creating a possibility through which to problematize and collectively learn through our experience. This of course did not eradicate closure to otherness and power-over relationships in the space but it did enable a shift in individuals and in the affective nature of the classroom space towards a commitment to multiplicity, otherness and care.

Reflections for pedagogical praxis

Writing this piece, which is inevitably incomplete – particularly the silence regarding the complicities and contradictions of my own practice – has nevertheless fostered a process of critical reflection. It has enabled a deepening of our understanding of the limits and possibilities of introducing critical pedagogy praxis committed to multiplicity, horizontality and 'otherness' into an elite HE setting. It has traced the epistemological logics that produce the knowing liberal subject within capitalist modernity, and which are often reproduced in dominant critical conceptualizations of revolutionary change and subjectivity. These logics reproduce an imperial knowing subject, symbolically captured in Rodin's statue, 'the thinker' who is able to separate himself from the 'irrationality' of emotions and unpredictable desires of the body. Such an epistemological politics writes over the knowledges of 'others', be they of the body, emotions, spirit, orally or visually transmitted and/or collectively constructed. The neoliberal subject represents thus, not a break, but an intensifying continuation of these epistemological logics.

We therefore found that resistances to a pedagogical practise that sought to decentre (importantly not eradicate) the imperial subject from his position of epistemological power and create an affirmative embrace of multiplicity in knowledge and forms of knowledge production came from both students with hegemonic subjectivities and those who identified with revolutionary and critical subjectivities. In the former case, the result was to dissociate from the course and teachers; an act of ambiguous resistance. For the latter, their embrace of multiplicity remained at the level of language but did not foster critical reflection on practice. Conversely those who came from non-traditional backgrounds or had arrived to the MA from a non-traditional route – who were marked as 'others' immediately on entering our elite HE setting – began with an openness to question these epistemological practices of producing the knowing subject. This enabled significant intellectual and emotional transformation and learning, particularly an opening towards others' knowledges, experimentation with collective forms of knowledge creation (in the classroom and other parts of their lives), increasing confidence in their right and ability to challenge the powerful and an intensifying awareness of dynamics of exclusion and silencing in the classroom.

However, some of the most powerful processes of collective and individual transformation occurred in acute moments of dissonance and discomfort. For Student D, his sensitivity to exclusion, embrace of multiple knowledges and yet political practice that reproduced epistemological closure and hierarchy created internal discomfort and dissonance. In his case the course helped him to forge an openness to critical reflection on this dissonance, and as he says 'on the contradictions and tensions in my practice as a student and activist'. The course's explicit embrace of multiplicity, of students' experiences and to inclusion and participation came into conflict with the gendered dynamics of exclusion and silencing in seminars. Here the role of the facilitator actively working with proactive ally students enabled the transformation of this dissonance into a productive pedagogical moment which made visible, in order to shift some of the closures that were structuring classroom practice.

I would like to conclude by offering five key points which I hope could be helpful for those who would like to develop similar projects such as those I co-initiated at Nottingham:

1. The need to actively cultivate compassion and generosity (key elements of the ethics of love and politics of care) towards the complexities and complicities of student subjectivities (and our own) to avoid alienating students that are other than ourselves or come into contradiction with our underlying educational philosophy.
2. Not to assume that by calling a space inclusive and participatory that it will be. Rather to create such spaces and relationships teacher-facilitators need to actively bring to consciousness to the student group the problematics of voice, inclusion and participation

at the beginning of the course so as to ground our commitment to these principles in critical reflection and shared experience.

3 To develop with more seriousness and depth processes of critical reflection about critical pedagogy courses with students. As opposed to merely undertaking an interview, the teacher-facilitator could for example then use this as a basis to draw out themes and questions with the student to facilitate further shared critical reflection.

4 To cultivate in teacher-facilitators using Andaluzia's concept of '*la facultad*' – an affective awareness of dynamics of power and a nuanced and acute practice of empathy. This will allow a more developed type of attentiveness to the dissonances and discomforts experienced by individuals and student groups which helps the transformation of such experiences into pedagogical moments not merely moments of reaction and conflict.

5 The body is the limit and the possibility of introducing critical pedagogy into HE. Many of the embodied and affective pedagogies that facilitate processes of internal transformation, or for Lorde the connection to our deep erotic knowing; 'an internal sense of satisfaction to which, once we have experienced it, we know we can aspire. For having experienced the fullness of this depth of feeling and recognizing its power, in honor and self-respect we can require no less of ourselves' (1984) would not be permitted in this space. They involve 'epistemological disobedience' (Mignolo, 2009) which would disrupt the essence of the epistemological norms of emotional behaviour and bodily practice of the University. This suggests that our commitment to this critical pedagogy praxis must transcend the limits and borders of the knowledge/power nexus of the University. Only by transcending the dualism between education and life can we hope to reconnect our minds with the knowledges of our bodies and emotions and create non-alienated social relationships against and beyond the epistemological logics of colonial patriarchal capitalism.

References

Anzaldúa, Gloria (2007) *Borderlands La frontera: The New Mestiza*. 3rd edn. Aunt Lude Books, San Francisco.

Boler, Megan (1999) *Feeling Power: Emotions and Education*. Routledge, New York and London.

Ellsworth, Elizabeth (1989) 'Why Doesn't this Feel Empowering? Working through the Repressive Myth of Critical Pedagogy'. *Harvard Educational Review* 59(3): 297–324.

Freire, Paulo (2000) *Pedagogy of the Oppressed.* (30th Anniversary Edition) Continuum Press.

Gillsepie, Diane, Ashbaugh, Leslie and Defiore, JoAnn (2002) 'White Women Teaching White Women about White Privilege, Race Cognizance and Social Action: Toward a Pedagogical Pragmatics'. *Race, Ethinicity and Education* 5(3): 237–53.

hooks, bell (2000) *Feminist Theory: From Margin to Center.* (2nd edn) South End Press, Cambridge, MA.

Lorde, Audre (2000) 'The Uses of the Erotic: The Erotic as Power', http://youtube.com/watch?v=xFHwg6aNKy0 (accessed 31 July 2012).

Mclaren, Peter (2000) *Che Guevara, Paulo Freire, and the Pedagogy of Revolution.* Roman and Littlefield, Maryland.

Mignolo, Walter D. (2009) 'Epistemic Disobedience, Independent Thought and De-Colonial Freedom'. *Theory, Culture & Society* 26(7–8): 1–23.

Motta, Sara Catherine (2012a) 'Teaching Global and Social Justice as Transgressive Spaces of Possibility', *Antipode* (early view) http://onlinelibrary.wiley.com/doi/10.1111/j.1467–8330.2012.00995.x/references.

— (2012b) 'Leyendo el anarchismo a través de ojos latinoamericanos: Reading Anarchism through Latin American Eyes', in Ruth Kinna (ed.), *The Continuum Companion to Anarchism.* Continuum Press, London: 392–421.

— (2012c) 'And Still We Rise: On the Violence of Marketisation in Higher Education'. *Beautiful Transgressions, Ceasefire (March),* http://ceasefiremagazine.co.uk/beautiful-transgressions-11/.

Scott, James C. (1987) *Weapons of the Weak: Everyday Forms of Peasant Resistance.* Yale University Press, New Haven, CT.

Zembylas, Michalinos (2003) 'Interrogating "Teacher Identity": Emotion, Resistance, and Self-Formation'. *Educational Theory* 53(1): 107–27.

SCHOOL OF POLITICS & INTERNATIONAL RELATIONS

Appendix: Social and Global Justice in Action

M14128/29 (20/15 credits)
Level 4

Taught:
Autumn Semester

Module convenors:
Prof. Andreas Bieler (C1)
Dr Burns (C5)
Dr Morton (C2)
Dr Motta (C14)

Email: Andreas.Bieler@nottingham.ac.uk
Office hours: Tue 11:00–12:00; Thu 12:00–13:00.

Email: Tony.Burns@nottingham.ac.uk
Office hours: Mon 15:00–16:00; Tue 15:00–16:00.

Email: Adam.Morton@nottingham.ac.uk
Office hours: Wed 10:00–11:00; Fri 9:00–10:00.

Email: Sarah.Motta@nottingham.ac.uk
Office hours: Thu 9:00–10:00; Fri 9:00–10:00.

Contents

Summary of content

This module is organized around problem-based learning and is informed by principles of 'critical pedagogy'. The content will stem from core issues in the field of social and global justice and teaching will be organized around a number of case studies, which will be presented as 'problems', for example 'What are the problems and issues surrounding 'food security' vs 'food sovereignty'?, or 'Why do social movements aim to challenge power relations outside of state power?' Each week primary sources relating to such 'problems' in the field of social and global justice will be presented. These may take the form of a newspaper article, pictures, quotes or an extract from a book. Students will generate questions on the basis of this 'problem', which they will seek to answer for the next session. For each 'problem' a list with suggested readings will be given, which evaluate the 'problem' in a variety of ways from different perspectives. Students have the task to engage critically with a range of different perspectives in order to generate potential answers to the problem.

Educational aims

Students are expected to

- think critically about 'problems' of social and global justice;
- think about the relationship between theory and practice and social justice;
- think about the relationship between education and social justice;
- develop inclusive/participatory ways of learning.

Learning outcomes

These will be:

1. Knowledge and understanding:

On completion of the module, students will be able to

- demonstrate in-depth knowledge of theories and themes of social and global justice;
- develop analytic tools that enable students to pursue complex empirical political analysis;

- demonstrate an understanding of the connection between education, different methods of learning and social justice.

2. Intellectual skills:

- ability to think about the connection between theory and empirical analysis in a reflective and critical way;
- ability to reflect critically on the conceptual frameworks that underpin different understandings of social and global justice.

3. Professional/Practical skills:

- evidence gathering and evaluation;
- organization of group work;
- independent learning and analysis.

4. Transferable and key skills:

Through active participation in the module students will acquire

- the capacity to engage in a structured and well-informed discussion about complex questions (to be practised in class discussions);
- the capacity to concentrate on core points and the ability to speak freely on the basis of a set of notes;
- the ability to work effectively in a group.

5. IT skills:

- ability to deliver a professional, word-processed document with accompanying bibliography and footnotes;
- ability to draw information and documents from the WebCT site;
- capacity to carry out focussed research on the internet.

Module evaluation

Evaluation and feedback are crucial to the success of any module. The School wants students to have their say on Politics modules. Therefore modules are formally evaluated on a biennial basis, so please use this opportunity to have your say. If you have any other comments or queries regarding this module, please contact the Module Convenor.

Lecture/Seminar titles

Under each lecture heading, a selection of literature is presented. It is divided in key readings and additionally suggested readings. Students are expected to do their own research for additional material on a weekly basis in response to the specific questions agreed upon.

The weekly seminar titles are as follows:

1) Why problem-based learning and critical pedagogy as a way of teaching social and global justice? [sm, tb, ab, am] [01/10/2010]

Readings to frame the methodology and pedagogy of the course

Amsler, S. (March 2009) 'Ethnographies of Critique: Critical Judgement as Cultural Practice.' *The Future(s) of Critical Theory*, Frankfurt Am Main, 19–21.

Boler, M. (1999) *Feeling Power: Emotions and Education*. Routledge, New York and London.

Canaan J. E. and Shumar W. (2008) 'Higher Education in an Era of Globalisation and Neoliberalism', in J. E. Canaan and W. Shumar (eds), *Structure and Agency in the Neoliberal University*. Routledge, New York and London.

Darder, Antonia, Baltodano, Marta P. and Torres, Rodolfo D. (eds) (2008) *The Critical Pedagogy*.

Freire, Paolo (2006) *Pedagogy of the oppressed*. London: 30th Anniversary Edition. Continuum Press, London and New York.

Harvie, David (2000) 'Alienation, Class and Enclosure in UK Universities', *Capital and Class* 71 (Summer), 103–32.

Kumashiro K. (2000) 'Toward a Theory of Anti-oppressive Education', *Review of Education Research*, 70: 25.

Motta, S. (2010) 'Opening Spaces of Possibility in the University – Critical Pedagogy in the Teaching of Social Justice.' *Critical Education for Critical Times,* 14 May, CSSGJ, University of Nottingham.

Reader. 2nd edn. Routledge.

Wink, Joan (2010) 'Critical Pedagogy: Notes from the Real World'. Merill.

2) Hegel's philosophy of history and its relevance for students of social and global justice today. Does the age of imperialism belong to the past? [tb, sm] [8/10/2010]

Key readings

Buck-Morss, Susan (2000) 'Hegel and Haiti,' *Critical Inquiry* 26(4): 821–65.
Fukuyama, Francis (1992) 'By Way of an Introduction,' in *The End of History and the Last Man*. Avon Books, New York: xi–xxiii.
Fanon, Frantz (1967) 'The Negro and Hegel,' in *Black Skin, White Masks*. Grove Press, New York: 216–22.
Hegel, G. W. F., *Selected Writings* (provided by course team).
Additional suggested readings
Bernasconi, Robert (2000) 'With What Must the Philosophy of World History Begin? On the Racial Basis of Hegel's Eurocentrism,' *Nineteenth Century Contexts* 22: 171–201.
Buchwalter, Andrew (2009) 'Is Hegel's Philosophy of History Eurocentric?' in William Dudley ed., *Hegel and History*. SUNY, New York: 87–110.
Chakravorty Spivak, Gayatri (1999*A Critique of Postcolonial Reason: Toward a History of the Vanishing Present*. Harvard University Press, Cambridge, Mass.
Cooper, Barry (1984) *The End of History: An Essay on Modern Hegelianism*. Toronto.
— (2003) 'Hegel's Racism: A Response to Bernasconi,' *Radical Philosophy* 119: 32–5.
Kojeve, Alexandre (1969) *Introduction to the Reading of Hegel: Lectures on the Phenomenology of Spirit*. Cornell University Press, Ithaca.
McCarney, Joseph (2000) *Hegel: On History*. Routledge, London.
McLennan, Gregor (2003) 'Sociology, Eurocentrism and Postcolonial Theory,' *European Journal of Social Theory* 6(1): 69–86.
O'Neill, John ed. (1996) *Hegel's Dialectic of Desire and Recognition*. SUNY, New York.
— (2003) 'Hegel's Racism: A Reply to McCarney,' *Radical Philosophy* 119: 35–7.
Said, Edward (1993) *Culture and Imperialism*. Knopf, New York.
Young, Robert (1990) *White Mythologies: Writing History and the West*. Routledge, London.

3) The Marxist theory of imperialism and its relevance for social and global justice today. Is today's world postcolonial? [tb, sm] [15/10/2010]

Key readings

Additional suggested readings

Bhagwhati, Jagdish (2007) *In Defence of Globalization.* Oxford University Press.
Brewer, Anthony (1990) *Marxist Theories of Imperialism: A Critical Survey*, 2nd ed. Routledge.
Callinicos, Alex (2009) 'Imperialism and Global Political Economy Today,' *Imperialism and Global Political Economy.* Polity Press: 14–22.
Callinicos, Alex et al. (1994) *Marxism and the New Imperialism.* Bookmarks, London.
— (2007) *A Brief History of Neoliberalism.* Oxford University Press.
Day, Richard J. (2008 [2005]) *Gramsci is Dead: Anarchist Currents in the Newest Social Movements.* Orient Longman.
Friedman, Milton (1979) *Free to Choose.* Penguin.
Hardt, Michael and Negri, Antonio (2000) 'The Limits of Imperialism,' in *Empire.* Harvard University Press, Cambridge, Mass: 221–39.
Harvey, David (2005) *The New Imperialism.* Oxford University Press.
— (2007) *Making Globalization Work: The Next Steps to Global Justice.* Penguin.
Marx, Karl and Lenin, V. I. *Selected Writings* (extracts to be provided by course team).
— (2002 [1962]) *Capitalism and Freedom.* University of Chicago Press, Chicago.
Panitch, Leo and Gindin, Sam (2004) *Global Capitalism and American Empire.* Merlin.
Panitch, Leo and Leys, Colin (eds) (2004) *Socialist Register 2004: The New Imperial Challenge.* Merlin Press.
Stiglitz, Joseph (2003) *Globalization and its Discontents.* Penguin.
Tormey, Simon (2004) *Anti-Capitalism: A Beginner's Guide.* Oneworld, Oxford.
Wolf, Martin (2005) 'Incensed About Inequality,' in *Why Globalization Works.* Yale University Press, Yale: 138–72.

4) Whose knowledge helps create social and global justice? Does how that knowledge is created matter? [sm, tb] [22/10/2010]

Key readings

http://eurozine.com/articles.

Motta, S. C. (2011) 'Notes Towards Prefigurative Epistemologies', in S. C. Motta and A. G. Nilsen, *Social Movements in the Global South: Dispossession, Development and Resistance*. Palgrave Macmillan Press. Politicising Development Series, London.

Santos, B. (2002) 'Beyond Abyssal Thinking: From Global Lines to Ecologies of Knowledges', Revista Critica de Ciencias Sociais, 80.

Wainwright, H. (1994) 'The Theory and Politics of Knowledge', in H. Wainwright, *Reclaim the State*. Verso, London.

Suggested further readings

Bevington, D. and Dixon, C. (2005) 'Movement-Relevant Theory: Rethinking Social Movement Scholarship and Activism', *Social Movement Studies*, 4(3): 185–208.

Chatterton, P. (2008) 'Demand the Possible: Journeys in Changing our World as a Public Activist-Scholar', *Antipode* 40(3): 421–7.

Chukaitis, S. (2009) *Imaginal Machines: Autonomy and Self-Organization in the Revolutions of Everyday Life*. Minor Compositions, London/New York. Autonomedia.

Diversi, M. and Finley, S. (2010) 'Poverty Pimps in the Academy: A Dialogue About Subjectivity, Reflexivity, and Power in Decolonizing Production of Knowledge', *Cultural Studies<->Critical Methodologies* 10(1): 14–17.

Emboaba Da Costa, A. (2010) 'Afro-Brazilian Ancestalidade: Critical Perspectives on Knowledge and Development', *Third World Quarterly* 31(4): 655–74.

Escobar, A. (1992) 'Imagining a Post-Development Era? Critical Thought, Development and Social Movements', *Social Text* 31–2, 20–56.

Foucault, M. and Deleuze, G. (1977) 'Intellectuals and Power: A Conversation Between Michel Foucault and Gilles Deleuze', in D. F. Bouchard (ed.), *Language, Counter Memory, Practice: Selected Essays and Interviews*. Basil Blackwell, Oxford.

Mohanty, T. C. (2003) *Feminism without Borders: Decolonizing Theory and Practicing Solidarity*. Durham and London, Duke University Press.

Situaciones, Collectivo (2003) 'On the Militant-Researcher', http://transform.eipcp.net/transversal/0406/colectivosituaciones/en.

Spivak, G. C. (1988) 'Can the Subaltern Speak', in C. Nelson and L. Grossberg (eds), *Marxism and the Interpretation of Culture* University of Illinois Press, Urbana, Chicago.

5) Can art and culture create resistances, rebellions and revolutions? [sm, tb] [29/10/2010]

Key readings

Da Costa, D. (2010) 'Subjects of Struggle: Theatre as Space of Political Economy', *Third World Quarterly* 31(4) 617–35.

Sengupta, M. (2010) 'Million Dollar Exit from the Anarchic Slum-world: Slumdog Millionaire's Hollow Idioms of Social Justice', *Third World Quarterly* 31(4) 599–616.

Wheeler, E. A. (1991) 'Most of My Heroes Don't Appear on No Stamps: The Dialogics of Rap Music', *Black Music Research Journal* 11(2): 193–216.

Further readings

Adorno, T. and Horkheimer, M. (1993) 'The Culture Industry: Enlightenment as Mass Deception', T. Adorno and M. Horkheimer, *Dialectic of Enlightenment*, Continuum, New York.

Anderson, B. (2002) 'A Principle of Hope: Recorded Music, Listening Practices and the Immanence of Utopia' Geografiska Annaler. Series B, *Human Geography* 84(3/4) Special Issue: The Dialectics of Utopia and Dystopia, 211–27.

Burns, T. (2008) *Political Theory, Science Fiction and Utopian Literature: Ursula K. Le Guin and The Dispossessed.* Lexington, London, especially chapters 6, 8–10.

Cole, K. (2010) 'Jazz in the Time of Globalisation: The Bolivarian Alliance for the Peoples of Our America', *Third World Quarterly* 31(2) 315–32.

Fernandes, S. (2003) 'Fear of a Black Nation: Local Rappers, Transnational Crossings and State Power in Contemporary Cuba', *Anthropological Quarterly* 76(4): 575–608.

Le Guinn, U. K. (1974) *The Dispossessed: An Ambiguous Utopia.* Harper and Row, London.

March, H. (2010) 'Writing Our History in Songs: Judith Reyes, Popular Music and the Student Movement of 1968', *Bulletin of Latin American Research* 29(1).

Swelbin, E. (2010) Revolution, Rebellion, Resistance: The Power of Story. Zed Books, London/New York.

Webb, D. (2005) 'Bakhtin at the Seaside: Utopia, Modernity and the Carnivalesque', *Theory, Culture & Society* 22(3): 121–38.

6) How do social movements change the world without taking state power? [am, ab] [05/11/2010]

Key readings

Esteva, Gustavo (2007) 'Oaxaca: The Path of Radical Democracy', *Socialism and Democracy* 21(2): 74–96.
Holloway, John (1998) 'Dignity's Revolt' in John Holloway and Eloína Peláez (eds), *Zapatista! Reinventing Revolution in Mexico*. Pluto Press, London.
Robinson, William (2007) 'Transformative Possibilities in Latin America', in Leo Panitch and Colin Leys (eds), *The Socialist Register: Global Flashpoints: Reactions to Imperialism and Neoliberalism*. Merlin Press, London.

Additional suggested readings

Day, Richard (2005) *Gramsci is Dead: Anarchist Undercurrents in the Newest Social Movements*. Pluto Press, London.
Dinerstein, Ana C. (2002) 'The Battle of Buenos Aires: Crisis, Insurrection and the Reinvention of Politics in Argentina', *Historical Materialism* 10(4): 5–38.
Esteva, Gustavo (2010) 'The Oaxaca Commune and Mexico's Coming Insurrection', *Antipode* 42(4): 978–93.
Holloway, John (2010a) 'Cracks and the Crisis of Abstract Labour', *Antipode* 42(4): 909–23.
— (2010b) *Crack Capitalism*. Pluto Press, London.
Lazar, Sian (2008) *El Alto, Rebel City: Self and Citizenship in Andean Bolivia*. Duke University Press, Durham.
Swords, Alicia (2010) 'Teaching Against Neoliberalism in Chiapas, Mexico: Gendered Resistance via Neo-Zapatista Network Politics', in Philip McMichael (ed.), *Contesting Development: Critical Struggles for Social Change*. Routledge, London: 116–31.
Tormey, Simon (2005) '"Not in my Name": Deleuze, Zapatismo and the Critique of Representation', *Parliamentary Affairs* 59(1): 138–54.

7) Exploding cities in the Global South: Is the prevalence of 'global slums' a threat to security? [am, ab] [12/11/2010]

Key readings

Davis, Mike (2006) *Planet of Slums*. Verso, London.
Eckstein, Susan (1990) 'Urbanisation Revisited: Inner-City Slum of Hope and Squatter Settlement of Despair', *World Development* 18(2): 165–81.
Menon, Gayatri A. (2010) 'Recoveries of Space and Subjectivity in the Shadow of Violence: The Clandestine Politics of Pavement Dwellers in Mumbai', in Philip McMichael (ed.), *Contesting Development: Critical Struggles for Social Change*. Routledge, London: 151–64.
Additional suggested readings
Bruhn, Kathleen (2008) *Urban Protest in Mexico and Brazil*. Cambridge University Press, Cambridge.
Koonings, Kees and Krujit, Dirk (2007) 'Fractured Cities, Second-class Citizenship and Urban Violence', in Kees Koonings and Dirk Krujit (eds), *Fractured Cities: Social Exclusion, Urban Violence and Contested Spaces in Latin America*, Zed Books, London.
Krujit, Dirk and Koonings, Kees (2009) 'The Rise of Megacities and the Urbanisation of Informality, Exclusion and Violence', in Kees Koonings and Dirk Krujit (eds), *Megacities: The Politics of Urban Exclusion and Violence in the Global South*. Zed Books, London.
Neuwirth, Robert (2005) *Shadow Cities: A Billion Squatters, A New Urban World*. Routledge, London.
Pansters, Wil and Berther, Hector Castillo (2007) 'Mexico City', in Kees Koonings and Dirk Krujit (eds), *Fractured Cities: Social Exclusion, Urban Violence and Contested Spaces in Latin America*. Zed Books, London.
Sassen, Saskia (2005) 'The Many Scales of the Global: Implications for Theory and for Politics', in Richard P. Appelbaum and William I. Robinson (eds), *Critical Globalization Studies*. Routledge, London: 155–66.
Satterthwaite, David (2006) 'Urbanisation and Third World Cities', in David Alexander Clark (ed.), *The Elgar Companion to Development Studies*. Edward Elgar, Cheltenham: 664–70.

8) Where are the workers? What role for transnational labour solidarity? [ab, am] [19/11/2010]

Case study: British jobs for British workers?

Good summary on Wikipedia: '2009 Lindsey Oil Refinery Strikes', http://en.wikipedia.org/wiki/2009_Lindsey_Oil_Refinery_strikes (accessed 01 September 2010).

Milne, Seumas (2009) 'Why British Workers are Angry', *Le Monde diplomatique* (September): 10–11.

Key readings

Bieler, Andreas, Lindberg, Ingemar and Sauerborn, Werner (2010) 'After Thirty Years of Deadlock: Labour's Possible Strategies in the New Global Order', *Globalizations* 7(1–2): 247–60.

Ferus-Comelo, A. and Novelli, M. (2009) 'Globalisation and Labour Movements: Transnational Solidarity and New Spaces of Resistance', in M. Novelli and A. Ferus-Comelo (eds), *Globalization, Knowledge and Labour: Education for solidarity within spaces of resistance.* Routledge, London: 21–48.

Lindberg, Ingemar (2010) 'Varieties of Solidarity: An Analysis of Cases of Worker Action Across Borders', in Andreas Bieler and Ingemar Lindberg (eds), *Global Restructuring, Labour and the Challenges for Transnational Solidarity.* Routledge, London. Chapter 15.

Additional suggested readings

Bieler, A. (2008) 'Trade Unions and the World and European Social Forums: A Move Towards Social Movement Unionism?' paper presented at the conference 'Trade Union and Social Movements – What Is in It for Us?', Oslo, 16–17 October, http://nottingham.ac.uk/cssgj/documents/working-papers/wp007.pdf (accessed 26 July 2010).

Bieler, A., Lindberg, I. and Pillay, D. (2008) 'What Future Strategy for the Global Working Class? The Need for a New Historical Subject', in A. Bieler, I. Lindberg and D. Pillay (eds), *Labour and the Challenges of Globalization: What prospects for Transnational Solidarity?*, Pluto Press, London: 264–85.

Novelli, M. and Ferus-Comelo, A. (2009) 'Globalisation, Neoliberalism and Labour', in M. Novelli and A. Ferus-Comelo (eds), *Globalization, Knowledge and Labour: Education for Solidarity within Spaces of Resistance.* Routledge, London: 5–20.

Taylor, M. (2009) 'Who Works for Globalisation? The challenges and Possibilities for International Labour Studies', *Third World Quarterly* 30(3): 435–52.

— (ed.) (2008) *Global Economy Contested: Power and conflict across the international division of labour.* London: Routledge.

Webster, Edward, Rob Lambert and Andries Beziudenhout (2008) *Grounding Globalization: Labour in the Age of Insecurity.* Wiley-Blackwell, Oxford.

9) 'Food security' versus 'food sovereignty': What is significant about struggles over food sustainability? [ab, am] [26/11/2010]

Key readings

Campesina, La Via (2008) 'An Answer to the Global Food Crisis: Peasants and Small Farmers Can Feed the World!', http://viacampesina.org/en/index.php?option=com_content&task=view&id=525&Itemid=1 (accessed 01 September 2010).

McMichael, Philip (2003) 'Food Security and Social Reproduction: Issues and Contradictions', in I. Bakker and S. Gill (eds), *Power, Production and Social Reproduction: Human In/security in the Global Political Economy*. Palgrave, Basingstoke: 169–89.

Panitchpakdi, Supachai (2005) 'Why Trade Matters for Improving Food Security'. Speech at the High-Level Round Table on Agricultural Trade Reform and Food Security at the FAO in Rome on 13 April, http://wto.org/english/news_E/spsp_E/spsp37_E.htm (accessed 05 January 2009).

Vigna, Anne (2008) 'Mexico: The High Price of Cheap Corn', *Le Monde diplomatique*.

Additional suggested readings

IUF (2004) 'Towards a Rights-Based Multilateralism for the World Food System', http://iufdocuments.org/www/documents/wto/rightsbasedmultilateralism-e.pdf (accessed 05 January 2009.

Kerr, Rachel Bezner (2010) 'The Land is Changing: Contested Agricultural Narratives in Northern Malawi', in Philip McMichael (ed.), *Contesting Development: Critical Struggles for Social Change*. Routledge, London: 98–115.

Mulvany, Patrick (2007) 'Food Sovereignty Comes of Age: Africa Leads Efforts to Rethink Our Food System', *Food Ethics*, 2(3) (Autumn), http://foodethics-council.org/files/magazine0203-p19.pdf: 19.

Pechlaner, Gabriela and Otero, Gerardo (2010) 'The Neoliberal Food Regime: Neoregulation and the New Division of Labor in North America', *Rural Sociology* 75(2): 179–208.

Wittman, Hannah (2010) 'Mobilizing Agrarian Citizenship: A New Rural Paradigm for Brazil', in Philip McMichael (ed.), *Contesting Development: Critical Struggles for Social Change*. Routledge, London: 165–81.

10) Round table: Social and global justice in action? [sm, tb, ab, am] [03/12/2010]

In Week Ten the class will be divided in two. With help from the module convenors both groups will work towards staging a 'round-table' event in the seminar. Presentations do not need to be formal and can include video clips; interactive methods used elsewhere in the module, or any other format deemed appropriate. The first hour time will be given over to start planning this exercise, which will not be assessed.

The themes from which the groups can choose for their round table can be drawn from the topics covered in the previous nine weeks

Method and frequency of class

Activity	Number of sessions	Duration of a session
Seminar	10	3 h

Location of seminar:	UP-TRNT-A46+
Day:	Friday
Time:	10:00 am – 1:00 pm

After each lecture, the lecture notes will be posted on WebCT, which can be accessed at http://webct.nottingham.ac.uk using your University network username and password. This will allow you to compare your own notes with the lecture notes and to go through the material learned in the lecture in an organized and systematic way. Once registered you can access the class at any time from any PC with an internet connection. You are expected to connect to the classroom at least once a week.

This 20 credit/15 credit module will be assessed on the following basis:

Assessment type	Weight	Requirements
Seminar presentation	20 per cent	1000/1000 word presentation
Coursework 1	40 per cent	2000/1500 words
Coursework 2	40 per cent	2000/1500 words

The first assessed essay should be submitted to the School Office by **2 November 2010** and the second by **10 December 2010**. You must submit an electronic copy of your essay via the module's WebCT site, taking note of the individual ID number that will be generated once you have successfully uploaded it. This process is self-explanatory.

After you have done that – and only then – you must submit **two** hard copies of the essay to the School Office by the deadline. A submission sheet should be completed and attached to the essay. You are required to enter the WebCT ID number on the cover sheet, as proof that you have already electronically submitted the essay. The submission sheet and the top of page of each copy of your essay should then be date stamped, and submitted to the essay chest outside the School Office. Please note that the School Office will be open from 10 am till 4 pm (Monday to Friday) on submission days. Essays handed in after 4 pm will be stamped as late and the usual University penalties will be applied.

The electronic copies will be scanned to detect plagiarism. It is therefore imperative that you consult the Student Handbook, which outlines what is counted as plagiarism and advises you how to avoid it. Failure to submit an electronic copy even if you submit two hard copies on time will mean that the essay will be counted as having not been submitted.

The standard University penalty for late submission should be 5 per cent absolute standard University scale per normal working day, until the mark reaches zero. For example, an original mark of 67 per cent would be successively reduced to 62 per cent, 57 per cent, 52 per cent, 47 per cent, etc. Normal working days include vacation periods, but not weekends or public holidays. Applications for extensions will not normally be considered retrospectively. Any student wishing to apply for an extension should collect and complete the necessary forms from the School Office.

Reading information

Recommended reading

Darder, Antonia, Baltodano, Marta P. and Torres, Rodolfo D. (eds) (2008) *The Critical Pedagogy Reader*, 2nd edn. Routledge.

Edkins, Jenny and Zehfuss, Maja (2009) *Global Politics: A New Introduction*. Routledge.

Wink, Joan (2010) *Critical Pedagogy: Notes from the Real World*. Merill.

Coursework support

The Hallward Library and Halls of Residence have a number of networked PCs to facilitate access to information on holdings.

As Module Convenor please do not hesitate to contact me if you have any difficulties with the module or assessed work. I will be available without appointment during my office hours. Appointments to meet at other times can be made by calling me on my direct line or via email. My contact details together with office hours are noted at the front of this module outline.

Guidance to essay writing

A short guide for students on essay writing skills and an outline of the marking criteria used by staff is available from the School intranet.

Assessed essay titles

This will be developed between the individual student and lecturers. The question must be related to the themes and topics of at least one of the weeks addressed.

Reminder: Submission dates are 4 pm Tuesday 2 November and Friday 10 December.

Method and frequency of class:

Activity	Number of sessions	Duration of a session
Seminar	10	3 h

Location of Seminar:	UP-TRNT-A46+
Day:	Friday
Time:	10:00 am – 1:00 pm

Method of assessment

PART TWO

Dialogues on Critical Pedagogy and Popular Education

Introduction to Part Two

Gurnam Singh

Part Two of this book is based on edited transcripts of six podcast critical dialogues that were done as part of a project undertaken in 2008/9. It was funded by the UK Higher Education Academy Subject Centre for Sociology, Anthropology and Politics (C-SAP), and the project was undertaken to develop a novel way for developing teaching and learning materials on the topic of 'critical pedagogy and popular education' based on the use of critical dialogue.

As Freire argues, at its core critical pedagogy aims to encourage progressive participative methods to deliver learning by breaking down the traditional power nexus between teacher and the students, by promoting reflexivity and critical consciousness, and by helping students question and challenge domination and the beliefs and practices that dominate. The critical dialogues that follow give many examples of how this can be done in practice. They also sought in the way they were carried and disseminated, in the form of podcasts, to demonstrate this as a process as well.

Critical pedagogy is also about developing certain dispositions among students that enable them to think, read, write and speak in ways that penetrates the surface of received wisdom, common sense or 'official versions of life', in doing so rather than being uncommitted, education becomes transformed into a vehicle for emancipation. Some of the discussions of critical pedagogy are related to classroom settings, while others are concerned with connect with those who, for a variety of factors, may not have access to formal education, and it is out of this that 'popular education' has emerged. Popular education is important for the way it has a more direct political imperative; it seeks to offer a framework for linking education with a wider political emancipatory project aimed at empowerment of oppressed communities through the creation of critically conscious political subjects.

Popular education is essentially problem based and begins with an issue, difficulty, need or aspiration identified by the community. In this sense it is very 'bottom up' and community led. But the pedagogical process is often initiated from outside and requires an external agent or 'popular educator' whose function is to facilitate learners to build 'popular power'. A crucial dimension of this is to enable learners to develop a collective history so that they can bring about the structural changes that ensure the fulfilling of their needs and wishes, both in their daily lives and on a broader social and cultural level. Broadly speaking, in relation to teaching and learning strategies, most accounts of critical pedagogy and popular education identify the importance of dialogue and horizontal relationships between the teacher and student or facilitator and participant.

The original project involved the production of a series of podcasts or recorded focussed conversations with radical educators who have sought to incorporate and develop critical pedagogy within their own practice. The podcasts that were produced were between 30–60 minutes in length and covered various aspects of critical pedagogy and popular education. Each conversation began with an exploration of the interviewees' personal education journey and how this had influenced their interest in critical pedagogy and popular education followed by a discussion on specific aspects of critical pedagogy. For each podcast that was produced a written information sheet with references, key concepts defined and links to further resources was produced to aid the learning experience of those listening to the podcasts. In total some ten dialogues were recorded, of which six have been selected for inclusion here. The podcasts were disseminated via the web and can be accessed at the following link: http://coventryuniversity.podbean.com/category/education/.

The six interviews which follow are not identical to the podcasts, but have been reworked by each of the authors so as to develop the materials contained in the original versions. Although each of podcasts which were selected for inclusion in this book address critical pedagogy, this is done in a different way. Stephen Cowden (Chapter Five) focuses on the way the ideas and concepts of Critical Pedagogy can be used in classroom settings. Joyce Canaan (Chapter Six), Michael Williams (Chapter Seven) and Jim Crowther (Chapter Eight) talk extensively about the interface between the university, schools and the wider community and seek to link critical pedagogy with activist education and action research strategies. Sarah Amsler (Chapter Nine) and Steve Wright (Chapter Ten) conclude this part of the book by looking at the significance of Critical Pedagogy through aspects of critical and political theory. The thread running through all of these different contexts is the way Critical Pedagogy opens up the emancipatory potential of education.

CHAPTER FIVE

Stephen Cowden on the Uses of Freire and Bourdieu

Stephen Cowden

Stephen Cowden is originally from Melbourne Australia, but has spent over half his life living in the United Kingdom. He worked as a Social Worker in London for over 10 years and while doing this completed his PhD in Australian Literature at the University of Kent. In 2001 he became a Senior Lecturer in Social Work at Coventry University. He is interested in applying the ideas and concepts of Critical Pedagogy for use in teaching as well as in Social Work practice, and he has also written about issues of ethics within Social Work (Pullen-Sansfacon & Cowden, 2012)

In this chapter Stephen Cowden, who works as a Senior Lecturer in Social Work at Coventry University, discusses how he uses Critical Pedagogy in his teaching. He explores the relationship between Critical Pedagogy, Social Movements and Marxian thought. Specifically, he highlights the way he synthesizes Paulo Freire's work with that of the French sociologist and public intellectual, Pierre Bourdieu. Stephen was interviewed by Gurnam Singh in July 2008.

GS: While radical movements that emerged in the 1960s are primarily associated with the struggle over workers' rights, women's rights, western colonialism and imperialism, the terrain of education was a hugely important area for these new social movements. Specifically motivated by Marxist analyses that education within capitalism primarily serves as a function of domestication, radical educators began to question the elitist nature of the education system. Along with demanding the abolition of privilege, they sought to challenge the curriculum that was being taught as well as the methods that were being employed to teach it.

It is within this context, that the idea of Critical Pedagogy as a teaching method, which intends to help students to question and challenge domination, emerged. One of the foremost advocates of such an approach was Ira Shor, whose definition of critical pedagogy has become a starting point for most explorations of it. Shor suggested that critical pedagogy is about '*developing certain dispositions amongst students that enable them to think, read, write and speak in ways that penetrates the surface of received wisdom, of common sense or official versions of life*'.

This encompasses the way critical pedagogy seeks to draw the learner's attention towards the social–political, discursive and ideological dimension, implicit in the production of knowledge, ideas and meaning. In doing so, rather than being uncommitted, education becomes transformed into a vehicle for emancipation. Stephen, if you were to start by expanding on some of Shor's conceptualization of critical pedagogy, how do you understand this idea yourself?

SC: I think it's a really interesting definition. I would bring it back to what you said at the start where you talked initially about the radical movements in the 1960s. I think inherent within any political movement is the question of pedagogy. Just as it was in the earlier period of the radical movements – the earlier moment of radical movements at the end of the nineteenth century, the 1890s, where you had things such as the Workers Educational Association (WEA) becoming important, the struggles around auto-didacticism . . .

GS: By 'auto-didacticism' do you mean a method of talking about your own life experience and situating that in a wider analysis?

SC: Essentially it is about the whole politics of self-educated working men and women who were claiming access to culture even though they were denied the formal means of education. So it was a specific movement, and organizations like the WEA are a remnant of that, but that was only one part of it during that period; there were Workers Musical Associations, theatres and a whole series of ways in which working-class people claimed accessed to culture. So I think Ira Shor's definition is excellent but I would also want to put that idea into a much broader context. The key point about the relationship between political movements and critical pedagogy is around the question of knowledge. Political movements which challenge the status quo have implicitly within them the need to question and open up the issue of what counts as 'knowledge' and I think this is a really crucial theme in critical pedagogy.

GS: Do you think its overstating the case to say that critical pedagogy has its spiritual roots, as it were, in a Marxist analysis?

SC: Yes and no; there are many people who appreciate the insights of critical pedagogy who are not Marxists, and equally there are many forms of Marxism which show very little awareness of the insights of critical pedagogy. One way of thinking of the relationship between Marx and critical pedagogy is that it picks up latent themes within the Marxist tradition and develops them. If you think of what Marx himself said on the issue of education there is not that much, though it is interesting to look at what he did say, for example in his third thesis on Feuerbach. Marx writes that 'The materialist doctrine concerning the changing of circumstances and upbringing forgets that circumstances are changed by men [sic] and that it is essential to educate the educator' (Marx, 1975:423). What I think Marx is talking about here is first that education is a dynamic process, based on the interchange between educators and educated, but also he is saying that if we are interested in social change we need to think of 'knowledge' itself as dynamic. For me this implies that radical education needs to be about educators who are always learning, always prepared to be challenged and be opened to be challenged – and it's that sense that I see critical pedagogy as having its roots in Marx's work.

GS: How is that different from a Hegelian perspective?

SC: A key issue in all of this is the concept of the dialectic, which Marx took from Hegel. The radical educationalist Paula Allman in her book *On Marx* (2007) characterizes Marx's use of the dialectical method as an approach which always rejects 'either/or' thinking. In other words dialectical thinking is a method and a means of grasping multiple realities. This is something I find very useful in classroom settings, where students will often put it to you that if something is one thing, how can it be the other? Dialectical thinking helps students to see how things are interconnected and enmeshed, but also contradictory and divided against themselves.

Coming back to Hegel and Marx, I think the key difference between them is that Marx emphasizes the centrality of the material changes in society as the basis of how people are themselves having to change, adapt and create these new forms of knowledge.

GS: Of lived experience?

SC: Yes the whole question of lived experience seems to be me to be behind all of what Marx is saying here. His whole conceptualization of the proletariat is of this group of people who had been farmers and peasants and were forced to move into these new cities where they had to become wage labourers – in England places like Birmingham, Manchester and London. I remember reading E. P. Thompson's book *The Making of the English Working Class* and being totally struck by the opening sentences where he writes 'The working class did not rise like the sun at an appointed time. It was present at its own making'. Thompson was really important for the way he reminded us that it isn't helpful to see 'class as a "structure", nor even as a "category", but as something which in fact happens (and can be shown to have happened) in human relationships' (2002:9). This means that we need to see lived experience and the responses of people to those experiences as crucial. It was this which threw up the kind of organizations that in time demanded the rights to education for working-class people. And equally you can understand the same process in relation to the suffrage movement and women's demand for education – these demands are a product of material changes and the lived experience of those material changes as you say.

GS: It seems to me that this gets at the fundamental basis upon which the elitist education system has historically been constructed within the West, going back to Greek times really. This is the idea that society has a select few 'philosopher kings' who need to be taken out of society and put into the monastery or the university out of the gaze of the public, free from the impurifying effects of common people. And through the power of their own intellectual endeavour, they produce the solutions for the rest of the world. It seems to me that the Marxist analysis is fundamentally challenging that basic premise of philosopher kings.

SC: I think that's right, yes. I mean there's obviously an egalitarian impulse within the whole of Marxism, but that's also true of radical social movements in general. I think what you're talking about also brings to mind Gramsci's analysis and I think he was the person who really kind of drew out this aspect of Marxist work with his discussion of traditional – organic intellectuals.

Traditional intellectuals are those people who you referred to in your question. They are those people who saw themselves essentially as disembodied and separate from the cut and thrust and the chaos of everyday life – it's this separation that is seen to make their form of knowledge legitimate. Gramsci is trying to say that's just one sort of intellectuality, but there are also what he calls 'organic intellectuals' – these are people who are organic in the sense of being rooted in the soil of particular groupings, of communities or sections of the community. He saw that as these social grouping formed themselves they threw up their particular spokespeople, their leaders, their 'theoreticians'. These sorts of intellectuals were a different kind of intellectual people; they were people whose lives had been shaped by those material changes and the lived experience of those material changes.

GS: So in a sense what you're saying is that the organic intellectuals have always been there. The other voice has always been there but it's always been silenced in official accounts and public discourse.

SC: Yes that's true, they have always been there and always will be. I think the other thing he is also saying is that though we have a sense of the traditional intellectuals as a kind of static group, its also the case that there is a kind of traffic between organic and traditional intellectuals whereby through societal shifts, and things like access to education, be that formal or informal, organic intellectuals become traditional intellectuals. I think one of the key things Gramsci is saying is that society is in flux and as groups acquire influence or hegemony that they come to articulate a new 'common sense'.

GS: In terms of university educators in the present day, are they organic intellectuals? Are they traditional intellectuals? Or are they non-intellectuals? How do you position yourself for example?

SC: I think that's a really interesting question and when I'm thinking of the people around me at Coventry University I often ask myself this question. If we are thinking about the social position of contemporary academics, particularly in the new university sector, are they just an expanded version of the traditional intellectuals?

Or do they represent such a 'proletarianized' version of these traditional intellectuals that they have become something else? What potentiality do these people have in terms of articulating different possibilities for themselves and their students? I think a key thing within all of this is looking at the actual material struggles taking place around education and looking at the role these people play in relation to that. If we look at that we do see many different forms of agency among academics, we see some resisting those changes in the name of particular conceptions of what it means to be an 'intellectual', while others are very passive in the face of those changes, and maybe would see ideas about 'intellectuality' as nothing much to do with what they do.

GS: So in a sense what you're saying is that educators in the massively expanded education system (whether that's universities or schools) have some kind of choice to make as to where they see themselves?

SC: I think that is very true. Paolo Freire puts this very well when he talks about pedagogy and says that 'education and education practice and its theory can never be neutral. The relationship between practice and theory in an education directed toward emancipation is one thing but quite another in education for domestication'. (1970:12). That is a really good way of understanding the way we are faced with choices.

If we put that into the contemporary context, what we see is – particularly coming from the Dearing Report that was initiated and responded to by New Labour to expand Higher Education – the target of 50 per cent of 18–30-year olds being in Higher Education. This in itself represents an enormous shift, probably from the time you were in university in Britain and I was in university in Australia, when it was about 8%. So in a sense there's a major change which has taken place. Now the question is: what is driving that? Is it simply that the government sees education as a social good, a collective good – an educated society? What seems to be driving this is this idea of the 'knowledge economy' where a more educated population is primarily about 'global economic competitiveness', but even if this is the main agenda, what other possibilities are to there to argue for that in a different way?

GS: One of the suggestions I would like to make is that throughout the seventies, eighties and nineties, we see a gradual decline of the Left. There are some important victories and some important developments but on the whole the Left have been waning throughout the seventies and the eighties and the New Right has been increasing its strangle-hold on government and institutions of power and on culture itself. Where has that left critical pedagogy? Has it simply fallen by the wayside or is there some kind of resurgence in the interest of critical pedagogy and the work of Paulo Freire?

SC: I think it's on the margins certainly but I nurture the hope that Paulo Freire will once again find a new audience. Most of the people who were influenced by his work the first time around are in their fifties and sixties. But I think there certainly is the opportunity that he will find a new audience in younger people, precisely because of the nature of the changes in educational institutions as they are taking place.

GS: In terms of those people who would have been fully fledged radical educators in the late sixties and seventies, have they just died off or have they changed their ideas? There is a view that a lot of those left wing intellectuals went heavily into post-modernism and that disconnected them from the very practical struggles that they were supposed to be promoting.

SC: Yes I certainly think that all those things happened. Some became demoralized and dropped out altogether, others became post-modernists, which as you say has shown itself to be simply another part of the process whereby intellectuals have abandoned any sense of an actual political practice. At the same time there have been those who continued to struggle away in the margins keeping those ideas alive and I think that's been important, even if they were on the margins.

GS: So what is the appeal of Paulo Freire? What's the appeal in someone who wasn't even a Marxist, who came from a Roman Catholic background, from a religious perspective? Is it some kind of emotive appeal or does he really give us some insight into the condition we're trying to deal with in education today?

SC: The way I see Freire is, he is doing several things, he's operating on several levels. I think as you correctly point out, he comes from this radical Catholic background. He was very influenced by the emergence of peasant unions in Brazil, which were themselves nurtured by radical priests who were working on the ground with poor people. The question of literacy was a very potent political question in Brazil in that you couldn't vote unless you were literate. This made the question of literacy a highly charged political question as the maintenance of the oligarchy in Brazil was contingent on people not being able to read and write. It is through these struggles that Freire develops his method of Critical Pedagogy, which is distinctive for the way it synthesises the practical skills of literacy development with a social and political critique.

Freire comes to Marxism in part through this radical Christianity, in part through an anti-colonial tradition present throughout Latin America and in part through an interest in existentialism, and this is why his writings have that strong emphasis on the idea of personal authenticity or truth. In this sense Paulo Freire stands at the opposite end of the spectrum from post-modernists who have relativized the question of truth. Truth for him is very real and he has no problem with this concept.

GS: But in his emphasis on language and metaphor, has Freire provided the landing strip for postmodernism?

SC: I think that may be one way of looking at it, and Freire's work certainly does rely heavily on metaphors – this is part of his very distinctive mode of expression and part of what makes him very appealing to me; its also something that makes him very different from say more conventional sociologists of education. But in general he is not someone who postmodernists have particularly sought to claim.

I think the basis on which I hope he finds a new audience is in reaction to what has happened to pedagogy in with the expansion of universities and what you could call the massification of education. Much of the pedagogy here has blurred the distinction between education and training. Many academics in many new universities see themselves not as people who are teaching students to think critically but as people teaching 'skills'. Therefore, the ethos associated I think with the massification of Higher Education is essentially dominated by the technical rationality and a very positivistic notion of knowledge, which is what Freire characterizes as the 'banking method' of education, and which he is very critical of.

GS: At the end of the day what people want is a successful economy. They want to enjoy life and their day-to-day consumer culture. We have to train people to serve the population and that's where the jobs are, that's where the expansion is, that's where the demand is. Yes, we should have thinking people where somebody is working in a department store or in a call centre or in a school. Yes they should be thoughtful people; they should be able to solve problems. Essentially that's where the growth is and the last thing they want is people who can ponder about the world – philosophize.

SC: Yes this is the argument which is used in new universities, where the critical reflective component of education is presented as a luxury that really can only be afforded to a privileged few. I think this brings us back to the fundamental question of what the purpose of education is. I think what Freire speaks to is this egalitarian impulse that says that part of our species-being as people is to understand the world; it's not a luxury, but instead its part of what it means to be human. The next part of the argument is that therefore that opportunity to understand the ways of the world is something that should be open to everybody, from all social classes, and not simply for instrumental purposes. That's not to say there is anything inherently wrong with teaching skills – what's wrong is the way this is separated off from critical thinking, and separated quite artificially in actual fact. The power of Critical Pedagogy lies in the way it combines social and political questions within the process dealing with very practical issues – as we said earlier Freire developed his ideas in the context of teaching literacy.

This brings us back to the basis on which his ideas could make a return; I sense a great sense of disillusionment people feel about the way everyday life is dominated by a technical rationality. I certainly feel in talking with students that there is a yearning for some more genuine form of engagement with what's really happening in the world particularly in relation to our political leaders, politicians and the media, about whom people feel really significantly disconnected from. Politics has adopted a commercialized language of customer satisfaction, which on one hand people are incredibly familiar with, but which doesn't really engage with the kind of problems that are around us.

I see Freire, as well as people like Henry Giroux who has developed a lot of Freire's ideas, as saying that critical educators have to be able to speak to these concerns, and understand and appreciate where people are at, but the process doesn't end there. You also have to place these issues in some wider context – so Critical Pedagogy isn't just accepting how people see things at face value – this has to be understood through what C. Wright Mills has called a 'sociological imagination' (Mills, 1959). Mills' idea here has an important pedagogical component that I see in my work with Social Work and Youth Work students. In terms of educating people who are the future public service professionals, it's crucial that we are able to see social problems in a broader context of the social structure in which we live; without that we have a very impoverished public sphere that largely reproduces victim-blaming. It's really important that these people need to know how to pose broader questions in the context of working with the immediate and the concrete; so if you're working with, for example, young offenders, its about finding a way of working that deals with the immediate issues that are in front of you, but also incorporating into that an understanding of why it is that so many young people end up in the criminal justice system and in prison.

Critical Pedagogy is about asking those questions, but also about developing forms of practice based on that understanding.

GS: I know that you've been influenced quite considerably by the work of Pierre Bourdieu, the French educationalist. In what ways do you think his ideas have helped to form your own practice of Critical Pedagogy?

SC: I think Bourdieu's great strength is in helping us understand the way social inequality is reproduced through 'class' – this whole emphasis has been particularly important in the wake of the way 'class' has been hugely de-emphasized within sociology in the last two decades. It's in this way that I think we need to understand what Bourdieu is saying about educational institutions. His concept of 'cultural capital' – the forms of knowledge that people have and which then enable them to make particular kinds of decisions and particular choices – the way he's used that concept gives us a very good way of understanding the way class, gender and 'race', and these in their particular interactions with each other, shape patterns of inclusion and exclusion. I often talk with students in class about how they were seen at school and I find this sense of inclusion and exclusion is felt at a very personal level, and really shapes how you see yourself throughout life.

One of things I think students really respond to in Bourdieu's work is the idea that people, that is themselves, often misrecognize the power of social structures in their own lives. I was discussing this with students, and a female student said to me that her teacher spoke to her at the end of school and told her that she'd be 'good for having babies'. What Bourdieu allows us to see is the way schooling reproduces these patterns of inclusion and exclusion, which then construct forms of subjectivity which are built around those – your teachers have told you you're 'thick, but don't worry you'll make a great mum!' Incidentally that student went on to do really well in her Social Work Degree. This is what brings me back to the question of Critical Pedagogy, because it gives voice to these sorts of experiences, but also contextualizes them in such a way that allows us to see where the ideas behind a statement like the one made by that teacher come from. Bourdieu gives you a framework for understanding this wider picture at a sociological empirical level, though it also needs to be looked at the level of values and ethics.

GS: In your discussion of the work of Bourdieu you use the word 'understand' quite a lot of times – that he helps us to understand the context, understand the processes. Perhaps one of the criticism of Bourdieu is that's all he does. He uncovers for us what's going on. Yes, that's really part of the solution, but he doesn't really offer us any solutions and one might suggest that one solution that one could extrapolate from Bourdieu's analysis is that working class children should have a bourgeois education. Would that be unfair?

SC: The point you're making is one that many critics of Bourdieu have made – that while he gives us a scientific approach to understanding what is happening within the system, he has said very little about what to do about that – about what forms of 'agency' that could be adopted. Rather than see this as a problem, I find it more useful to place Bourdieu's analysis of what's happening in the wider social structures of education alongside the work of Paulo Freire – the two together make a powerful combination. I can give an example of this in my teaching on Bourdieu where I get students to examine the concept of 'symbolic violence' through looking at a quote from Bourdieu. Bourdieu's concept of symbolic violence is about the way inequalities are reproduced by working-class people, ethnic minorities, women, people with disabilities, internalizing through their socialization, lower expectations of themselves. One of the interesting features of Bourdieu's work is he's an incredibly convoluted writer; he writes in these long sentences that are often quite difficult to follow – they're complex for lecturers to understand, and so are of course even more so for students. I give students the following passage from *The Purpose of Reflexive Sociology*:

> "Symbolic violence, to put it as simply and tersely as possible, is the *violence which is exercised on an agent with his or her complicity*
>
> . . . To say it more rigorously; social agents are knowing agents who, even when they are subjected to determinisms, contribute to producing the efficacy of that which determines them insofar as they structure what determines them. And it almost always in the 'fit' between determinants and categories of perception that constitute them as such that the effect of domination arises. I call *misrecognition* the fact of recognising a violence which is wielded precisely inasmuch as one does not perceive it as such". (1992:167–8)

I ask the students, working in groups, to figure out what this passage means and to put it in their own words. The students will often protest and ask things like 'Why does he have to use all those big words? Why is the way he writes so complicated? Why is it necessary to write like that? Can't he talk in plain language?'

I acknowledge that it is difficult, but I still ask them to go through the passage sentence by sentence. When they do that they find out that they actually can figure out what it means – it's as though they have surprised themselves with what they are able to understand, and they share this as a group. Then, reflecting on what it was like to have done that, I say to the students 'So what was it about that passage that made you think that you wouldn't be able to do understand it?" This is a difficult question because I'm asking students to, if you like examine the impact of this misrecognition in their own lives, and of course challenging this is part of understanding the impact of the way symbolic violence works. In that sense the power of this exercise resides in the way it has a kind of mirroring effect in that it's the very power of symbolic violence in lowering people's expectations of themselves which is on one hand what the passage is about, but also what is also being demonstrated through the exercise. I developed this exercise to try to use Freire's idea of teaching a practical skill – in this case how to read a difficult passage by going through it line by line – with a social and political critique of power – in this case the power of language both to exclude, but that also when you can overcome that sense of exclusion, to use. I find that teaching in this way engages students much more effectively that just by teaching abstractly about Bourdieu's ideas.

GS: So, in a sense what you're saying is that part of the role of the teacher, the critical pedagogue, is to work with people's identity; whether they see themselves as being part of some educated elite or they see themselves as part of some lumpen uneducated mass. That you're challenging both of these identities and saying that both can be thinkers and both can engage with social life, both can make sense of their worlds and in that sense it's neither a call for elitism for everybody or a call for dumbing down. What it is is a call for critical educating throughout.

SC: And this brings us back to the quote from Ira Shor you gave at the start; that the fundamentals of critical pedagogy lie in the idea that education is a process whereby we critically apprehend the world around us. We come to understand ourselves as products of history. Our choices are not simply our individual choices but are made as a result of our social position, our position within the family, our gender, what community we come from, and of course all of this needs to be located within a wider process of history.

GS: In conclusion then I think we can say that education is arguably one of the most precious commodities that any human being can possess. While one cannot deny that educational provision has expanded dramatically over the past three decades, the efficacy of what and how students are taught is a moot point. Henry Giroux, the radical educationalist, in reflecting upon what he sees as a crisis in universities, makes a powerful argument that in a world marked by increasing poverty, unemployment and diminished social opportunities, educators must vindicate the crucial connection between culture and politics and defending public and Higher Education as sites of democratic learning and struggle. Essentially to do such a task, he suggests we need to provide students with the knowledge, skills and values they will need to address some of the most urgent questions of our time. Educating for critical citizenship and civic courage means, in part, re-defining the role of academics as engaged public intellectuals.

References

Allman, P. (2007) *On Marx*. Sense Publishers, Rotterdam.

Bourdieu. (1992) *An Invitation to Reflexive Sociology*. Polity Press, London.

Freire, P. (1970) *Pedagogy of the Oppressed*. Penguin, Harmondsworth.

Marx, K. (1975) 'Theses on Feuerbach' in *Early Writings*. (Introduced by Coletti, Translated by Livingstone and Benton)Penguin Books, London, pp. 421–23.

Mills, C. W. (1959) *The Sociological Imagination*. Penguin Books, London.

Pullen-Sansfacon and Cowden (2012) *The Ethical Foundations of Social Work*. Pearson-Longman, Harlow.

Thompson, E. P. (2002) *The Making of the English Working Class*. Penguin Books, London.

CHAPTER SIX

Joyce Canaan on the Neoliberal University, Critical Pedagogy and Popular Education

Joyce Canaan

Source: Photo by Kevin Hayes.

Dr Joyce Canaan describes herself as a 'Public Sociologist and Popular Educator'. She is Professor of Sociology at Birmingham City University, United Kingdom. She completed her PhD in Anthropology from the University of Chicago in 1990, and has published extensively on Critical Pedagogy and teaching and learning in the neoliberal university. Previously she has worked at the Centre for Sociology, Anthropology and Politics (C-SAP) based at the University of Birmingham. Joyce's current research concerns the challenges students and lecturers face in their efforts to engage with the process of 'class' and students' perceptions of the current crisis in Higher Education.

In this chapter Joyce Canaan, Professor of Sociology at Birmingham City University, offers an analysis of the impact of neoliberalism on university life and the way she is seeking to respond to this in her own work (Canaan and Shumar, 2008). This discussion is prefaced with brief reflection on her intellectual and professional journey and how she became committed to Critical Pedagogy and popular education. She then goes on to outline some of the political and pedagogical strategies she has developed within her work as an academic activist. Joyce discusses some of the various activities she has supported and participated in, including the links she developed with Venezuelan popular educators. Last, in reflecting on her own teaching practices, Joyce ends by offering a series of suggestions as to how university academics can inculcate the principles and methods associated with critical pedagogy and popular education into their own teaching practices.

GS: I am a firm believer that one can get a better appreciation of somebody's ideas and thoughts if one has some insights into their personal biography, and in the context of our discussion on pedagogy, their educational experiences. I would like to start with this before we go on to talking about how you have sought to translate the underpinning ideas associated with critical pedagogy in your own academic practices.

JC: The first significant moment for the purposes of this discussion is probably when went to the University of Chicago to commence my postgraduate studies in the Department of Human Development. By the end of my first year I was an absolute wreck. My first piece of work was described as 'interesting'; by the time I got my third piece of work, I had got a C, which I never had in my life. C's were simply not allowed at Chicago and the comments next to the grade were to the effect 'your work has been consistently mediocre', which to somebody who was an aspiring intellectual was devastating. It shook my sense of self profoundly and forced me to rethink my motivation for grad school. I later realized part of the issue was that I was going down the road of Human Development when in fact Anthropology was my true passion. By moving into the Anthropology Department I was being allowed to ask questions that were troubling me. I remember reading Durkheim who was a huge influence in the department; not the version that is read by sociologists but the '*Elementary Forms of Religious Life*' and I was fascinated by learning about the way people attached meaning to symbols of life. Clifford Geertz was another key influence in helping me with questions relating to how people interpret and understand their lives and how we, as researchers, can never stand in the shows of the people we study but we talk to them; stand alongside them.

Later on I was also extremely taken by the literature coming out of the Centre for Contemporary Studies (CCCS) at Birmingham in the United Kingdom in the late seventies and eighties. The work of Paul Willis, Angela McRobbie, Chris Griffin and Stuart Hall began to provide me with both a critique of Anthropology and an alternative framework for studying so-called third-world 'exotic' others. This brought me to a realization of the importance of resistance and the Gramsci's idea of hegemony.

GS: So how did you get from Chicago to the United Kingdom?

JC: It was through the interest with the work coming out of CCCS that I came to the United Kingdom, for what I felt at the time would be a year of a life-time. I wanted to get more engaged with feminism and Marxism. What was great about the CCCS was its focus on the everyday; what was not so great was that it didn't engage as fully as I would have liked with the political world around it and this is what led me to work outside in the 'informal education' sphere. I remember meeting cultural workers and activists who were not speaking the language of academics but were intensely engaged in politics and critique. I was taken aback by this and what it did to me was to think about the questions, to whom do I want to speak? Was it to elitist academics, or was it to my students, my peers and to the world? I chose the latter.

GS: In more recent times, and particularly through your work at C-SAP you have been involved in a number of initiatives for developing critical pedagogy and popular education in universities: what kind of strategies/ways could people include some of these ideas and principles into their teaching?

JC: One way is by rethinking what the purposes of learning and teaching are – really very profound but also very simple *in part*. Should we be giving lectures or should we engage in dialogue with students? I have been able to shift from lectures to discussions so that I am no longer the great sage on the stage. I have been able to set up, with students, a beanbag room where we all sit 'at the same level' as students put it and that encourages dialogue among us – a dialogue that at least somewhat builds on students' prior knowledge.

GS: That seems like a luxury in the massification agenda where you might have 100–200 students enrolled onto a module.

JC: It is a luxury, but ironically in the current era when we're supposed to be enabling student learning to build on students' own experiences, one could very easily argue for and justify such spaces. It won't always be possible but I would suggest that we try to break out of the massification as and when we can. This kind of learning and teaching moves towards Freire's ideas about posing problems based on what students say to help them expand their current frameworks, if they wish, beyond what Freire in the *Pedagogy of the Oppressed* (1970) called their 'limit situation' or the obstacles directed at negating people's liberation. He suggests 'it is not the limit-situations in and of themselves which create a climate of hopelessness, but rather how they are perceived' (1970:80).

GS: Would you describe this as moving away from the 'banking principle' as one of those obstacles that negate liberation, which possibly predominates the lecture method to a dialogical method.

JC: The move to the beanbag room has encouraged me to engage with critical academic literacies, which takes us from the discourse of derision about students, in which all of us have engaged, asking, '*Why don't students today do things the ways students used to do'?* That is one way to frame students – as being dumbed or dulled down. Another way is to consider that we have a widening participation agenda that encourages more students to come into the university than previously. Maybe we should ask, as the critical literacies literature suggests, asking 'What is it like for these students to come into the university'? Why would the way that we were taught as students be appropriate for those from backgrounds so different from ours? How can we reorganize learning so we support these students better, so that they engage more fully?

GS: That's very interesting; I also feel the need to defend intellectual work. I feel a profound sense of the value of the intellectual enterprise. Although not withstanding some of the problems with the traditional forms of intellectual practices. It's trying not to throw the baby out with the bath water, which I think often happens with some of the ways in which widening participation agendas are configured.

For example, a lot of universities are now setting up academic writing centres/academic literacies which really seem to be a re-hash of the old remedial kind of support that would be given in secondary education and primary education. And I like this notion of critical academic literacies and would like you to explore how that is different to remedial support to teaching people how to write sentences, paragraphs and referencing. What's behind the notion of critical academic literacies?

JC: First of all, literacies rather than literacy is the appropriate concept, which is to say that you can't have generic teaching of academic skills because each discipline has different ways of reading, writing and arguing, of engaging theoretically and methodologically. So there are multiple academic literacies rather than one. We can't have a generic literacy for all disciplines.

Second we must ask, '*Why are we encouraging these students to engage in learning? What's the purpose of it?*' Is it to produce more entrepreneurial people for the future or to produce people (who, given the current world crisis economically and politically, need considerable critical skills) who will be able to negotiate this world and work to make it a place that's at least humanly habitable and just in 50 years' time?

GS: One of the things that profoundly struck me in thinking about students and their academic prowess/abilities is that these capacities might be about what they possess within but often it's about how you feed yourself to be embodied without. If you feel that you're not a clever person, unsurprisingly one tends to underachieve and it does seem to be in our education that we are falling for that trap. We're giving mixed messages to these students, on the one hand we're saying '*you're in higher education, you're in university, you're capable of higher learning*' and then we start to do remedial work and send them to these places to be interviewed.

It's a paradox and there's not an easy way out but what I've tried to do is to try to enable students to see deficiencies in literacies as partly to do with the way in which they have a self-concept. An example would be where students often complain about difficult writing/reading and rather than saying it is difficult and confirming may be the fact that they may not be capable of engaging with that text alone. I would say well, 'Let's work together and climb the mountain together'. And the sense that students then can have of achievement, of self-ability is immense. So I feel it's partly to do with process and embodiment as much as with the technical skills.

JC: I agree completely. One thing I've done when teaching someone like Baudrillard, for example, was to say '*let's look at a paragraph, let's just look at one paragraph*' in his essay. They read the first sentence together and then we had a discussion something like the following:

> '*What do you think it means?*'
> '*I don't know.*'
> '*Well let's read the next sentence. What does that mean?*'
> '*I'm not sure.*'
> '*Ok let's go back and look at the first sentence again*' and then the third sentence. '*Does that help you understand the second sentence, the first sentence?*'

So then you go through it and at the end of the class almost all students were really engaged because they were doing it themselves. They could see they weren't the only one who found the text hard. By reading together, we deconstructed 'hardness'. Students could also recognize that they couldn't read it in one go. First we need to read with other people and recognize that you not understanding doesn't mean you are stupid, it means actually that you need to think and maybe think somewhat differently than you have thought before. And that's ok, it's scary but it's ok and we can do it together to make it a bit more ok.

GS: Another dimension of popular education and critical pedagogy is the relationship between the personal and the professional and we've already talked about the political. To what degree do you use your own biographical sense or biography in teaching students or do you think that's appropriate for critical pedagogs to share self?

JC: Because I've come to critical pedagogy through feminist pedagogy, I already recognized the feminist point that the personal is political; our own experiences speak to larger issues.

For example when I teach students to deconstruct the idea of a stable gendered self, I tell students about how, in recent years, when the phone rings, people sometimes say to me, '*Is that Mr Rogers?*', which is my partner's last name. And for a while I would get really upset, '*why is my voice so low?*' Clearly my gender identity is less secure than I thought. Last night my stepson rang and said '*Hi Dad*' and my first reaction was to say, '*Oh no, you think I'm Dad*'. He said '*Well, you sounded like Dad*'. My point is to show students how my gendered identity, after all these years, is still changing. So, as Judith Butler (1990) so powerfully demonstrates, gender is performative, it shifts as we produce it and others and we respond to its production. Examples from my life show that I, too, am vulnerable, sand that linking theory and practice, using theory to understand my vulnerability and my practices more generally. Maybe they can do the same.

GS: It seems to me 'role-modelling' imperative behind what you're doing is not a sycophancy or installing hero worship but actually using yourself as a resource/a template, a sounding board as a way of enabling your own subjectivity to enable students to locate their own subjectivity.

In your book 'Structure and Agency in the Neoliberal University' you talk at length about the neoliberal university and some of the issues that academics are now facing. But do you see a future for popular education and popular educators in neoliberalized higher education?

JC: This is some of the things we are talking about in our Critical Pedagogy and Popular Education group [to which you and I, and Sarah Amsler, Stephen Cowden and Sara Motta, belong]. We recognize, building on Bourdieu (1998a,b) and Santos (2003), that at the current juncture, the university must be connected to the world outside. So for example, Michael Burawoy's (2004) idea of public sociology is that sociology is already and must be more fully linked to the world outside. We must have public intellectuals and we must encourage sociology students to bring the analytical and critical skills they learn at university to the world outside and to see space outside the university as potentially informing university knowledge. But also the university must recognize that learning for the sake of earning is not the name of the game. We need learning for the sake of transformation!

GS: And with the global economic crisis, do you see the beginning of the end of neoliberalism or another phase?

JC: I think that remains to be seen and I think this is actually an opportune moment for those of us who are critical pedagogues or popular educators to work together. To say '*ok, let's encourage our students to see the world outside and see how their skills that they're learning here can be used out there. Let's bring people from outside, who are doing really interesting and compelling things, into the university.*' We talk about employer engagement – why not do as some activists at Leeds University do, bringing together activists inside and outside the university. Recognizing that 'scholarship with commitment', as Bourdieu put it, means recognizes that academics have certain analytical skills. However, there are practices going on outside, praxis going on outside. For me critical pedagogy and popular education are two complimentary sides of the same strategy that is crucial at the current moment.

GS: The current situation of our higher education system is pretty challenging for all of us and maybe more so for critical pedagogues. Nonetheless, what progressive strategies do you think could develop?

JC: I think there are strategies that some people are already adopting. One is for lecturers in their own classrooms doing things that they think of as critical pedagogy. This is to help to develop the next generation of students to be critical thinkers and is an important first step. But this should not be the last step because the systems functions and flourishes by allowing little bits of subversion to operate at the particular chalk-face. And management are happy for us to do these acts of mini subversive as it shows that there's diversity among lecturers.

GS: But we have increasingly commodified students who are very strategic and often come to university to get a job whereas critical pedagogy argues that there are more important things than getting a job, like engaging politically with the world. How do you persuade students that this is a good option?

JC: When I have said to my students that they are acting instrumentally, their response is *'Oh no we're not; you just think we are'*. So I have to listen to them and discuss with them what we mean. We don't recognize that we're instrumental. We don't own our own instrumentality. The ways in which are trying to get through the day, the week, the year, the rest of our working lives. We have to recognize that we are part of the problem, and therefore they and we need to be part of the solution, rather than have us demonize them.

Also, I have found that our students often have an inherent hope – perhaps hunger is a better word – because when you ask students about the world, they believe it is in bad shape; they're rightly depressed about the future – they're pessimistic rather than optimistic. So if you talk with students, you can try to encourage them to see and imagine beyond the horizon, to the wider world. The keenness for learning that students often express is staggering. This means partly believing in our students.

GS: And maybe also we should ask about them seeing their lives in different ways; not negating their social lives but getting them to see their lives from a different perspective.

JC: I agree. If you say to students, *'What are the problems you face right now'?* They may say, *'Debt; I don't know if I'm going to get a job'*, and then you can ask in a Freirian way, *'Why do you have that debt? Where did that come from'?* It came from the government introducing student fees. So it's about starting where students are at and encouraging them to see beyond themselves to the ways that government policy created the problem. 'Why do you think you're not going to be able to get a job? What's happened to the world of work'? Again raising questions that place their most immediate issues in a wider context.

GS: And is that also about offering them alternative idealisms than those offered by the market, which is like their imprisonment as much as anything else? There's a pointlessness of what their lives have become which links in with Freire's notion of the Pedagogy of Hope (1994). This can feel quite religious in the way it proposes a different world and a different place. I'm aware Freire's work is replete with these ideas around liberated spaces/liberated worlds and of course about socialist ideas around socialist societies. What about enabling them to see another world? Is that too grand a project to contemplate with these students?

JC: I think it is in a way. Let's start at a concrete level. Let's listen to the comments that students make to our module evaluations, which is often that students say 'my eyes were opened by this module'. What does this metaphor mean? It a means that you see more of the world; you see more of the connections that are there but were not apparent to you before. Then the question is what you do with that. And maybe in the course of a module (if I don't think beyond a module, it would be hubristic to assume we can take it far beyond) when students see things more fully there's an understanding, an excitement, a possibility that, *'It doesn't have to be this way'*. Maybe that's the most we can ask for an undergraduate degree but then it does allow you to work with the students to help them to understand more fully the world that they're in and hopefully begin to ask questions – so they can take that question asking/ problem posing into the future.

GS: It might be wishful thinking to expect students to get involved in large-scale social movement projects. It might be nice but wishful thinking. But what might be possible is for them to transform some of these micro relationships that they have – in the family, with partners, within their local communities to small-scale campaigns. It feels like there are possibilities of social change without some big grand project, which is probably one of the mistakes we made in the past where we felt it was 'all or nothing'. What kind of projects do you think could emanate from some of this work? What work have you been involved in on the ground?

JC: I started by talking about issues in class. If you want to create an alternative you need to know how the world at present is organized. So it's important to speak truth to power, to understand the factors operating in the present situation to get beyond this situation. I also talk about what other people are doing and what I'm doing, to change the current situation.

GS: That seems very Hegelian in a sense that the starting point is to understand the world better but Marx was a bit sceptical about that kind of thought process. For him, the whole job of radicals is to change the world.

JC: I agree with Marx that understanding should serve to help us get beyond critique to transformation. So we need to critique different parts of the neoliberal agenda. For example, one thing I'm doing through my post as the national coordinator of learning and teaching at C-SAP is to fulfil the Higher Education Academy agenda about employer engagement and employability. My tongue sours as I say these words. So my thought is, '*What do these mean? What kind of employment do our students get'?* I remember a decade ago, a joke was to ask, 'What does a sociologist graduate say most frequently? Do you want chips with your burger'? So what notion of employability do we mean?

I'm organizing a day through C-SAP on employability after the economic crash. This subjects this notion to scrutiny, which is still the first step of critique, and to take this a little further. One speaker is going to do a discourse analysis of the concept of employability. I'm hoping they explore the particular meanings government place on the concept of employability and the ways that it imposes the onus on the individual to find a job themselves and ignore the wider social world, which is one of the things Bourdieu talks about in his discussion of neoliberalism, which is the erasure of the social.

GS: My sense is that the government has a completely different conceptualization of community engagement, community cohesion and employer engagement than we do. Things may have changed with the crash but it seems to me that all roads lead to one thing: how can we supply the neoliberal society with cannon fodder really? So what you're saying feels like this is a radical departure from the ways in which those in power might conceptualize these things.

JC: Yes, this is something a past colleague of mine said to me once. She had been getting loads of grants and she's on the Left and I said to her, 'How do you get these grants? She said that the terms government use are slippery and, as Judith Butler and others said, we can destabilize this usage by using their terms differently. So perhaps if they used our terms against us, why shouldn't we say there are more possibilities in these concepts. That's a pretty modest step in the right direction that allows us to explore what we want.

GS: An image of dancing with the devil comes into my mind but this is a form of subversion isn't it? It's trying to take the devil away from hell, as it were, so you dance them towards some other place. Presumably there are possibilities here and there are success stories.

JC: Yes, there are success stories. I was able to set up, with my colleague Matt Badcock, a BA in Public Sociology. In the School of Politics at the University of Nottingham there's a Centre for Social and Global Justice which does really excellent work. There's an MA programme on Activism and Social Change in Human Geography at Leeds University. Alongside resistance within, there are new important developments outside the neoliberal university in the form of for example, the Free University of Liverpool, Birmingham Free University, the Social Science Centre, Lincoln and the London Free University, Tent City and the Bank of Ideas, which all were sparked off by the Occupation of St Paul's Cathedral on 15 October 2011, as part of the global occupy movement of autumn 2011.

GS: It feels as there's something very exciting and new emerging here. In the sixties, seventies and eighties universities were replete with similar kinds of courses, such as women's and ethnic relations programmes. I was very much a product of those educational possibilities and then the neoliberal agenda kicked in saying we need employment-orientated vocational programmes.

Some of these programmes that talk about changing the world or whatever seem to have very little relevance to the practical needs of society in late modernity. But it does seem to me, as you were saying earlier on, with the crash new questions are emerging in people's minds about there maybe being a window of opportunity now to offer an alternative curriculum which gives meaning to their lives, in a way in which, prior to this, a commodified neoliberal curriculum gave meaning to a neoliberal society. In a post neoliberal society, maybe this is what is needed.

JC: Yes, the question is whether we are in a post neoliberal society or whether neoliberalism is continuing; right now there's an immense effort to bolster the neoliberalism, despite the financial collapse. For example, Noam Chomsky has argued that the purpose government funding of banks is to allow these banks to get rid of their dodgy debts, which is why no money is circulating in the wider economy. What do I hear this morning on the news? Exactly that point. So some things are beginning to slip out. But the Right is clever. This is a possible moment of opening up and they will do all in their power to close it down. We really need to be using this moment.

GS: My sense is that there is clear distinction between the political class and the mercantile class – the bankers and stockbrokers. I'd like to think the vast majority of working- and middle-class people (e.g. professionals and civil servants) are really seeing a powerful rejection of the ways in which these ruling classes – the political elites and the economic elites have been working hand in hand. So I do think there are opportunities, although you're right as that doesn't mean there won't be any resistance to what we might want to do in universities because the people who control the purse strings are still very much linked into the political and economic ruling class. But it does feel like we need courage now to step forward and offer these alternative programmes.

JC: Yes. What I find staggering is when I said at my individual performance review that I'd like to set up a new MA programme in Education and Social Justice, I was told, *'Go ahead and try'*. This reminded of what Liam Kane from Glasgow University said; 'We often push against open doors – we don't imagine we can do these kinds of things'. So I'm now going to try to develop this one. And what's interesting about this moment of possibility is that we're legitimated by key theorists in the Social Sciences; both Santos (2003) and Bourdieu (1998b) have both talked about the fact that the university among other places is being radically transformed. Santos says that the university is now being opened up to top–down neoliberal forces and this opening up enables the opening up to bottom–up, progressive, democratic, socialist forces. So we can have an MA in Activism and Social Justice where students are working with campaigning groups. It's not only opening up the university to these bottom–up forces but importantly having the students work with groups in the community outside the university – linking scholarship with commitment, which is what Bourdieu talks about. Linking the university to the world outside and having the world outside as a necessary partner in the educational process.

GS: I think that's really interesting. Where I work, I'm leading an Applied Research Group (ARG) on Social Inclusion in Social Care and certainly there is a top-down agenda there around bringing research money, prestige and everything else to the programme. But the group and the people involved in the group have been clear that our agenda is about social change and social transformation and ethically we will not take on projects unless we can fulfil those criteria. We're not getting huge grants but we are getting a lot of important engagement. So like you say, taking things out there is again about linking the university to outside. This is another employment engagement agenda – employer engagement for social change rather than for the accumulation of capital.

I just want to share an experience, as earlier you were talking about the possibilities of setting up alternative programmes of study that could begin to connect with other agendas that are obviously critical for citizens of today. For example, agendas concerning the environment and political issues around human rights and refugee issues. My colleague Stephen Cowden and I did a workshop about 2 weeks ago on a Post-qualifying Social Work Programme' at Northampton University, which is for professional workers, social care workers and managers. The person who runs the programme asked us to do something bold and something different. So we said yes, we will do a day on 're-claiming radical social work'. This is something that's dropped off the agenda of undergraduate education, let alone of postgraduate competence-focussed education, which is supposed to be about practice issues.

So we went with some trepidation, wondering whether the students would ask what's the relevance of this to enabling us to work with children? But to our pleasant surprise, the students are asking for another day, saying we wanted to spend more time looking at these issues, and a number of students in their feedback said this was transformative – these are senior managers. And feedback; later from the course leader said a number of them have initiated work-based meetings to discuss these ideas.

This does feel like something important is happening. Something about people's consciousness shifting, even if it's only temporary, it has been destabilized. But I do think there's a moment now where radical educators, critical pedagogues and popular educators need to offer some ideas and interpret some people's concerns with some concrete steps. So I think its fantastic work that you're doing.

JC: I think we need to be guided by others. I'm guided by an experience I had a couple of years ago when I went to Venezuela. Seeing what is possible and not just possible but happening on the ground in other countries. Four of us went – we didn't know anyone but had a couple of contacts to look up. We happened to bump into a talk that Hugo Chavez was giving. We spoke to the people sitting in front of us and behind us and they each invited us to their communities.

One of those conversations led us to go to this amazing community in the middle Caracas. We were waiting for the people we had met at what they called a community centre and I suddenly realized what a community centre actually is – a centre for the community, for people of all ages – little children were playing outside, older people were waiting to get medical care and we saw classes training people to become chefs and cooks. Also, there was a medical centre down the road with a Cuban doctor who was dedicating two years of her life to help this community develop medical knowledge and knowledge of health prevention to prevent illness. So we could see a community working. The people themselves were organizing activities, and from that visit came a visit to another community.

In this other community an Anglican priest, who was very warm and engaging, took us around the new community being built. The community are building a school, not just for the children, but for the mothers coming back from work in the evenings, where they can be taught literacy. So the schooling space is a community space.

One day I went to the sociology department at Caracas University, a department located in the formerly privatized petroleum company of Venezuela. This is now where the free, public university is located. One of the sociologists spent three hours talking with me. He said that the university isn't just located in the university, but goes to communities like the one I had seen, and they work with community members. To do a BA in Sociology you cannot enter this free university unless you have a project usually agreed upon by your community. So the project is not for you as an individual yourself, but for you to work with your community, to help them improve themselves. So immediately it's a social rather than an individual experience.

Another guy we met, Edenis Guilarte, was a mature student at the other free university in Caracas, working with a popular educator in the School of Education. He took us to the community where he had been doing work, a community that had previously been located in a slum. We saw the slum and a few families still lived there but most of the community, with the help of Edenis and his lecturer, Alejandrina Reyes, had built a new community. Edenis had worked with this community and we saw that they really loved and respected him.

They showed us where they had lived and what they had built. Edenis and Alejandrina had used a Latin American popular education idea, called diagnostification. To ask people in the community to consider what problems they faced and to list them in terms of their priority. They had been asked to explore what they needed to do to solve this problem, what skills they needed to be able to solve this problem. So when the community said that they needed funds, Edenis, Alejandrina and others asked, '*Does anyone here know how to apply for grants? Let's work together to figure out what the government criteria for a grant are (because Chavez is using oil money to give to communities to come up with projects). How can you get these projects going?*'

It was just staggering. They built their own houses, their own schools, they built a community centre. I mean it was imperfect, it is not a dream social estate, it never could be. There were problems in it and in Venezuela in general. There are two parallel systems running: the old system, which has been running on corruption and greed and benefiting the old guards who run Venezuela. But there are steps being made in this parallel system to set up an alternative ad hopefully they can replace the old one.

GS: If we think about the last 20–30 years or even longer of neoliberalism, both in terms of how society has been re-configured and the impact on education, my sense is that those people that advocate and campaign for those kinds of alternative systems, talk about capitalist systems and not about neoliberalism. Neoliberalism in many ways is the critique that's been developed. So is it necessary to talk about socialism or do we just get on with the project?

JC: What you're saying is Freirian really because we work with people where they're at. If words like *'socialism'*, *'feminism'* or *'anti-racism'* scare them, then these aren't appropriate words to use. It's not that we're being deceitful, we're actually being respectful of where people are at. One thing Merleau-Ponty (2004) talks about when reflecting on radicalism is where he says if people knew where they were going to get to from where they started, they might not make the journey. We need to recognize that. I remember the first time I recognized that I was a feminist, which was my first area of radicalism. I phoned up a friend and said *'I think I'm becoming a feminist'*. I was terrified because I had this image of bra-burning, radical women who didn't take care of their appearance; I had bought the media ideas at that point in time and eventually I became to see that the reality was more complex than that. So we work with people from where they are at and help them to develop.

GS: It might mean forming new forms of reflexivity, I think as you're saying. I think Freire is consistent, he says that in his pedagogy of hope, his ideas around transformation, that critical pedagogues have to be bold to go into unchartered territory and spaces. As you were saying earlier on, we already know what that space is; then what's the argument? What is there to be learnt?

JC: We need to work with groups that we wouldn't have imagined working with before. There are popular educators in this country, for example, green activists, who are part of activist networks and bringing activists from outside into the university. In my own teaching, a couple of years ago I brought a theatre production on asylum seekers by the radical theatre company, Banner Theatre Company (www.bannertheatre.co.uk), to my students. Afterwards some students said that the production, in which there were video extracts from interviews Banner conducted with asylum seekers projected onto a screen, said that their ideas about asylum seekers were really changed after seeing that production, because they heard about asylum seekers, as one of them said, 'from the horse's mouth'. So hearing asylum seekers speak of their own experience made my students think about issues of asylum in ways that I could never have done.

When students say, 'What can I do to make things better'? I talk about what I've been able to do, not individually, but with others. I have been talking to the students about my own political activism, guided again by Liam Kane (2007) who says that one way to inspire the next generation isn't just to say, 'We must go out and do things' but to say, as I have, given my activism around asylum seekers and refugees, '*last weekend I was helping to stop a family from being deported*'. The group I am part of have helped to save a family fleeing from death in Iran. If I do nothing else in my life of significance, I've done that. So Kane is saying that we can and should use our own political experience to show students they can make a difference.

GS: That's really interesting and I think you're were also saying earlier on that the way in which you share your own political activism, your own biography in a sense, does create a different relationship between the teacher and the student. It's not that they need to have the same experience as you, but you give them permission then to legitimize and value their lived experience. Because what happens in formal educational pedagogies, is that lived experience becomes de-valued. In fact not only de-valued but seen as part of the problem, and of course it excludes the learner completely from the whole process. I think that for me, that's what critical pedagogy and popular education are about. It's saying that there are lots of different kinds of knowledge. They all have value, it's not about competition and saying this is of more value than that but that they all offer you an opportunity to make sense of yourself and the world in which we live.

JC: And this takes us back to the beginning, to the idea that we need to work with students from their own experience. We need to find out what their understandings are, what feels real to them. Help them to see that it makes sense that it feels real and that there are also additional connections and insights that can be had if we can encourage them to expand their framework.

On widening participation and academic literacies

Lea, M. R. (2004) 'Academic Literacies: A Pedagogy for Course Design', *Studies in Higher Education* 29(6): 739–756.

Leathwood, C. and O'Connell, P. (2003) '"It's a Struggle": The Construction of the "New Student" in Higher Education', *Journal of Education Policy* 18(6): 597–615.

Lillis, T. and Turner, J. (2001) 'Student Writing in Higher Education: Contemporary Confusion, Traditional Concerns', *Teaching in Higher Education* 6(1): 33–42.
Street, B. (2004) 'Academic Literacies and the "New Orders": Implications for Research and Practice in Student Writing in Higher Education', *Learning and Teaching in the Social Sciences* 1(1): 9–20.

References

Bourdieu, P. (1998a) 'The Essence of Neoliberalism', in *Le Monde Diplomatique*, English edn, http://mondediplo.com/1998/12/08bourdieu/ (accessed 10 July 2012).
— (1998b) *Acts of Resistance: Against the New Myths of Our Time* (trans. R. Nice). Polity Press and the New Press, Cambridge, UK.
Burawoy, M. (2004) 'American Sociological Association Presidential Address: For Public Sociology', *American Sociological Review* 70(1): 4–28.
Butler, J. (1990) *Gender Trouble: Feminism and the Subversion of Identity*. Routledge, New York.
Canaan, J. and Shumar, W. (eds) (2008) *Structure and Agency in the Neoliberal University*. Routledge, New York.
Freire, P. (1970) *Pedagogy of the Oppressed*. Penguin Press, London.
— (1994) *Pedagogy of Hope: Reliving Pedagogy of the Oppressed* (trans. Robert R. Barr). Continuum, New York and London.
Kane, L. (2007) 'The Educational Influences on Active Citizens: A Case-study of Members of the Scottish Socialist Party (SSP)', *Studies in the Education of Adults* 39(1): 54–76.
Merleau-Ponty, M. (2004) Part 5: Selection from "The Visible and The Invisible" in *Maurice Merleau-Ponty: Basic Writings*, in T. Baldwin (ed.). Routledge.
Santos, B. S. de (2003) 'The University in the 21st Century: Towards a Democratic and Emancipatory University Reform', in R. Rhoads and C. A. Torres (eds), *The University, State, and Market: The Political Economy of Globalization in the Americas*. Stanford University Press, Stanford: 60–100.

CHAPTER SEVEN

Michael Williams on Indigenous Pedagogy

Michael Williams

Michael Williams was born into the Goorang Goorang peoples of the Southeast Queensland area. He has had a long career in public life, mainly in the tertiary education sector, and has recently retired as Director of the Aboriginal and Torres Strait Islander Studies Unit at the University of Queensland after almost 20 years. He was also a long-serving member of the Council of the Australian Institute of Aboriginal and Torres Strait Islander Studies (AIATSIS) in Canberra.

In this chapter Dr. Michael Williams, former Director of the Aboriginal and Torres Strait Islander Studies Unit at the University of Queensland, offers a unique insight into the ways in which Indigenous Knowledges can contribute to pedagogy, as well as discussing the pedagogical strategies that he has developed to address the silencing that takes place in traditional teaching and learning. Michael explains the way he expresses these ideas in his own research and teaching practice, and how the Unit which he once headed has became a centre of excellence and expert opinion on teaching, research and consultation in Aboriginal and Torres Strait Islander cultures, including their role in maintaining a committed system of personal and academic support for Aboriginal and Torres Strait Islander students. Michael Williams was interviewed by Stephen Cowden in November 2008.

MW: I'd just like begin by telling a story to set the scene: on a course that I teach on, a couple of years ago, I was working with a colleague and a friend, a member of my staff, team teaching it. Also visiting at the time was one of my brothers from Central Australia where I'm also a man in our Aboriginal Law from the desert of Central Australia. My brother from the desert was visiting and he was working with the class and he posed this idea or this thought to them: '*Imagine a fish jumping out of the water; that fish has no knowledge of the world above water. He just gets a glimpse of it for a few seconds*'.

He then posed a question to the students: '*You're in a room with 2 doors. One door leads to life, the other to death. In this room there are twins, one twin always lies and the other always tells the truth. These twins know where each door leads, how do you find out which is the right door?*'

The students pondered this question and one student came up with a solution and he said ask either twin which door his brother would tell you to go through and then go through the opposite door. My brother from the desert then replied that's a good answer but what if I told you one twin was your mind and the other was your perception. How useful is your solution to the problem now? With the silence that followed, it became apparent that the question posed was not an abstract mental game type problem, it was a fundamental life question that addressed what we are and what is real in the world.

He then said, '*In my country I walk and I know about what everything is. It is my university – all the knowledge is there. It's much bigger than your university; it takes me weeks to walk it.*

Your university has thousands of books, more than anyone could read. Maybe you can see through this question. I've got a glimpse of your world and you've got a glimpse of mine – just like that fish'.

Now that is taken from the draft PhD thesis of one of my staff, Dr Norman Sheehan, and he's written a thesis on Indigenous Knowledge and Indigenous education but it sets the scene and that comes from an Aboriginal man who's in his 40s, who grew up in the desert and has been in our Law all his life in the old traditional ways and who didn't see Europeans until he was in his teens.

SC: That's an amazing story. As many of the people reading this book won't be all that familiar with the kind of key issues of what Indigenous Approaches to Knowledge are about, how would you provide a way of people getting a sense of this?

MW: I think the key is in the expression of 'approach to knowledge'. In the class that I work with, with students, this is about how our knowledge is managed as Indigenous people. And as a central part of that, it acknowledges that people who own knowledge or are bosses for knowledge (that's the way we express it), who carry that Law/that knowledge, they pass it on when they deem it appropriate. So the idea that we face in most educational settings in the Western world certainly, the idea of asking a question to gain knowledge doesn't necessarily work because you can ask the question, and unless the person deems it that you're ready to receive the knowledge, you won't get that knowledge. And if you persist with asking questions, their response will be to walk away from you or to tell you a story. And the story may sound very plausible but it's not necessarily the truth.

The anthropologist, Margaret Mead, who worked with and wrote about people in the Pacific and Samoan communities, found out in later years that people who she had worked with as young women weren't necessarily telling her the whole truth and nothing but the truth as such. So approaches to knowledge from our point of view have to be about learning the protocol and the respect that's associated with managing knowledge within our societies so that it is protected.

SC: You mentioned the word 'respect'. Why do you think respect is such an important concept in terms of this question of the Indigenous approaches to knowledge?

MW: Well again in what we do, the first thing we say to any new class is that respect is important in the sense of respecting yourself, taking the time to self reflect on what you know and who you are and then respect others and respect knowledge as it's managed through the process. And that means that we open up a dialogue process where people know that when they speak they'll be respected and their voice will be allowed to be heard.

SC: I see an affinity between the way that you're talking about that whole question of respect and dialogue with the critical pedagogy tradition of Paulo Freire in his book *Pedagogy of the Oppressed*. One of the things that Paulo Freire thought was very important was that education should be based on dialogue between teacher and student rather than seeing students as simply empty vessels who are filled up with knowledge. Do you see a resonance with those kinds of ideas that Paulo Freire has and the kind of material that you're working on with your students?

MW: As I understand Freire, there is a lot of resonance because part of the respect comes from a recognition that each of us has different responsibilities. The native American scholar, Greg Cajete, who's written one of the definitive texts on the American–Indian Native American education (Cajete, 1994) talks about the way Indigenous teachers look for 'moments of teachability'. And I've twisted that a little by saying that students have to look for 'moments of learnability'. We're all learners in that class. I learn as much from people that come into these classes and as I hope that they learn from me. So we all take responsibility for getting an outcome that is enriching for all of us and part of it is respecting the person and the feedback we get from students is that they actually feel that they are learning something. Another fascinating comment is that students will say with some surprise that we're actually interested in what they think. That's a fundamental aspect of respect. If you take it out of the adult education domain into the service delivery domain of government, etc., and a whole range of other domains, if you could go in with the task of trying to resolve a social issue, if you don't sit down and listen to the person articulate how they see the issue that they are surrounded with, you're not showing respect. If you go and impose a model of healing (or however you wish to describe it) that's imposed from the outside doesn't matter who you are, if you don't sit down and also hear. That's a fundamental part of Aboriginal ways of engaging with knowledge.

One anthropologist friend of mine, and indeed a man I call grandfather through our Law because he lived for a long time in an Aboriginal community, he said '*Aboriginal people are very common sense people. They are quite happy to work with the knowledge that they have and as they work with that knowledge they pick up other knowledge*'. Again, if a teacher goes in and starts from a platform based on what they've bought with them, that they've got from other theorists from other examples from other countries where Indigenous people have faced a similar problem, then you're not allowing the person that you're working with to be part of the process. It's like walking into somebody's house and saying '*well you got your kitchen disorganized, it's not the same as I organize it at my home*'. It's as fundamental and as simple as that.

SC: But that sense that teachers are there to be participating in the process is fundamental to approaches you adopt. When you were describing some of the things you do when teaching students about Indigenous Approaches to Knowledge, you mentioned some of the ways you tried to get students to think differently about all this. One of the things you did was told students here is the Module Outline, but what you actually showed them was an Aboriginal bark painting. Now, students come into a module these days expecting to see the curriculum – these are when the lectures will be, this is where the lecture theatre is, this is the assessment and this is what we want you to cover on the module. Instead, you put up a picture of a bark painting. Just summarize why you did that and what you were trying to get across to students by doing this .

MW: What motivated me was that I wanted to move people away from the notion of linear time and the idea that you can compartmentalize knowledge because relationship is an important part. Back to respect, by showing respect you are developing a relationship and therefore you have a relationship with knowledge and that relationship is not something that you can control. The only thing that you can control inside of that is yourself. So I wanted to move people away from this idea that week 1–13 in a semester and that we do topic *x* this week and topic *y* the next week so that people could then compartmentalize it and say that '*look I did this topic with another lecturer in another class last semester or last year. I won't come to this one because I've done that*'.

So what I say to people is that when we were working through this course, '*there are pots of knowledge that are floating. Imagine it's here in the room here with us*'. My task as an Indigenous teacher looking for moments of teach-ability is to give warning or notice that these pieces of knowledge are floating around. The student is there to look for moments of teach/learnability and pick up on my signals and together we'll make sure that they go into this given part zone. Any one week we might be covering several topics.

The bark painting, I said to one of my staff who is an artist and indeed is the man I mentioned before, Dr Norman Sheehan, that I want a bark painting and he drew this painting that is based on an artistic or graphic representation of an Aboriginal world view. Aboriginal culture, which many people would appreciate, which has been written about is, that it's a culture that is intimately interwoven with the natural world. So we have the sky world, the human world, the sacred world and the physical world. And all that goes on in the mind set and the world view of Aboriginal people (ceremonies, land, marriage, rules of behaviour, dreaming stories, etc.) is all there and this painting represents that.

I show this to the class for 5 or 10 seconds, maybe a minute and watch their eyes glaze over. Then I put the artistic or graphical representation, which is diagrammatically drawn which is adequately drawn with English words (sky world, physical world, sacred world, etc.) so that it then makes sense to them. Then of course I do hand out, as its part of the requirement of running a course within a university that you have a set of objectives and a standard course outline. But the precursor at the beginning is putting people into another space and place and that part of the process is saying that you can look at this from outside of your comfort zone but from a position of respect. My respect for you and your respect for me and others, etc. And from a position of safety – you're not thrown out to dry so to speak if they understand that expression.

SC: That's really interesting. This idea of moments of teachability and your own adaptation of that, moments of learnability, comes from Greg Cajete, who is an American–Indian scholar. This illustrates that you're taking ideas from traditions of other Indigenous peoples and you're applying them in Australia in an Aboriginal Australian context. Is there much work looking at these kinds of Indigenous Approaches to Knowledge? Is there much written down or is this a developing body of knowledge?

MW: There's a developing body of knowledge and if I could just backtrack a second, this comes from a fundamental principle that we apply in our cultural domain, if you like. There's a nice text published back in Australia about tracing your family and it's called *Lookin' For Your Mob* (Smith and Halstead, 1990) and we do that all the time when we're walking down the street, we're looking for other Aboriginal people and there's an immediate engagement and resonance if we see someone that looks like an Aboriginal person. In the same way when I travel, when we travelled, and from my understanding of other Indigenous Australians, we are looking for Indigenous people from all over the country. In fact, whenever I speak, whatever country I'm in, my words are the same as I would apply in moving through country in Australia and that is to acknowledge the traditional Indigenous owners of the land.

So this idea of engaging with Indigenous people and Indigenousness is a fundamental part of what we're doing in the development of Indigenous Knowledge and engaging with other scholars. It's our contention that Indigenous Knowledge exists everywhere. Everyone is Indigenous, everything is in fact Indigenous and that if you look for it, you will find it. So yes, there is a growing body of knowledge. There are certainly Indigenous people writing about this but also non-Indigenous people.

Also, there's been a dialogue between scholars from various disciplines within the Western Academy. For instance, a number of staff from the Aboriginal and Torres Strait Islander Studies Unit at the University of Queensland have travelled to Albuquerque in New Mexico some 10 years ago now or more, and this has been arranged by Native American scholars. It was a dialogue circle in the middle, where if you're invited to that circle you had to speak and participate according to Native American dialogue circle tradition.

Others who attended the conference sat outside the circle and observed and were occasionally invited into the inner circle where they could speak. There were two quantum physicists, both non-Indigenous people. So we had Indigenous and non-Indigenous scholars. One of the quantum physicists said '*when you speak of the quantum, our language and our paradigms have taken us as far as we can go and we are looking to Indigenous scholars to look further*'. So there's resonance within the scholarship of quantum mechanics and chaos theory that recognizes that there is currency within the Indigenous worldview.

SC: I know when we've spoken earlier you've said that you feel a greater affinity with the scientific side of western knowledge. Alongside this you've expressed dissatisfaction with the way a lot of Indigenous knowledge is framed within the 'softer' humanities. Could you say more about this?

MW: Well indeed with my experience if you go to the 4 central points of our assessment domain of what we're doing at the University of Queensland, is developing this Indigenous knowledge paradigm it's respect, engagement, mobility and relationship. Now, if you're looking at those concepts and the fit and mobility of knowledge, you're working with knowledge in a different way. When I've engaged with people from a science or mathematical background, I sense a kind of adrenaline rush from both sides that there's a connectedness that I don't observe often in engaging with people from the soft sciences/the social sciences, for example, anthropology, history, etc.

SC: Why might this be?

MW: In part I think it's that Aboriginal studies has been for a long time and probably still is in lots of peoples' mind, a sideshow for the real disciplines of anthropology, history, sociology – that of the western scholarly domain. And if it's considered to be secondary, you're not showing respect. The other thing that's important in this is that Indigenous people are human beings and human beings develop intellect, they develop philosophy, they develop religion, they develop science. How can you live in any part of the world for a long time, in the case of Aboriginal Australians for 60,000–50,000 years at least; you must develop scientific understanding of that domain.

To relegate it to only a social science area of the western academy is being disrespectful, so I think the relationship is flawed from the start. Again it's not rocket science at one level, in the sense that if you go into someone's home or you go into someone else's country you show disrespect by doing certain things. So you observe their conventions, you try to speak their language however badly, etc. but you're showing 'I respect you' – it's your country, it's your house. You don't barge into your neighbour's house and reset the table or rearrange the furniture or whatever it might be. But essentially that's what I think the Western Academy to some extent has done, as they've institutionalized knowledge. They've taken it and made it fit their paradigms. They may have listened but they have not heard in a deepest way, what Indigenous people are saying when they're talking about our knowledge. Whereas I think science and that of hard science minds, it has the capacity to do it in a way that I haven't observed on a large scale.

SC: Nonetheless you're saying that you're talking about that affinity. I think that's very interesting as that very much challenges where people, both in the Western Academy but also in popular culture where Aboriginal and First Nations' people are seen as a spiritual adjunct to the western consumer lifestyle – in some respects as a kind of antidote to it, but one which still leaves Aboriginal people very much as the kind of sideshow. The real event is of course where the power lies. I think that's very interesting and that really gives something for people to really think about.

MW: I think perhaps sometimes there's a subliminal inclination to think of Indigenous people talking about things in a spiritual way as being 'New Age'. I remember talking about this with colleagues and friends some years ago. And they said 'if you go back 2008 years ago, there would have been someone walking around then who would be considered as new age'. So I have some trouble with this notion of 'new age'. It's an opportunity to put something in a box that you're not prepared to understand, won't understand or can't understand.

SC: Earlier when you were talking about some of the principles in the indigenous approach to knowledge, you mentioned the idea of mobility. Could you say more about this idea of mobility?

MW: It's how knowledge is moved through time, what our responsibilities are for that and indeed in our articulation of Indigenous Knowledge as it's emerging in scholarships across the globe. There's an acceptance within Indigenous peoples' way of thinking in our minds that of course knowledge exists in its own right – it has its own soul and it doesn't need the intervention of humans to transport it through time.

A nice example of that is out of a book called 'Blackfoot Physics' by an Englishman, David F. Peat, who I think is a chemist, he's certainly a scientist. He's writing about black-foot Indians/Native Americans and I gather he's of the age where the old Hollywood cowboys and Indian movies were very popular and he was fascinated by Native Americans and found himself one time in a Blackfoot reservation in North America and visited several years and grew to know and form friendships.

One day he was asked to write the knowledge of that particular reservation, the Blackfoot Indian peoples. In that book he's talking about knowledge and he tells this story of this Native American man who was going to a ceremony, I think a Sweat Lodge ceremony. And he came out and said to one elder of the community '*about 3 or 4 weeks before I came here this tune came into my mind and it's just kept in my mind*'. You know the way you hear a tune and it just sticks with you and it takes you a day or two to get it out your head and you're singing it all the time. He said '*I thought I'd come to the Sweat Lodge and thought it would be part of the ceremony but it wasn't in the ceremony*'. And the old man said to him '*well sing it*' and so he sang the tune and the old man says '*ah, that's old Joe's song. Joe died 30 years ago, it must have been tired of waiting around for someone and so it decided to introduce itself back into this domain, this dimension*'. That resonates, that sits easy with my understanding of the world. I see it from an Indigenous mans' point of view.

SC: There's an interesting resonance with particular ideas in art and music. The jazz musician John Coltrane used to say that he was simply the vessel for the music he played, and that he saw that music actually coming from, as he called it 'God'. In other words, he was just playing the music, but he saw this music existed in its own right in much the same way that you're talking about. He didn't see himself as the owner of the music, simply the vessel through which that music came.

MW: Sure, in that sense, when I started at the University of Queensland in 1992, in the first two-and-half weeks I was at a retreat for senior people appointed to the university and you had a two-and-a-half day retreat where you were briefed on the university. In the morning of the second day (with another afternoon and morning to go), I realized that I started to remember stories that I hadn't thought about since I was a kid – probably hadn't thought about them for about 30 years in any kind of stark way. And the message for me as I read my world from my cultural standpoint is that my old people wanted me to say something. So I got the opportunity to talk about story.

Story is very important to Indigenous people and it's very important to Indigenous Knowledge in the way that we run our learning environment within our classes – we're telling stories. We respect the innate ability of people who come into the class, to be able to work this through, take responsibility for skilling themselves up and we tell stories that facilitate, that stimulate their thinking, their thoughts so that they can establish their relationship with the knowledge based on their terms.

SC: Could we move the discussion forward now and could you talk to me about some of the difficulties facing young Aboriginal people in conventional schools throughout Australia. The kinds of schools where they are likely to be educated in what we can imagine to be a very conventional, western or in Freirian terms banking paradigm, where the traditional knowledge is not discussed. The respect that you indicate is so important to your own approach to knowledge is not present. What kind of impact is this having on the generation of young Aboriginal people who are currently at school in Australia?

MW: I have three children, two daughters in their early 30s and a son in his mid-20s. The eldest one took to the system of education, as it is offered within the Australian schooling system, quite well and achieved quite well and went through to grade 12 and then went on to university. My other 2, the daughter being headstrong and the middle child, she withdrew herself after grade 10. Anyway she had other interests. But more particularly to your question, my son. I made the decision to pull him out after 2–3 years of high school – after grade 10 which was the minimum you can do, or had to do albeit at a certain age. I took him out because the system was essentially destroying him. It didn't fit. He's very intelligent. My view is that I would rather have a healthy young human being on my hands without a grade 12 education and he can pick that all up later on. He can learn when he was ready. As far as the system is concerned in Australia certainly I don't think it's a very good system. It's too much of a 'one size fits all' approach to education. And it's systematically failed and persistently failed Aboriginal Australians/ Indigenous Australians since its inception.

I used to work in a former career of training secondary teachers and early childhood teachers. And working with principals in in-service training with a colleague, two remarkable things were said to me. This was in the 1980s and this is working towards their end of career-principals and some early career-principals. They said two things that fascinated me. They said '*if they had someone like me to work with when they were young teachers or certainly new principals, they would have treated Aboriginal kids and Aboriginal education differently*'. But the other more sinister thing they said was '*for any child to succeed at school, they have to be able to look into the school and see themselves and their society and culture reflected back at it*'. They said, *there's more chance of that happening for a child of a migrant background than an Indigenous child*'. Every parent is told, if you want your child to succeed, you involve yourself with the school. Now that to me is quite a powerful observation by the principals yet they weren't able to do anything about it as principals working from within the system.

Yet in recent years, in the last 10 years, we've had a revolution beginning in Australia in my view. With a young nephew of mine, taking over an Aboriginal school, an Aboriginal community primary school. This is Cherbourg; it's about a 3- or 4-hour drive North West of Brisbane. It's been remarkable what he's been able to achieve. He's an immensely talented young person. He went into the first assembly, one of the Aboriginal teacher aids was telling me, on the day it was being announced he was going to be the permanent principal after being there for about 3 or 4 months. He addressed the children and he said '*you're strong and smart because of not only the knowledge you get through this education system and schools like your school but also because of your culture*'. And that was the fundamental turning point for those kids and for the community in fact.

SC: And my understanding is that previously prior to his arrival as head, the children at that school were almost being written off as un-teachable.

MW: Indeed they were. The participation rates of Aboriginal people in all levels of education in Australia is appalling – right at the bottom end of it. Yet in 18 months he was having grade 2 kids reading what grade 7 kids couldn't read when he started there. Now in his time, he moved the levels and the key indicators to equal and sometimes better the state and the national averages as far as achievement in primary school. And part of it goes back to the earlier point that we've been making in this interview: respect.

Because he did something remarkable on the day it was being announced. Knowing that this was going to happen he worked with the school community, the teachers and the students and the administrative staff. They identified all men and women who were senior in the community and they made a little message stick, which in Aboriginal traditional terms is symbolically saying this 'it's your passage through country and right to enter country or going on through country'. And he attached to it a basic 50-cent door key. And he gave it to every senior man and woman in the Cherbourg community and said '*this is symbolically saying the old way, it's your right through the country. The key is saying in the modern way, your right to enter the educational domain of this school anytime you wish*'. Which comes back to the fundamental principle: if you want your child to succeed, involve yourself in the school and they were given for the first time absolute respect and acknowledgment of their place within the school domain as senior men and women of the community. And that to my mind is one of the most important steps he ever made. And he did it knowingly and the other thing he said to me is that '*it's not rocket science – again. If you've got 35 kids in the class, and you have to find 35 different ways of instructing them and working with them, you have to do that, it's your responsibility*' and that's essentially what he did.

SC: I think again there's a resonance with the work that Paulo Freire did when he was working with peasant people in Brazil. He found that again you had these children completely written off as hopeless cases. One of the first things he did was he brought their parents into school and worked with the parents. He realized that the parents either had no education themselves, or had rejected education due to the oppressive atmosphere in the classroom, and so they didn't value education. But by actually opening that up to them he was able to bring about significant change; and you can see this same theme of respect – the fundamental question of respect.

And you look at the difficulties in terms of the instrumentalization of education in Britain, we see how significant things like School League Tables have become. While these claim to measure a school's success, which is questionable in terms of what is being looked at, they do this in such a way that further entrenches the existing divisions between different schools, undermining children, parents and teachers at the bottom end of the league tables.

This suggests to me how relevant those ideas of respect, and of children seeing themselves and their community reflected in the school, are to the way these issues present in Britain. Without this sense of respect, a process develops where teachers come to have incredibly low expectations of the young people they are working with, and of themselves as teachers, leading to situations where working-class young people are being written off as un-teachable, or referred to Pupil Referral Units, which can so easily become dumping grounds for children from the bottom end of the social structure. It seems that these ideas about respect, while they're very fundamentally rooted in Indigenous tradition in terms of the way you're approaching them also have more universal relevance. Would you like to comment on that?

MW: Well I believe as a paradigm for teaching or for managing knowledge what my nephew has done and what we're talking about, Indigenous Knowledge does have a much greater currency for all of society. In fact, my view is that it's a revelation in Australia and I hope that the administrators and the politicians all see that it is what it is and that it is worth moving that to be in part of the main paradigm that drives education in Australia. I had the privilege a few weeks ago of witnessing the launch of an institute which was housed within the Queensland University of Technology in Brisbane and headed up by my nephew who was principal of Cherbourg School.

He runs an institute that brings principals from around Australia, mostly from schools that have got large Indigenous Australian student populations – but not only. And they work with him for 5 days. At this launch there were principals from Western Australia, New South Wales and Queensland and there are a number of schools who have taken up and applied the same principles in their own interpretation of it – this notion of being strong and smart and focus on respect and culture, etc. And it was remarkable to see people, teachers, principals in the twilight of their careers, in their late fifties/early sixties saying that 5 days with this institute they had gone through this brain shift and now in the last 2 years have been able to achieve with the school what they have been trying all their careers to achieve. In simple terms of what they're doing, they're not putting the teachers above anyone else. They're working with the parents and the kids and the community to say it's all our responsibility to bring about the best possible outcome out of our school.

There was a young, beginning principal who took over a school and in the first 3 or 2 months expelled 40 per cent of children but went to the parents and met every parent and said this is what I'm planning for the school, these are the standards I want to achieve and these are the standards and principles of behaviour, etc. and every parent said we agree. And then they systematically worked at it and they made a school that's part of the community where everyone walked through it freely with respect. Now 2 years later, there's a 100 per cent satisfaction with going to school and no expulsions, etc.

There's one school in New South Wales, where there was one very highly regarded private school and 1 state school where parents would bust their boilers to have their children to go to the private school but now are busting their boiler to get their kids in the state school. Simply as a result of this principle of respect. Again a principal in the twilight of his career, having this brain shift and now he's attracting families to the school. I mean it's quite amazing and it's based on some very basic principles of regard for each other, not trying go set up hierarchies. Because everyone's interested in education. Another thing my nephew said is '*you show me a kid who is not interested in learning*'. He said '*there's no such creature*' and it's absolutely true. You know the curiosity in children.

SC: Yes, it's said by many people that it's what it is to be human. One of the things that really comes to my mind is again Paulo Freire, this idea that it's about 'humanizing the curriculum'. So much of what we have seems to have forgotten the joy, pleasure and excitement of learning, and of how important it is for us as a society to teach people how to think for themselves. The sad thing is that so many people go through the entire education system and they'll turn round and say that no one ever taught them how to think.

MW: Indeed, this comes down to one of my fundamental beliefs that education should be interested in developing the human being or working with the individual human being to be the best that they can be as a human being because it's their responsibility. And if you create an environment that is supportive of that, you will have that result. My view is that my university should be about graduating better people. Now becoming degreed in Law, Sociology or Medicine, you would think that there is a spin-off effect that you are a better person but often it's the overt actualization and acknowledgement of the process of becoming a better person that is the most powerful of any, and it comes down to the basic principle of education. If you have low expectations of someone as has happened in Indigenous education in Australia, you're going to have low outcomes. It's the idea that you have a deficit theory approach to it.

Whereas the paradigm that we're talking about in Indigenous Knowledge, of respect, of the relationship of engagement of mobility of knowledge, acknowledgement of knowledge existing in its own right, respecting each other, respecting yourself. That's a paradigm of affirmation. When you're working in that environment, everyone's enthusiastic about learning something because you know you can say anything and you don't get this instance of what we all go through in the system that we've gone through in secondary and primary and in tertiary; too frightened to ask a question because you think you might be making a fool of yourself. In our paradigm, you can say anything and we've had amazing discussions. There are no no-go zone discussions. You can talk about things – as it's part of the human condition and you don't leave it out because it's too politically incorrect or whatever it might be. You actually speak it and you learn from it.

I think there's something I want to draw from Norman's thesis which has come out of some of the work that he and I did together. I want to pay respects to his immense skill as a learner in putting this PhD thesis together. It's just a simple line in Indigenous Knowledge: '*there is no superior or emotive observer standpoint from which to have knowledge of things because all things are intermeshed, enmeshed in knowledge relations*'. And in some ways that sums up a lot of what we're talking about.

The closing comments I would like to say is in this marvellous quote from an old man from South Australia, an Aboriginal man, who said something like: '*if you cannot understand an Aboriginal person's silence, you'll never understand their words*'. In my view too much of what goes on in the name of education in the Western paradigm silences people and what I think goes on in the name of Indigenous paradigms is that we don't silence people, we allow voice. It's our responsibility to think about as individuals, whether we are self-silencing or whether we are silencing.

References and further reading

Cajete, G. (1994) *Look to the Mountain: An Ecology of Indigenous Education* Kivaki Press, Durango Colarado.

Smith, D. and Halstead, B. (1990) *Lookin For Your Mob: A Guide to Tracing Aboriginal Family Trees*. Aboriginal Studies Press, Canberra.

F. David Peat (1996) *Blackfoot Physics: A Journey into the Native American Universe*. Fourth Estate Limited, London.

Another recent book which develops this theme about the relationship between Science and Indigenous Knowledge is:

Don Four Arrows, Greg Cajete and Jongmin Jongmin (2009) *Critical Neurophilosophy & Indigenous Wisdom*, Sense Publishers, Rotterdam.

The work of Dr Norman Sheehan is discussed in the interview. For further material by him see Sheehan, N., Martin, G. and Krysinska, K. (2009) *Sustaining Connection: A Framework for Aboriginal and Torres Strait Islander Community, Cultural, Spiritual, Social and Emotional Wellbeing* published by the Centre for Suicide Prevention Studies, University of Queensland.

Dr Sheehan gave a seminar on the subject of 'Aboriginal and Torres Strait Islander Social and Emotional Well Being: A Critically and Culturally Grounded Social Issue' at the Faculty of Design, Swinburne University in Melbourne in March 2010. This can be viewed at http://vimeo.com/10513930.

CHAPTER EIGHT

Jim Crowther on Popular Education and Higher Education

Jim Crowther

Jim Crowther has been a practitioner, researcher and academic in adult and community education since 1980. His PhD focussed on adult learning in and through popular protests. He is the co-ordinator of an international popular education network (PEN) for academics and researchers in higher education.

His main research interest is in the contribution of adult education to furthering democracy and social justice, and more recently has undertaken research on the educational use of information and communication technologies, and social media, in struggles for environmental justice. Jim is currently Senior Lecturer in Community Education at Edinburgh University.

In this chapter Jim Crowther discusses ideas associated with popular education and their relevance to higher education. Through reflecting on his working class roots and educational journey as an adult learner, Jim offers a unique insight into the ways in which the underpinning ideologies and practices associated with critical pedagogy and popular education can be deployed by academics in their role as teachers and researchers. Jim also talks about how he has harnessed new information technologies to nurture and support environmentalist social movements in Scotland. Jim was interviewed by Gurnam Singh in May 2008.

GS: As co-founder and coordinator of the Popular Education Network (PEN) I know you have a long-standing interest in critical pedagogy and popular education at local, national and international levels. A cursory scan of your work reveals a deep interest in connecting popular and higher education and the transformative role that university educators can play and are playing to support wider struggles for social justice. Before we explore this, perhaps we can begin with your own education influences and your journey as to how you've got to where you are at the moment.

JC: I'm probably very typical of a certain category of working-class person growing up in the fifties/sixties. I didn't do well educationally, I failed the 11+ school exam and was turned off education. My father was a fish dockworker; my mother worked in a typewriter factory and I was one of five children. My parents were very strong Labour Party supporters, and both were lay union activists at one time or another at their workplaces. They were interested in education for their children but did not have much understanding of the education system. I eventually became the first member of the family to go to university. Of course in my early teenage years I wasn't interested in education at all and was very antagonistic to schooling (being expelled when I was 14). I suppose it wasn't until I was 17 years of age when I started to get an interest in studying during a period when I was unemployed. I took a liberal adult education class at Hull University which was taught by the Marxist historian, John Saville. I later found out he was very well known for his work as co-editor of the Socialist Register as well as being Professor of Economic History at Hull University, although I didn't know anything about his reputation at the time. It must have helped and kick-started a process of thinking because I also went onto study for O and A levels and eventually, after 2 years, acquired sufficient academic credentials to apply to study for a sociology degree.

GS: How do you theorize that important moment for you? Was it something from 'within' or some external influence of a combination of the two?

JC: Well probably a few things. Later on, jumping ahead a bit, I read the book by Paul Willis *Learning to Labour* which was spellbinding as it seemed to capture my own experience. His argument showed how young working-class lads in resisting the authoritarianism of school rush head on into another form of oppression at work – this seemed to be my line of travel too. After experiencing two uninspiring apprenticeships, and various short-term, dead-end jobs I began to want something more for myself. I was also stimulated by political discussions and these two interests seemed to come together when I found sociology. I went on to study this subject at undergraduate and postgraduate level. Ironically, I was never really interested in the sociology of education until much later when I found myself in Edinburgh working for a research centre on a project about community schooling. I worked in a 'deprived community' in the north of Edinburgh and that was my first introduction to the idea of community education. It was an action research project which turned into a really important learning experience for me.

GS: It seems like your own personal struggles with education keep taking you back to some of those roots. Would it be right to say that?

JC: Moving on to the area of what is popular education, I suppose I feel quite strongly that it is grounded in material realities. There is that kind of sense that social class creates a fundamental structure in inequality in society – I've always held that view although in some people's experiences other forms of exploitation, through gender, 'race' or other forms of identity issues may be more significant.

GS: Would it be too crude to say that for you then, that education is an important terrain of the class struggle and that your work as a popular educator is in effect taking that struggle for transforming the class system.

JC: Absolutely, I would say transforming the class system is fundamental to creating a more socially just order. Education is politics – Paulo Freire told us that. In a sense my experience told me that too. It seems to me that educators know this to be the case but seldom talk about it. So I see education as a part of that struggle of cultural politics in which the educator has a key role to play in making visible the forms of exploitation and oppression that occur in society. I think this applies to all levels of education: schools, community education and higher education. For educators who share this perspective on education there may be different opportunities and different issues that arise, working in different contexts, nevertheless the general analysis is relevant.

GS: Let me put it another way. Someone who is doing Physics, who is a Physics lecturer or engineer as supposed to be someone who might be teaching Social Work. Surely there are these differences here?

JC: Well I'm sure that the nature of the subject area does create different issues but if someone is working in engineering, what are they engineering for? Who benefits from the engineering? Who can afford what they design? What are its environmental implications? I mean there are issues to do with purpose really, which are always issues of politics, so that designing something for a third world country, which maybe helps people to improve their water supply, is different to designing a facility for very few rich people to enjoy.

GS: So what you're saying is that education is never neutral.

JC: Education cannot be neutral. There are different degrees of politics in education. We have subject areas like English or History, where these issues are more obviously to the fore. And there are other areas like Mathematics where it's not so apparent. But of course there are debates around different types of Mathematics, different knowledge systems and the dominance of a particular system of Mathematics.

GS: How do you conceptualize popular education? There are different terms that are talked about. Some people talk about informal education, some talk about emancipatory education and you call yourself a 'popular educator'. Are these terms synonymous or are there important distinctions to be made between them?

JC: I think it's important to try and clarify what we mean by popular education, as far as possible, because there are different traditions which are bound up with historical and cultural conditions in different societies. I talk to people in Sweden, Norway and in Denmark about popular education and it seems to me that they generally mean something entirely different. Then speaking to people in France or Spain about popular education, it clearly has a different history and also in European countries like Germany and Italy.

The history of popular education in Latin America has obviously been very influential but we do have very different traditions in the United Kingdom. Popular education may be a synonym for radical adult education in my language or emancipatory education but the choice of terms often involve differing ideological influences and intellectual resources. For me, popular education is a collective educational project based upon the lived experience of people acting together for social and political change. It's about linking, where possible, the local and global in order to ally education and action.

GS: I know Freire talks about and uses the word 'liberation' quite a lot. Again not quite certain whether he's talking about political liberation, in terms of the structures or whether he's talking about psychological liberation, expressing a sense of human agency or if he sees this as the dialectical relationship between the two.

JC: Well he's an eclectic thinker. He has different theoretical, political and religious influences that he draws upon. I would personally take from Freire's thinking the bits that are most valuable for helping us understand and act on our present circumstances. I believe that his work sensitizes us to the dialectic between our unfreedom, that we live in situations that constrain us, and that it is through exercising our agency that we begin to enlarge our freedom. Dialogue is fundamental to knowing and acting on this dialectic and that education is a resource which can help enlarge our ability to be free.

GS: Would it be helpful to maybe disconnect the goals of popular education with maybe outdated conceptions of socialist societies.

JC: Well I think there's a political 'baggage' with socialism but we should avoid 'throwing the baby out with the bath water'. Maybe we have to struggle for the same values under a different name. I think William Morris made the point that these things happen that way. It's the values and aspirations – equality, social justice, freedom – that are important rather than the label – and sometimes the label gets in the way of achieving these values. For me popular education is linked to socialism. I would think of socialism in an open, non-doctrinaire, sense. My colleague Ian Martin once expressed it in three ways:

1. that it involves a fundamental essential equality of being;
2. that we are social and political animals and that our humanity reaches its highest expression in relationships and caring for others; and
3. that society, including its material and cultural resources should be organized to honour this equality of being and this enhances our capacity to live useful and meaningful lives.

I think this way of thinking about socialism captures what popular education is seeking to achieve. It's about creating the kind of society where these values are recognized and enacted. We seem to be a long way from these now and heading in the opposite direction.

GS: I'll come back to popular education in terms of some of the methods we might employ. I just want to link this partly back to your own work. You mentioned earlier, that you were instrumental in establishing PEN. When did that come about? Why? What was your involvement in that?

JC: It came about through discussion with one of my colleagues here, Ian Martin, who has now retired. It was 1997 and on a bit of a wave of seeing the Conservative Party lose the general election, and feeling that the time was ripe for some more progressive interventions, we agreed to send a letter to like-minded colleagues working in universities to set up a network to encourage and support our interests. So, in a sense it snowballed from that particular development over 10 years ago.

The main contribution PEN makes is through its conferences. One distinctive characteristic of these events is that they are low cost, with subsidies to students, which aim simply to cover expenditure rather than generate income. One way this has been done is to strip out the usual conference paraphernalia of bags, pens, books and CDs so that the fee simply has to pay for the basics of meeting and eating. Local organizers have also done their best to acquire institutional support. This practice of keeping the conference fee low is itself becoming a subversive activity in a context where, increasingly, conferences are expected to be profit-making ventures that have financial targets to meet. A remarkable fact is that PEN has never had a budget in 15 years of its existence.

A further distinctive aspect of the conferences are that there are no conference proceedings and academic papers are not required. While this helps to keep costs low it also works pedagogically in that it serves to create a more flexible and dialogical space; contributors are invited to open up discussion, present accounts of research or practice, reflect on their experience or a particular theme and work in this more open-ended way rather than to present and defend an academic argument presented in a text. The latter is not barred but it is not usual – although some academics have to present papers to legitimate their participation with their institutions. Moreover, encouraging participants to meet for social activity, to eat and drink together helps to break down barriers and facilitate challenging and good-natured discussion. The unprogrammed space of a conference is as important to the experience of those who participate as well as what happens inside the conference programme. The culture of the conferences has also been enhanced by the shared nature of the commitment to popular education. Participants are provided with a history of the network and a definition of popular education, which does not claim to be the only way of thinking about it as an educational and political practice. But it does help to frame what the purpose of the conferences are and generally speaking brings together ideologically sympathetic participants even if, at times, individuals do not subscribe to PEN's definition of popular education. The aim of providing a definition also seeks to avoid academic navel gazing, so instead of analysing what we mean by popular education more energy can be spent on what we do in its name.

GS: I would now like us to focus on the role of academics that might be sympathetic to the broader aims of critical pedagogy and popular education. How can those academics that are subject to the constraining forces of the neoliberal university work, to borrow a phrase work, 'in and against the state' within the context of the global commodification of HE?

JC: If I could give an example, which is a type of public education rather than popular education but it gives some insights into what is possible. It's a project called *'Renewing democracy in Scotland'*, which was inspired by the devolved government in Scotland that happened after the 1997 general election in the United Kingdom. This is a publication which was developed collaboratively with Ian Martin and Mae Shaw. We decided we would try and exploit the resources of the university to help engage in a project in public education.

We elicited support for the publication from 60 academics across the whole range of faculties within this university. We asked them to write very short pieces which linked their area of academic interest with the subject of enhancing democracy. We asked them to write about 1000 words, to make the text simple and accessible, and to identify two or three questions which they thought were worth discussing. We created an educational source book on the theme of renewing democracy which could be used within and outside the university particularly in communities of disadvantage. We were pleasantly surprised at the support we received and people waived copyright so that material could be reproduced, and the overall cost of the document was low. So this became a public education resource which the university supported. It wasn't radical in the sense of asking academics to take a particular educational and political stance but it did help open up resources of the academy to individuals and groups outside it.

GS: How would popular education be manifested in the classroom?

JC: It depends on the number of students you have for one thing. The greater the number of students the more difficult it becomes. I think a really fundamental starting point to quote an old sociologist,

Basil Bernstein, is his view that *"for the culture of the teacher to be in the conscious of the child, first the conscious of the child has to be in the head of the teacher"*. The teacher has to learn where the students are coming from, their experience, their kind of aspirations, their kind of reference points, and their connections. Now if you have a group of 300 students it's very difficult to do that, if you have 30 it's possible. It's the starting point that the educator has to be to put themselves in the position of the learner first, which is fundamental and that seems to me to connect with the notion of dialogue and engagement.

GS: And empathy would be there and by in large with some exceptions, most university educators still come from a particular stratum in society. And again with some exceptions, the students can be a pretty mixed group nowadays, so how does one transcend these ontological barriers?

JC: I think building a culture of engagement with ideas is really something that you can draw people into and I think we've been fairly successful in this institution in doing that in our courses. But that's partly because a number of us share a similar point of view so things get reinforced over a period of time.

I was impressed by Michael Collins, who wrote a book '*Adult Education as Vocation*' and he made the point that it's not simply putting theory into practice, although that's one way of thinking about things, it's also we put ourselves into practice. In a way we have to change ourselves by being able to draw upon experience but also to step back from it at the same time. Our experience is relevant and a good starting point but the essential thing is to examine it critically. Students find this difficult until they connect with critical ideas, so encouraging them to read critical literature is important.

GS: Does that link in with certain notions of praxis or Dewey's notion of reflexivity?

JC: Yes, well I think that if we change ourselves, we change our understanding. If our values begin to change then we embody that, it's a form of embodied practice in a sense. So getting students to engage with a core range of critical ideas – and some will connect with traditional Marxist ideas, or a post-structuralist, Foucauldian type, or of a feminist persuasion – anything that gets people to stand back and look again at their experience in a different light can provide a starting point for critical reflexivity.

GS: One of the ways it seems to me that in the critical pedagogy/popular education paradigm that one can build commonality as it were, capacities to enter each other's realm, each other's ontological space, is through this idea of common humanity – of this humanitarian conception.

JC: When I made that point earlier about the essential equality of being, I think that is making a similar point. We have one race, we have sort of intrinsic kind of rights and equalities and I think that is an important way in which we began to see beyond any particular differences and differences are difficult to find their kind of common ground. In the United Kingdom at the moment it is not an easy kind of issue to address and see a way through.

GS: Can we explore a bit more about the popular education principles methods in terms of teaching? Can you give me some insights into how we could employ some of these into teaching?

JC: Could I start by saying I think popular education/critical pedagogy is always a matter of purpose rather than process. Participatory methodologies are useful but for what purpose? The focus on purpose and principle has to be reflected in the curriculum and then there are different ways this can be taught. I think the fundamental need is to introduce materials which allow students to engage critically with their common sense, to transform it into 'good sense' through a more critical appreciation.

Primarily critical in this context refers to trying to make explicit/visible the way in which power operates in our lives. Now that might be a kind of discursive power or, it maybe economic power or, a form of cultural power but I think it was Alberto Melucci who said something like "*power that is not visible is not negotiable*." If students, if people in communities, if educators are going to make some difference or some changes then they have to make visible where power influences their choices and actions. So being critical is about making visible the operation of power.

GS: That's very interesting. If you look at most textbooks or most references to criticality and higher education it tends to be much more instrumental kinds of definitions around students' ability to reference work or to be able to look at two sides of an argument. But here you're taking much more the critical social theory approach to understanding criticality.

JC: Can I relate that to some of our teaching? For instance, I organize a course on adult education and the course is structured around the argument of being 'in and against the state'. How people in the current context are either employed directly by the state or through the voluntary sector – indirectly by the state because the state generally provides funding to these kinds of organizations.

So first some theoretical analysis of what does that argument mean and how it has changed in the current context because clearly the state has changed. We have the European state; we have globalization – big things that have taken place since the 1970s when the original argument was formulated.

I have 'witnesses' in terms of a panel of practitioners who are carefully selected in terms of being able to talk about their work in terms of policy context, in terms of ideas and in terms of analysing how power influences their work. But at the same time, the agency of the worker involves developing the unintended outcomes of policy – to relate the work to the more kind of lived experience of people's lives in communities. So their attempt is to develop both individual and collective autonomy/power of people living at the sharp end of inequality and oppression. The 'witnesses' are a way of embodying theory–policy–practice and the students task is to interrogate them.

GS: Anything else about teaching that you want to share?

JC: I think increasingly it's important to look at where we come from and to see how options have been closed down and to look in the past for possibilities of different futures. Here's an example of a project – a very straightforward project called *'Learning for Democracy, Ten Propositions and Ten Proposals'*.

A group of students and staff produced a list of ten statements; ten propositions of what democracy is about in relation to things like freedom, equality, justice, solidarity and so on plus ten proposals – so what does that mean for taking action, what does it mean about acting, taking up risk, working up the grassroots and so on. It is very useful when working with groups because the propositions provide a structure for examining what freedom, for example, might mean. It is amazing some of the discussion this can open up. Discussion of the proposals can then lead into what can be done to change the constraints, what resources are needed, who can help and so on. The framework itself can be challenged, expanded, adapted or transformed if necessary.

GS: So far we've talked about some of the really interesting strategies one can employ in teaching, using the principles of popular education and critical pedagogy. What about in terms of research? Maybe in terms of the methods of research but also the question, the purpose of research.

JC: I've done various bits of work on adult literacy in the Scottish context and I think the type of questions you ask, the type of issues that you focus on, reflect your interest as a politically committed academic as it were. Not to distort things but simply to highlight what is often overlooked. This can be because funders want to know for example how successful some literacy initiatives might be, but are not interested in some of the wider issues, or the different ways in which the idea of literacy could be expanded – which are important to people's lives. You know you can use those opportunities to develop things that may not be developed if it wasn't you involved in that kind of research.

We were fortunate in getting some money for the research to do with informational technology and the environmental justice movement. I think research should be tied, where possible, with the issues and concerns of social movements and this to me is fundamental to kinds of popular education. One such project I was involved with is called *'Learning through Information Comunication Techonologies (ICT) and the environmental justice movement in Scotland'* and it involves three case studies. It started in May 2007 and it finished in September 2009, so in a way we've gone through most but not all of the data collection and we are in the process of analysing, writing up research findings.

The initial ideas were to look at how informational technologies are either aiding or getting in the way of movement activity. How do they have an impact on participation, what kind of political strategies do they influence? What do people learn through social processes of learning mediated by information technologies? One case study was of women involved in the microchip industry.

Social movements and information technology

Case study 1:

It was news to us and news to the women that the production process of microchips involves the use of arsenic in what they call 'clean rooms' (which can be seen on the library pictures on news reels) where people walk around in suits and look like Michelin men, but in fact these suits are there to protect the micro chip not the workers involved in the industry.

And so lots of spillages occurred and lots of people got cancers and so on from work in the microchip industry. The struggle has been for recognition and against the social construction of ignorance really. So the women have led their own campaign but a crucial ally in this campaign is a group in California, a microchip industry, where exactly the same companies, multi-nationals, the same kind of processes, the same illness happens. And they were able to internationalize their struggle and get a lot of support partly through international labour organizations but also by making direct contact with similar groups – information technologies have facilitated rather than created these opportunities.

Case study 2:
Another one is of a place called Scoraig on the far Northwest side of Scotland; it's a peninsula where in the eighties they started to put fish farms on the seabed. Initially the fish farms were supported because of potential for work and employment. But of course these things are not very labour-intensive. When salmon grow to a certain size they come up and are scooped up in these great big boats, hoovered out of the nets and are taken away. But if you ever see one of these fish farms, you'll see the salmon jumping up and down, which is caused by sea lice. This means the fish then need to be treated with chemicals which in turn damage the sea bed. The campaign in that area was to remove the fish farms and informational technologies again have helped internationalize that campaign because it connected those individuals with groups in different parts of the world who have been involved in a similar struggle. So it's bringing out a wider perspective. It's been quite a successful campaign; in fact the major multi-national has now pulled out, though this is partly for economic reasons as more profits can be made elsewhere.

Case study 3:
The third case study is of Friends of the Earth Scotland (FoES), which is a national organization committed to environmental justice, which uses information technologies – web pages, e-mails, e-petitions – all these kinds of things to inform and engage their members. Again these technologies can help sustain a sense of collective purpose and common commitment particularly among distributed communities where people are geographically separated.

GS: So you used these case studies to illustrate the facilitative powers of ICT for the development of social movements?

JC: What the above cases suggest is that information technologies help to connect people in ways which can begin to transform their identity and what they're struggling for. Local actions by small groups of relatively powerless groups can be enhanced when actions are scaled up from local to national and international campaigns. Information technologies can help this happen.

GS: This usefully leads me onto the last area that I would like for us to touch on. Reflecting on the geo-political, the global situation that we're all facing, confronting, experiencing. Taking all these things together where does it leave higher education and the whole possibilities of popular education?

JC: I started a lecture the other day and quoted a Wall Street banker who said he had just read Marx and didn't realize that Marx was right. I thought that was a neat insight from a Wall Street banker or the fact that he read some of Marx. The opportunity needs to be exploited now and unfortunately there's not a kind of political force to create an argument around the politics of finance. I think that's missing so we need to be able to look at the kinds of choices and challenges for an alternative kind of agenda. I don't think we have that at the moment.

The politics of higher education are changing; on the one hand we have teaching universities who are going for the widening access agenda, bringing money through students – they are not going to get the big slices of the pie in terms of research. Then there are the research-led universities who see their market in international terms, and who look to the Shanghai Index about where their position is (are they in the top 100 or whatever). These universities are moving away from undergraduate programmes in order to promote Masters and PhD students because that's where the money is – so we're facing different kinds of crises really. I think for the teaching universities, there is a crisis of funding. Can they sustain themselves? Are they going to have the resources to do that? The academics in the richer, research-led universities are being pushed towards bringing in money to pay their salaries. There are some universities where academics do that, they have to at least bringing in a third of their salary a year. So it's a new agenda.

GS: I want to just finish really where we began because what you said at the beginning was how you became involved in political action, in discovering your own agency through work with trade union movements and Labour movements. Again, I think there is an opportunity and need for movements to emerge now – large-scale movements almost in the mould of traditional social movements – but those structures don't seem to be there. What can/should we do about that as popular educators? Do we go back to the trade unions?

JC: I think the trade union movement always awakens when there's real crisis among its members. The biggest membership turn out in my own union in this university is over pension funds – and pension funds are threatened because of the financial crisis. Now these things are not necessarily going to lead to a radical reworking of the Labour movement but at least there are spaces where people can begin to, even if it's only for personal interest, engage in some of these wider issues. So I'm not pessimistic in the sense. I think there are movements, like the environmental movement, which has been hugely influential in bringing onto the agenda neglected issues and challenging the dogma of growth. In the current crisis without sustained growth capitalism is in big trouble. We need to capitalize on it.

References

Bernstein, B. (1971) *Class, Codes and Control Volume 1*, Routledge and Kegan Paul, London.

Crowther, J., Martin, I. and Shaw, M. (2003) *Renewing Democracy in Scotland: An Educational Source Book*. NIACE, Leicester.

Hemmi, A., Crowther, J. and Scandrett, E. (2011) 'Environmental Activism and "Virtual Social Capital": Help or Hindrance?', in A. Fragoso, E. Kurantowicz and E. Lucio-Villegas (eds), *Between Global and Local: Adult Learning and Development*. Peter Lang, Frankfurt am Main.

London Edinburgh Weekend Return Group/Conference of Socialist Economists (1979) *In and Against the State*.

Martin, I. (2003) 'Adult Education, Lifelong Learning and Citizenship: Some Ifs and Buts', *International Journal of Lifelong Education* 22(6): 566–79.

Melucci, A. (1985) 'The Symbolic Challenge of Contemporary Movements', *Social Research* 52 (4): 789–816.

Willis, P. (1977) *Learning to Labour: How Working Class Kids Get Working Class Jobs*. Ashgate Publishing, Aldershot.

CHAPTER NINE

Sarah Amsler on Critical Pedagogy, Critical Theory and Critical Hope

Sarah Amsler

Sarah Amsler is a Senior Lecturer at the University of Lincoln, where she works in the Centre for Educational Research and Development. She previously held lectureships in sociology at Aston and Kingston universities. She earned her PhD in sociology from the London School of Economics and Political Science in 2005.

Sarah's work bridges the critical social sciences, philosophies of knowledge and educational studies. This interdisciplinarity is vital for facilitating forms of knowledge and pedagogical practice that maximize critical consciousness, imagination, autonomy and collectivity in the service of both struggles for justice and human. Her academic research centres around the critical theory of knowledge, the politics of cultural work and education and theories of transformation.

In this chapter Sarah Amsler, shares some of her own praxis in the area critical pedagogy and critical theory, focussing specifically on the relationship between critical pedagogy, critical theory and the sociology of 'hope'. In doing so she talks about how critical pedagogy comes to life in her roles as a teacher/researcher/activist/citizen. The first half of the dialogue concentrates on some aspects of Sarah's own pedagogical and intellectual journey. This forms the backdrop of a discussion around some of thoughts about the Contemporary University and the challenges and possibilities of developing critical pedagogy. Sarah was interviewed by Gurnam Singh in June 2008.

GS: You've been exploring potential synergies between critical pedagogy and critical theory, and trying to develop a pedagogy that connects educational practices and activism (Amsler, 2008, 2011a, 2011b). Could you summarize some of the influences on your academic and intellectual and personal development that have brought you to these ideas and related questions in your writing?

SA: On reflection, I think that my intellectual journey has been somewhat – if not meandering, at least surprising. But I have been an educator for as long as I can remember. There are a number of teachers and scholars in my family; I had long wanted to be a teacher and began working with nursery school children when I was 11. I went on to study education as a first degree during the 1990s and was at that time strongly drawn to the liberal traditions of North American progressive education (e.g. Dewey, 1916, 1933, 1939).

GS: How did you come across these traditions?

SA: I think I first encountered them seriously while at university, though they were probably present throughout my childhood in various ways as well. I was initially interested in how early childhood education could contribute to liberal democratic life. Ultimately, I did not find many answers to this through my professional teacher training. What I did gain was an understanding of how even these quite basic beliefs about what education was for and how it could work in practice were not terribly prevalent in the schools. I left teaching rather abruptly, and obviously temporarily, before I even finished my undergraduate degree. In retrospect, this was probably an early step towards developing a more critical philosophy of education, leading me then to the earlier work of writers like Michael Apple (1982), and Stanley Aronowitz and Henry Giroux (1993), as well as to an interest in the history of informal feminist education (Addams, 1994; Hill Collins, 1990).

GS: I went to university in the late 1970s and early 1980s. I suppose I was at the back end of the 'counter-culture' movement and the radical education movements that emerged then. But your schooling was very much situated in the neoliberal period, no doubt shaped by the ideas of the Thatcher–Reagan Right and those that succeeded them. How did you actually become engaged with some of these debates – or, has your engagement been more retrospective?

SA: When I first began working in education, these debates weren't really visible to me. Many of my professors at the university were critically oriented within the parameters of the American liberal traditions, but as far as I remember there was little discussion of more radical critiques or alternatives. These emerged rather more through practice; for example, in the recommendations of a teaching mentor who paradoxically advised that I not work in schools because I enjoyed teaching, or in my experiences of being discouraged from teaching anything but a sanitized and standardized history of American slavery to elementary school kids. But it wasn't until I actually left the United States in 1998, after having completed a Masters degree in Sociology (in order to interrogate the politics of public education and knowledge) that I discovered people like Paulo Freire (1970, 1994, 1998), Ira Shor (1996) and bell hooks (1994, 2003) – and not until much later that my awareness of other philosophies and practices of critical pedagogy began to stretch beyond this canon.

GS: When you left the United States you went to Kyrgyzstan, and this is where some of the ideas you talk about began to influence you. Can you share some of the impact this process had on you at that time?

SA: The conditions under which I moved to Kyrgyzstan to teach Sociology at a new university during the late 1990s – working under the auspices of an Open Society Institute programme which was then called the Civic Education Project – ultimately became the theme of my doctoral research on the politics of culture and education, and on intellectual colonialism. Shortly after I arrived, I began to sense that my presence there, in what was by then post-Soviet Central Asia, was the effect of politically problematic assumptions about the universality of social scientific knowledge, and of understandings of education as a thing, or a set of socially neutral skills, that we can transport from one context to another. In my first year there, working with young people from Iran, Kazakhstan, Kyrgyzstan, Russia, Tajikistan, Ukraine and Uzbekistan, my unexamined faith in much of my own knowledge about education and society that had guided my pedagogical and political practices was entirely disrupted. My students and I seemed to have different epistemological and experiential starting points for virtually every discussion; my 'sociological' knowledge often seemed abstracted at best and imperializing at worst; and my formal pedagogical training had not prepared me to facilitate engagement with the politics of knowledge in learning situations or taught me how to create for inter-epistemological dialogue. I often assumed I had nothing of relevance to offer these people, and feared they felt they could say nothing of importance to me. I did gradually discover that this was not the case. At the time, however, I needed to find ways of making learning possible and meaningful, and to find ways of encourage student–teacher relationships that were non-dominating and non-alienating. I found Paulo Freire's work in this way; I needed it, without knowing what 'it' was, and went looking for it.

GS: You say the problem was one of 'universalizing education'. Does this suggest you felt that universalism was in and of itself a kind of imperialistic move? You said that there were possibilities of conversation – but could you not say that conversation itself can be universal, a human condition?

SA: I don't think I would have articulated it as imperialistic at the time. I did later, and with some critical caveats relating to the special position of post-Soviet societies in the history of post-colonialism, would articulate it this way now as well (Amsler, 2007, 2009). I think universalizing is very dangerous in a lot of ways that probably need not be rehearsed here. However, I agree that there are dangers in over-particularizing as well, presuming that certain kinds of knowledge can only exist in certain places for certain people, and so on. But, as establishing dialogue among people that occupy different and perhaps conflicting material, social or epistemological positionalities can sometimes take years of committed work, I am not sure the dualism of universality and particularity is always useful. It risks reifying into categories relationships and ideas that are actually, or potentially, in various states of flux and transformation.

GS: Perhaps one way of reconciling this problem of cultural imperialism is to distinguish between cultural imperialism as the enforcement of a worldview within a dominant hegemonic relationship by a dominant power, and dialogue, which may enable you to overcome this relationship through coming to some consensus. This may well be similar to the imperialist consensus, but it is the process of coming to those conclusions that would be important. For example, it seems to me that in human rights culture, you could argue that United Nations declarations are 'western' and imperialistic. But some of those ideas are very important to people in non-western societies as well. So in the way that for Martha Nussbaum (2011) articulates in her work it's about including people in a dialogue towards some conclusion through which you can come together.

SA: I agree with the point that ideas are neither necessarily enemies nor friends; that they are complicated, ambiguous things to be problematized, developed and explored. But what are the conditions for the kinds of dialogue that make these relations to ideas possible? For such dialogue to happen, everyone participating in a conversation needs to have a certain way of understanding of what ideas are and what they're about.

And what then happens if this critical form of dialogue isn't equally desired by all those who want to be part of the conversation? You can't simply make power structures disappear because you want them to. Shor's (1996) reflections on his early attempts to negotiate curriculum offer a beautiful exposition of this problematic. Relations of power can be deeply rooted, including in people's desires to maintain them, even to maintain conditions of self-domination. In my early encounters with such desires when working with students in Central Asia, I remember trying to de-legitimatize my own authority almost by coercion, not understanding how to actually disrupt my positionality or transform my relationships, and ending up in what felt like – and perhaps often was – a completely paradoxical position.

GS: This sort of emotion that you've expressed – this desire to de-legitimize yourself and trans-distance yourself from people who are quite privileged; from your own background – is not uncommon. Audrey Lorde's work reverberates around the tensions for 'white radicals' or 'white liberals', whom she says often experience feelings of guilt. Sivanandan (1985) also talks about the guilt of powerfulness, suggesting that it should be transformed into the emotion of shame. The argument is that shame inspires and motivates you to act, whereas guilt simply turns you into a victim. Within my own tradition, shame is a real virtue. There's a word, '*barsham*', which means 'without shame', that my mother used when telling me off when I was young. I suppose that shame is connected to agency, because it suggests that we have agency and need to exercise it. I am wondering whether at some point, perhaps when you left the States, you were struggling with your role in these spaces.

SA: Yes, this led to many anxieties and lots of soul searching. Of course I'm only one person, but I do try to see myself as part of much larger processes and understand the role I play in them. I went through periods of feeling guilty, but this is not a word I use to describe my feelings now, partly because I can only hope to have learned something from Lorde. I am aware that I am a white person born into a professional-class family; I am aware that I am a woman. I try to be conscious of the complexities of my positionality and my identities, including my many privileges. I am not ashamed of my embodiment or the circumstances of my birth; I feel that to be so would to be in a strange relationship with myself; to have the sort of guilt that Lorde criticized as being so destructive of dialogue and solidarity (1981). But I am ashamed whenever I don't struggle enough against the power of the privileges I have, or work to challenge the inequalities and injustices that I encounter in my everyday life. As Lorde once spoke, 'privilege is not a reason for guilt, it is part of your power, to be used in support of those things you say you believe. Because to absorb without use is the gravest error of privilege' (1989:215). I believe it is for my political failings that I should feel ashamed. And yes – as they are many, at present, I do.

GS: It seems that your academic work is located in the realms of critical theory and theorizing. I want to explore the links between critical theory and critical pedagogy, but before discussing this, let's unpick some key ideas. How do you understand critical theory?

SA: I suppose my approach to critical theory is cobbled together from different traditions that I find useful: critical philosophy, heterodox Marxisms, feminist epistemologies, post-structuralist theories of knowledge and language, philosophies of radical democracy, and more recently some anarchistic work. It is not a form of neo-Marxism or a tightly parameterized school of thought, as the Frankfurt School of critical theory is sometimes mistakenly understood. I understand it as an approach to the critical analysis of social relations which illuminates how the conditions of human experience – particularly the causes and consequences of injustice, inequality, violence, suffering and unhappiness – are contingent, relational and impermanent. It offers tools for understanding the relationships between culture, consciousness, bodies, political forces, economic relations and physical matter; and in this way can disclose otherwise invisible possibilities for naming and challenging power, and for transforming subjective and social life. For me, critical theory is an interdisciplinary way of knowing the world that is oriented towards both understanding and improving it.

GS: So are you saying that critical theorists try not only to grasp the grand historical trajectories of social life, but also to understand better the micro-processes of oppression, resistance and negotiation? Would it be correct to say that early critical theorists in the classical Frankfurt School tradition rejected the orthodox Marxist proposition that economics determines all action and must therefore be the basis for revolutionary change? That they argued, in a sense, that ideas – the ways in which people make sense of their worlds – are equally as important? Is there a stronger dialectic between agency and structure, culture and economy?

SA: Possibly, at least for the inheritors of the Frankfurt School tradition. For many reasons, the interests of new critical theorists take this dialectic somewhat for granted and have, to some extent, shifted the attention to problems of discursive power, forms of cultural participation, the crisis of liberal democracy, the meaning of radical democracy, and the ethics and politics of recognition (Wilkerson and Paris, 2001). But the normative project is still critical interdisciplinary analysis, liberation from all forms of domination and from capitalist rationalities and practices in particular, and societal transformation.

GS: Let's move on to critical pedagogy. You say that critical theory is a way of thinking about your place in the world. Some people might rather argue that critical pedagogy is an approach that takes critical thinking into action. How do you understand critical pedagogy?

SA: I think it is possible to speak on the one hand of a kind of critical pedagogical thinking that inheres in theoretical work, on the one hand, and a more bounded tradition of critical pedagogy that is understood as being specifically related to education as a social practice and developed from particular authors – above all, Paulo Freire – on the other. Freire himself drew on a wide range of humanist Marxist critical theorists and philosophers to develop his critique of authoritarian education and his analysis of learning itself (Hyslop-Margison and Dale, 2010). But the notion of critical pedagogy as a specific kind of educational practice, or unfortunately more often as a set of techniques for facilitating learning, developed later, in many ways departing from these critical philosophical foundations and charting other paths.

For me, critical pedagogy is an approach to forms of education in which people learn in order to be freer, in which acts of learning aim to be acts of liberation, and in which learning to learn critically for emancipatory purposes is itself a kind of pedagogy for democratic life. It offers tools for conceptualizing how we can come to understand the world in critical, autonomous ways that enable us to liberate ourselves and one another emotionally, intellectually and socially.

GS: That's an interesting take. Again, drawing on my own tradition, there is a notion that the teacher is the student; that we are embodiments of each other. It seems as though you are saying that in the process of helping others to be transformed, you are seeking to be transformed yourself. Is that right?

SA: That's how I understand it. I also believe that critical pedagogy must be linked to concrete problems, desires and struggles. I think the approach makes the most immediate sense to those people who have clear reasons for needing to know the world differently; who have clear limit situations to explore, critique, re-imagine and transform.

GS: One interesting question running through both critical theory and critical pedagogy is the role and possibilities of human agency. What, for you, is the place of agency in these traditions?

SA: I see agency as central – indeed, perhaps some too central at times, or prioritized in uncritical ways. I am fairly critical of assumptions that simply re-imagining the world, understanding the power structures that shape your life or recognizing the possibilities of your own future, necessarily increases the power to act with effect. This is not necessarily so. Take, as an example, the work of C. Wright Mills, which has been very personally influential for me. The *Sociological Imagination* (1959) has become something of a sacred text for critical sociologists in the Anglophone world, and for some good reasons – Mills' defence of critical, humanist scholarship and social research; his critiques of grand theory and abstracted empiricism; his analysis of the slide into bureaucratic anti-intellectualism are still relevant today. But his thesis that understanding the symbiotic relationship between history and biography empowers people to live more autonomous and agentic lives is also extremely individualized. Mills does not really offer an adequate account of how my empowerment and liberation are linked to yours. In other words, the desire for change does not just emerge from a critical analysis of the conditions of one's existence. The possibility of agency seems to me to be a question for critical research and collaborative action; a problematic, rather than a fact.

GS: I know that when Freire speaks about the link between agency and action, he often invokes notions of alienation and learned helplessness. Some would say that one problem with traditional Marxist approaches is that agency become elusive, whereas for Freire, agency is central to the very idea of working to transform individual consciousness. Individual consciousness is here understood to be in dialectical relationship with social consciousness. Does critical pedagogy offer the possibility to work at the local or even individual level?

SA: I think we need to be doing both in practice, asking how we can be more autonomous and how we can contribute to expanding the autonomy of others, situating both within broader processes of social life and social change. The whole theory–practice distinction often doesn't make sense for me, really.

GS: One of the promises of autonomy is that we can do things differently, creatively; that we can produce culture in new and alternative ways. Would it be right, therefore, to suggest that enabling individuals to be creative is in and of itself a form of agency?

SA: Absolutely. Creativity, autonomy and spontaneity are connected. Thinking together and being together can create spaces of possibility. I see these as spaces where agency becomes possible, but do not think it necessarily inheres within them.

GS: Where is the place of ethics in all of this? For example, we can create at the point of destruction. In other words, a person could be creative in ways that deprive others of creativity. So we need some kind of ethical framework to evaluate these practices. Does this take us back to where we started? Within revolutionary movements, do you still need to have the possibility of some universal basis upon which you can determine ethical action?

SA: Again, I would be hesitant about using the word 'universal' in a sort of a hegemonic way . . .

GS: Let me propose something very concrete. It is possible for someone to argue that in conditions of extreme oppression, such as that of Palestinians in the occupied territories, without recourse to legitimate forms of defence, suicide bombing is legitimate. It would also be possible to argue that suicide bombing should be regarded as an act of conscious agency and a creative solution to these particular conditions of oppression. That it is a creative act, even if absurdly so. But I would find it difficult to say that this is a kind of creativity I would want to nurture.

SA: But surely not all creativity, and not all action, is necessarily progressively humanist or democratic? Analytically speaking, suicide bombing is an agentic act. Is it creative? I don't think it's terribly creative. It actually seems ritualized. But to acknowledge that something is an act doesn't mean it is progressive, and does not mean it is morally justifiable. This elision is why I have difficulty with some of the more activist notions of critical pedagogy – those that regard critical pedagogy *per se* as always-already justified and 'progressive'.

GS: One strands of Freire's work is his profound commitment to universal humanism. This is rooted in his grounding in a radical

Catholic tradition, that arguably influenced his ideas that we are all connected as human beings, that there is sanctity of life, and love. Freire talks a lot about love, about how the oppressor needs attention just as much as the oppressed need nurturing. Maybe there is an ethic there?

SA: Indeed, if we have forms of education that do not prioritize ethical pedagogies and pedagogies of ethics, then what else can we imagine but a society of self-interested individuals who may feel free to act, but who have no collective knowledge about, conception of, or commitment to any larger visions of social justice and human freedom within which their actions might make sense?

GS: Thus far, we've been talking about the relationship between critical theory and critical pedagogy in a somewhat abstract sense. Let's now discuss the institutions in which critical pedagogy and critical theory are practiced, which for you and me is the university. It is indisputable that neoliberal forces have sought to engulf the academy in contemporary times, and many radical educators are very frustrated about this. What sort of problems and possibilities have you experienced while working in universities? Do you feel frustrated working in a university under the conditions of neoliberalism?

SA: This does take us back to the beginning of our conversation. I have always felt frustrated working in universities, whether in the United States, Central Asia or the United Kingdom. The fact that I'm still here suggests that I also believe there is huge critical potential in these spaces. However, I don't think that most of us have an adequate analysis of the neoliberal university, our role within and against it, or its alternatives. The sort of theoretical and practical ideas that we need are just now beginning to emerge in force, not primarily from the traditional academic routes but through the theorizations and experiments of the new radical education movements in the United Kingdom, Europe, United States and Middle East.

GS: You've been writing and speaking about how the university is potentially a site of political action. How can it become so – by students and lecturers protesting in a 1960s sense, or are you talking about a new kind of politics here?

SA: I tend to make some distinctions between political action and political activism. I think the university is inherently political because it is a social institution; politics being defined as the everyday struggles for justice, autonomy and recognition throughout all of social life. When I speak about possibilities for activism within the university, I am therefore thinking about a broad field of struggles over the social conditions of learning, the social conditions of teaching, the politics of knowledge, of organizational administration and so on. But I don't necessarily see universities as inherently radical sites of social transformation; baring unusual circumstances, this is not my understanding of the history of the university.

GS: So the experiences of radical educators within formal institutions such as universities are, in a Gramscian sense, a war of position, with members seeking out and exploiting spaces of action, all the time realizing that those spaces can close again?

SA: That's one way of looking at it. I think it depends on the specific conditions within particular institutions; even within localized departmental politics, power networks and so on. But I also think there are potentially valuable spaces for critical work in theorizing, in conversations, and this perhaps distances me from many radical educators who see cultural and intellectual practices as superfluous precursors to 'real' political action.

GS: This raises broader questions about the relationship between theory and practice. Some people might argue that spaces for critical conversation and engagement are simply theoretical spaces that have little connection with action. Does it depend on how you define action? What is your take on this?

SA: I would rather not fetishize action, as if what matters politically is to be permanently on the barricades, with all other social, cultural and intellectual forms of action devalued as either expressions of bourgeois idealism or pseudo-politics. This seems to me to be an impoverished analysis of the possible relationships between thinking and doing. In his essay on 'Resignation', Theodor Adorno (1991) offers a provocative set of arguments for why direct action is not necessarily more critically political than thinking, and why it may sometimes play a reactionary role. I understand education to be always-already a form of political action, and I thus tend not to think of my teaching, at least within the university and at least in the abstract, as a necessarily activist practice. First of all, I don't presume to know the relationship between thinking and action in any particular situation prior to experiencing it, or to know whether certain learning practices will fall into these categories. Second of all, when working in the constraints of a professional role within formal institutions, I don't always feel that I can create the kind of spaces that could make more explicitly activist pedagogies meaningful, collaborative or democratic. Although my classrooms are certainly spaces in public, they are not necessarily always spaces in which political publics meet or form. Michael Burawoy has argued that students are in fact our 'first public'. While this is an ideal that I aspire to, many of my classrooms and students are not organic publics – at least not in the sense of a group of private individuals who come together to deliberate a common purpose. Some classrooms barely even seem publics in the more general sense of people being thrown together into a space for broadly similar reasons. In these circumstances, it seems to me that work to transform groups of atomized individuals (and even more so 'student-consumer' subjects and 'service-provider' teachers) into publics, and classrooms into spaces where practices of genuinely critical thinking and action can be developed collectively, is really the activist moment.

GS: I think this is a question we will have to explore further in the future, as I'm sure other people may have a different view. But let's move on to the last theme that I would like to discuss, which is linked to the theoretical work you've been doing around the conception of hope and its relationship with critical pedagogy. What do you mean by hope in your work?

SA: For me, hope is the possibility of possibility . . .

GS: Do you see this notion as bridging ideas that might be offered to us as barrier opposites between spirituality and materiality; as a transcendent notion? Can you explain how this notion helps to transcend different realms?

SA: I don't yet know how it transcends different realms of human experience. But it does relate to our earlier discussion about the relationship between theory and practice, and thought and action. One of the conditions of possibility for political action at the most subjective level is the hope that it might have some effect; in other words, the hope of human agency. Thus, while hope is often treated as a psychological phenomenon or emotional state, I think also has a material force in political life. Ernst Bloch (1959), for example, very nearly substituted the principle of hope for the materialist dialectic – which I don't do, but I believe Bloch was on to something in conceptualizing hope as a driving force of agency. I am also inspired by his idea that hope is an active practice that can be learned and taught.

GS: You've talked about the relationships between reason and faith, contemplation and action, imminence and transcendence, and ideology and utopia, and say that you see the concept of hope as bridging these. What do you mean?

SA: I have seen people paralysed by desperately hopeless circumstances, not because they had pessimistic personalities but because the conditions of their everyday lives were experienced as immutable and inevitable. I want to understand what role education can play in interrupting that paralysis; how it can contribute to both transforming subjectivities so radical hope grows in conditions that are defined by their impossibility, and to transforming those conditions in a material sense.

GS: You talk about the idea of critical hope – what does this mean?

SA: I suppose using the concept of critical hope is one way of trying to distinguish a certain kind of critical anticipatory consciousness from more conservative future orientations. The notion of hope is vague, and particularly within the orthodox Marxist and traditions often associated with political passivity and a lack of robust knowledge about the limits and possibilities of one's own conditions of existence. The notion of critical hope opens space to produce alternative definitions of hope as a kind of agentic action or process, rather than a disposition that you possess.

GS: I wonder, then, whether the danger of uncritical hope is that it might be an acceptance of some kind of false consciousness.

SA: Hope is often dismissed as a type of false consciousness. This is precisely why Bloch took such pains to elaborate a theory of '*educated hope*'. This is not without problems – who might be educating hope, and for what purpose? The politics of education are here as well; however, the potential uses of the ideas of 'critical' or 'educated' hope for critical pedagogies are perhaps best indicated in their application (Giroux, 2002) and in the elaboration of actual pedagogies of hope (hooks, 2003; Waghid, 2008). More generally, though, I think we must find some way of talking about hope without being trapped in the binaries of ideology and utopia, truth and false consciousness. What else does it mean to make a difference in the world? You must have a working theory of action, and some conception of what is wrong and how you'd like it to be otherwise. If education is not oriented in this way; if there's no critical analysis of where we are specifically located in the world and imagination of our theories of action and future desires, then it seems to me that enabling people to articulate this for themselves both individually and together is an important kind of pedagogical work.

GS: I think that's really useful advice: keep talking about these issues, and never lose hope.

SA: Never lose hope, and never lose your sense of discomfort either. Never lose hope, and never lose the fear that you need to learn something more – and then hope again that with this you can create even more space for genuine conversations to emerge, because if we don't create and defend space for them they tend not to happen. Making critical pedagogy into a public issue and a social practice in everyday life is a political project in its own right, and we need to be doing more of it.

References

Addams, J. (1994) *On Education*. Transaction Publishers, NJ.

Adorno, T. (1991) 'Resignation' in *The Culture Industry: Selected Essays on Mass Culture*, with an introduction by J. M. Bernstein. Routledge, London, pp. 198–204.

Amsler, S. (2007) *The Politics of Knowledge in Central Asia: Social Science between Marx and the Market*. Routledge, London.

— (2008) 'Pedagogy against Dis-utopia: From *Conscientization* to the Education of Desire', *Current Perspectives in Social Theory*. 25: 291–325.

— (2009) 'Promising Futures: "Education" as a Resource of Hope in Post-socialist Society', *Europe-Asia Studies*, special issue on 'Polities of the Spectacular: Symbols, Rhetoric and Power in Central Asia' 61(7): 1189–206.

— (2011a) 'Revalorising the Critical Attitude for Critical Education', *Journal for Critical Education Policy Studies*, 2011, 9(2), online at: http://jceps.com/?pageID=article& articleID=224.

— (2011b) 'From "Therapeutic" to Political Education: The Centrality of Affective Sensibility in Critical Pedagogy', *Critical Studies in Education* 52(1): 47–64.

Bloch, E. (1959) *The Principle of Hope*. MIT Press, Cambridge.

Apple, M. W. (1982) *Education and Power*. Ark, Boston.

Aronowitz, S. and Giroux, H. (1993) *Education Still under Siege*. Greenwood Publishing, CT.

Dewey, J. (1916/1966) *Democracy and Education: An Introduction to the Philosophy of Education*. The Free Press, NY.

— (1933/2009) *How We Think*. Blackwell, Oxford.

— (1939/1997) *Experience and Education*. The Free Press, NY.

Freire, P. (1970) *Cultural Action for Freedom*. Harvard Educational Review, Cambridge, MA.

— (1994) *Pedagogy of Hope: Reliving Pedagogy of the Oppressed*. Continuum, NY.

— (1998) *Pedagogy of Freedom: Ethics, Democracy and Civic Courage*. Continuum, NY.

Giroux, H. (2002) 'Educated Hope in an Age of Privatized Vision', *Cultural Studies — Critical Methodologies* 2(1): 93–112.

Hill Collins, P. (1990) Black Feminist Thought: Knowledge, Consciousness, and the Politics of Empowerment, Routledge, NY.

hooks, b. (1994) *Teaching to Transgress: Education as the Practice of Freedom*. Routledge, London and NY.

— (2003) *Teaching Community: A Pedagogy of Hope*. Routledge, London and NY.

Hyslop-Margison, E. and Dale, J. (2010) *Paulo Freire: Teaching for Freedom and for Transformation – The Philosophical Influences on the Work of Paulo Freire*. Springer, NY.

Lorde, A. (1981/1997) 'The Uses of Anger', *Women's Studies Quarterly* 25(1/2): 278–85.

— (1989/2009) 'Commencement Address, Oberlin College' in R. Byrd and B. Guy-Sheftall (eds), *I Am Your Sister: Collected and Unpublished Writings of Audre Lorde*, Oxford University Press, Oxford, pp. 213–218.

Mills, C. W. (1959) *The Sociological Imagination*. Free Press, NY.

Nussbaum, M. C. (2011) *Creating Capabilities: The Human Development Approach*. Cambridge, MA: Belknap/Harvard University Press.

Shor, I. (1996) *When Students Have Power: Negotiating Authority in a Critical Pedagogy*. Blackwell, Oxford.

Sivanandan, A. (1985) 'RAT and The Degradation of Black Struggle'. *Race and Class* 26(4): 1–34.

Waghid, Y. (2008) 'Higher Education Transformation and a Pedagogy of Hope: Editorial', *South African Journal of Higher Education* 22(4): 745–48.

Wilkerson, J. and Paris, J. (2001) *New Critical Theory: Essays on Liberation*. Rowman and Littlefield, NY.

CHAPTER TEN

Steve Wright on Autonomist Marxism, Social Movements and Popular Education

Steve Wright

Source: Photo by Ginevra Wright.

Steve Wright lives in Melbourne with his partner Rosa, children Ginevra and Sean, cat Tiger and dog Bonnie. He works in the Caulfield School of Information Technology at Monash University, where he teaches information management. His first book Storming Heaven (2002) is an introduction to Italian workerism, and his current research interests concern the creation and use of documents in radical social movements.

In this chapter Dr Steve Wright, the Australian Marxist academic, develops the themes he discussed in his book *Storming Heaven* (2002), relating Italian workerist/Autonomist theory and the influence of social movements in Italy to questions of popular education. As well as referring to what he sees as the distinctive contributions of writers such as Antonio Negri, Sergio Bologna and Mario Tronti, Steve goes on to discuss the relationship between the Italian Social Centre movement and the traditions associated with critical pedagogy and popular education. Steve was interviewed by Stephen Cowden in London in November, 2008.

SC: Steve, I want to start by asking about your book *Storming Heaven* (Pluto Press, 2002). This was a book which sought to provide a broad outline to an English-speaking audience of the Italian workerist tradition, which is also known as Autonomist Marxism. This was an interest you developed out of your political activism and work in Melbourne, Australia. What was it about the Italian Workerist tradition that appealed to you in the light of the other left wing Marxist political currents that were available in Melbourne at the time of the nineteen seventies and nineteen eighties?

SW: Thirty years ago while I was an undergraduate studying history and politics, I came to identify with a tradition known as 'council communism'; a political movement based on the idea of workplace self-organization, rather than unions or political parties, as the basis of radical social transformation. What appealed to me about this kind of Marxism was that it took most seriously the notion that workers needed to emancipate themselves, and that nobody else could help them do so. In fact I moved from being an anarchist to being a council communist precisely because there seemed to be continuity in many of the political perspectives, but council communism had a political and economic critique that seemed far superior to anything I encountered within anarchism at that point.

But I also harboured a probably not-so-secret ambition as an undergraduate to be a historian of the Australian working class. I really wanted to understand class politics where I lived – where it had come from and where it might be going – so I was searching around for different frameworks that could help me make sense of what had happened in Australia in terms of class politics. Somehow I stumbled across some writings of Sergio Bologna and other people about cycles of struggle in Europe and the United States across the first third of the last century.

SC: Sergio Bologna was one of the significant theoreticians of the Italian workerist movement.

SW: Yes, he's one of the most prominent and influential of them, who continues to write, less about history now, although he does talk about historical research. I discovered a paper he had written in 1967 about the council movement in Europe which also talked about the Industrial Workers of the World (IWW) in the United States. Bologna was one of first workerists to apply the category of class composition in some detail, and I was intrigued by the work that he had done. And also because in Australia the IWW had been very significant, and it made me wonder whether there were ways in which his work might be relevant in Australia.

Not long after, I started to find things in English about what was happening in Italy at the time, and discovered that people like Sergio Bologna were not only writing interesting historical pieces, but were also politically active and were involved in a number of movements. I decided I had to try and make sense of this if I actually wanted to be a historian – and then I became so immersed in it that I never really found my way out. So I never did get to writing much about Australian working-class history, although I'm hoping that's going to be changing more and more in the next few years.

SC: You've mentioned that what you attracted to the Italian working-class tradition was this notion that the working class must liberate themselves. That would strike me as a fairly central idea within Marx's work – could you say why this idea is such an important idea?

SW: This really concerns the relationship between pedagogy and political activity. It used to fascinate me when I discovered that a number of the original council communists, such as Otto Rühle (1874–1943), had themselves been educationalists. Many of the issues about the different ways in which people can learn parallel those of political engagement, so that at one extreme you have a transmission theory of knowledge, what you might call the Banking Method in Paulo Freire's work, where the teacher or the expert knows everything and either they share it with the pupil or sometimes they don't, and that creates all sorts of problems, particularly in establishing and maintaining an authoritarian relationship that reproduces dependence. But there are also different sorts of educational practices, for example the notion of *scaffolding* and the ways in which it is accepted that one party knows less than the other but together perhaps those who know more to start with can support the other so that they can learn as well – and even in the process that both parties might learn, which as you said is perhaps something which is central to Marx's work. And I think the two sides of political activity and education can be linked partly in that notion of emancipation – the working class can only be the work of the working class itself – alongside Marx's throwaway line about how the educator themselves must be educated.

I've always been unsympathetic to the kinds of Leftism that were common in the late seventies and the early eighties when you and I met in Melbourne, which were different forms of Leninism. These always implied that there was a small group of people with some sort of revealed truth who knew better than everybody else, and so from the beginning there was an assumption that workers had to be led along, and if there was going to be any knowledge created it would only move in one direction, from the expert to the novice. The novice was always the worker and the expert was always the political person, and I found that problematic.

SC: One of the things you've also written about and discussed in your work is the movement of Italian social centres. Could you say something about their relationship to workerism, as well as their role in political activism and political education – what we're describing as pedagogy?

SW: I'm not sure how well known the social centres in Italy are, but there are similar spaces also in Spain and Germany and the Netherlands, Denmark and the United States, as well as even Australia occasionally. In the mid-to-late seventies there were new generations of young people, particularly in Italian cities, who had become very frustrated with the Leninist politics they encountered. They had also encountered the feminist movement which influenced their politics. What was interesting in Italy at that time was that lots of the young people then left the main far Left groups, but rather than just drop out of politics, which is what often happens in some way where I come from, they decided to continue working with their friends outside the formal structures of the far Left. And often in the process they would take over some abandoned building in their neighbourhood and use that as a base for getting together with friends, socializing but also trying to engage with the local community or have the space as a base for a political campaign.

SC: Could you give some examples of the kind of political campaigns that were run from some of the social centres?

SW: In Venice some of the occupied or squatted spaces also involved petrochemical workers at the big plants near the port there. There were campaigns in neighbourhoods to try and stop increases to utility bills, increases in charges to electricity and for gas. That was a movement that actually predated the social centres, but continued into the second half of the seventies. If the price of electricity had gone up they would refuse to pay the increases, and neighbourhood by neighbourhood people would get together and organize to hand their bills in at the old rate, and sometimes they would even say 'we'll pay what the employers pay', maybe a third or a quarter of what households paid.

There were campaigns to find spaces for people to live in because housing was a real issue. Whole blocks of apartments would be occupied and squatted by people, and sometimes these were run through the social centres. There were also campaigns against heroin and heroin dealing, to the point of people going out and physically dealing with heroin dealers as well.

SC: The latter kind of thing might be what you would associate with more right wing vigilante activism in England.

SW: In the late seventies, at least from within the far Left, dealing heroin was often seen to be bound up with some of the fascist groups. So to fight against heroin dealers also meant confronting parts of the far Right, because it was argued that heroin was deliberately being brought into working-class communities as a way of trying to break up the communities that were being formed.

In any case, the movement of the seventies was smashed at the end of that decade, and thousands of people ended up in prison. The broader far Left in many ways had collapsed at that point, and campaigns in workplaces had almost disappeared. All that seemed to remain were the social centres, and these tended to be either autonomist or anarchist: there are other sorts of cultures there as well, but the former two were the most common. During much of the eighties, many of the social centres retreated into themselves and became little ghettos. The positive side of this was that they kept up certain sorts of communities that were able to link up with each other and engage and campaign against, for example, the construction of nuclear power plants, which was a big campaign in the eighties.

When things did start to stir in other parts of Italian society in the second half of the eighties, some of the social centres found it hard to relate to this. Only really at the beginning of the nineties, when there was a new movement in the universities, did the social centres started to find some new life and more and more centres were established.

Today the social centres seem again to be in a crisis in Italy, but certainly by the mid-nineties there was a real vibrancy, something like around 150 of them around the country. Then they offered a space in which musical groups that couldn't find a place elsewhere were able to win an audience. In Italy then, the social centres were the only places where certain kinds of alternative music, whether it was industrial music or hip-hop, could actually find a place, so that some of the best-known Italian bands of the nineties in Italy actually came out of and explicitly identified with the social centres.

SC: The link between political activism, political education and culture is very important here.

SW: There was an Italian writer who unfortunately died about 10 years ago, Primo Moroni. He was very active in workerist politics all through this period, and he was also closely associated with a particular social centre in Milan. He was one of the people who wrote about and thought the most about what was distinctive about many of the Italian social centres. He argued that at their best, the centres could bring together overtly political people and a more counter-cultural network, and that when the social centres worked really well, they actually melded these two experiences together. Although as he also pointed out, what was more often the case was that in many of the social centres the two would more commonly co-exist – and not necessarily so easily – alongside each other, with one element typically dominant. Moroni argued that with hindsight, you could see how counter-cultural movements in the Italy of the early- to mid-sixties anticipated the political upsurge that came in the late sixties. He further suggested that this relationship was worth exploring in contemporary societies, and that often counter-cultural movements which don't appear at all to be overtly political in the way we tend to define that word, can actually be the precursors of something new.

SC: What kind of reasons did Moroni offer for why those counter-cultural movements can prefigure the more overtly political movements?

SW: In the sense of being transgressive, of trying to challenge the daily rhythms in which we find ourselves. In Italy the *'beats'* in the sixties were a small minority of people who wanted to somehow live differently, in a way that carried an implicit critique of what was seen to be normal in a capitalist society. To the extent that such circles found an audience and could engage with other people, this suggested there might be a broader disquiet about the apparently acceptable and normal routine of things. Perhaps there were undercurrents where more and more people were dissatisfied with their lives, and didn't know yet how to find an outlet for their dissatisfaction. I don't want to labour the point, but of all the people in the workerist movement, Moroni is one of the most interesting and important, and his works have almost never appeared in English.

[Steve has written in more detail about Primo Moroni, and this is available at *http://libcom.org/history/cattivi-maestri-some-reflections-legacy-guido-bianchini-luciano-ferrari-bravo-primo-moroni*].

SC: In terms of the current state of the Italian workerist current, why do you feel there is a renewed interest among the work of people like Toni Negri? I'm asking you this because of the influence of the book *Empire (2001)* which Negri wrote with Michael Hardt and which gained a significant readership among activists in the anti-globalization movement. This has meant that Negri has become a well-known figure in the English-speaking world. Does this suggest that there is there something in the Italian workerist current that needs to be or is being re-discovered?

SW: What's most striking for me about the discovery of people like Negri is that they had been part of the workerist and autonomist movement of the sixties and seventies, but by the time there began to be a broad interest in their work, particularly in the English-speaking world, they saw themselves as having moved on in significant ways from their work of 20 years before. There's been a fascination with their work and I think one of the reasons is that it dovetails well with a style of activism which, rather than using a traditional party, seeks to develop networks for example. But at the same time I suspect there is very little interest, particularly in the English-speaking world, about where people like Negri come from. This is different from the present situation in Italy where there has been something of a revival in interest in the workerism of the sixties; people in Italy are publishing books on the topic now, on the assumption that they will be able to recover the costs that they've laid out, so there's a belief that there's some sort of a market there.

I've been asked by some Italians how I can explain the way in which *Empire* seemed to be such a hit at the beginning of the decade. It wasn't so much that they were saying this book was not valuable, but that they didn't understand why it so influential in the English-speaking world: all of a sudden many people seemed to be carrying it around.

SC: I found it very curious actually, because Negri was very significant in the sixties and seventies, and then he appeared to sink without trace – he was in prison for a significant amount of time. Then he came out of prison and he seemed to speak to a particular moment. At a time when I think people on the Left felt very demoralized, he appeared to be quite an inspirational figure.

This may be because he speaks about class in a way that is new and that appeals to people who were perhaps – certainly in

Britain – bound down with quite traditional definitions of class and class identities, after the defeat of the miners and the print workers in the mid eighties. A lot of people found a traditional language of class that came out of British socialism to be no longer quite relevant, and possibly Negri was someone who able to speak to that new moment. On the downside, Negri is much less good at defining actual political projects and real things.

Coming back to this idea of Marx's that the liberation of the working class has to be done by the working class themselves, do you think that this libertarian current, also running through Negri's work, could be an alternative to the Labour traditions of socialism in Britain which are very top down?

SW: If you look at the experience of the workerists themselves, you find that there's a constant tension between that libertarian emphasis on self-organization, and then moments in their political practice when many of them become so frustrated that when workers do move, they don't move in the direction that they're supposed to. There were always attempts then by some of the workerists to try and force things and push things along, and there was often a return then to some kind of Leninism.

But the workerist tradition at its best in the sixties and seventies – and here it has influenced some contemporary political activism as well – involves something that they took from some other people close to them such as Danilo Montaldi, who had come up with the notion of what they call *co-research*. In other words, that the knowledge of the situation, which workers find themselves is something that can be developed by workers and others who want to work together with them politically. This is a political project, but in the same time it's a form of collective self-education. At its best workerism has been very much about co-research, and sometimes quite detailed analyses by workers about the kinds of situation in which they find themselves, and trying to identify the ways in which they can overcome the divisions that they find imposed upon them in the workplace and in the community.

SC: I'd like to mention a particular article, 'Conricerca as political action' written by Guido Borio, Francesca Pozzi and Gigi Roggero, which appears in a book called *Utopian Pedagogy (2007)*. The authors of this article raise a lot of important questions about what they call 'counter-subjectivity'; this means that research is not simply about finding out what people are thinking, feeling and doing, but looking for the ways in which people's live are ambivalently located – in the world but also against the world.

SW: Those authors are also interesting because in 2002 they produced the first serious book in Italian about the workerism of the sixties and seventies. They interviewed dozens of people who either participated in that movement, or were involved in other parts of the Left and wanted to offer their own perspectives on workerism as well. What's also important about Borio, Pozzo and Roggero is that they've been active in the social centres, so that article can be seen as one of the better texts that the movement has produced in Italy. Some of the social centres have been quite innovative in the political culture that they have tried to generate, whereas others have been more concerned with preserving something from the last cycle of struggles.

SC: These authors are critical of a kind of rhetoric of class in which working-class people are heroic and sacrificing everything and always engaged in very significant struggles. They argue that we need to put aside what they saw as a socialist–communist mythology of the working class, and tried to investigate what workers were actually thinking, feeling and doing. This is linked to the radical pedagogical tradition within Marx – the idea that political movements are about peoples' self-emancipation, that they come to an understanding themselves. This leads me to the question of the role of the political activist, which is obviously important.

One of the ideas that has always appealed to me in terms of radical pedagogy/critical pedagogy is Antonio Gramsci's notion of *organic intellectuals*. But I understand that within the Italian workerist tradition, Gramsci hasn't appeared as such a positive figure.

SW: The workerists had a very peculiar relationship with Gramsci, who had virtually been enshrined in Italian communist culture after the Second World War. But the particular reading of Gramsci that was dominant within the Italian communist party in the fifties was of a figure who looked to a national-popular road to a new society. It was precisely that kind of notion that the workerists were most critical of, because what they wanted to emphasize was certainly not what Gramsci and others had called the *southern question* – the apparent backwardness of the south of the country when so much of the traditional militancy of the Left was concentrated in the north, even in the countryside. What the workerists said in quite a cheeky way was 'we want to explore the *northern* question', which is that of the formation of an industrial working class and its practices. And particularly in the fifties of the new industrial working class that often had migrated from the south in search of work, and which the Italian communist party and the Italian socialist party, and the unions associated with them, had much difficulty in trying to understand.

So in the first instance, the reason why workerists turned their back on Gramsci wasn't necessarily about Gramsci himself, but a particular way he was read. But rather than trying to salvage him, they wanted to start from scratch and do something new. Only in the seventies did some of the workerists realize that perhaps they might have been a bit hasty in throwing Gramsci away completely, and went back to reconsider some of his work concerning the factory councils that appeared after the First World War. That's a different kind of Gramsci to the one that the communist party emphasized, the Gramsci of the late twenties and early thirties who was puzzling over what radical change could mean within the national context of Italy. So partly Gramsci was rejected because of how he was used, and there wasn't a similar communist party or socialist party reading of Marx, since although everyone on the Left apart from the anarchists said they were Marxists, there was very little reading of Marx in Italy during the late fifties and early sixties.

The workerists were not the only ones, but they were among the first in the postwar period in Italy to seriously attempt to read Marx, and above all the Marx of *Capital*. They found that certain things in Marx's work resonated with what they were seeing in the new factories with the introduction of mass production processes into factories at the time. Finally, there were Gramscian categories – above all that of organic intellectuals – that the workerists were sceptical of, since they saw such figures as only organic to the communist party, as the trained intellectual seals of the communist party. They weren't organic intellectuals anymore in the sense that Gramsci had described: they weren't organic to the working class itself: they were functionaries, whether they were paid or not, there to justify and enhance and glorify what the party and its bureaucracy meant.

SC: Whereas the way the term *organic intellectuals* is understood in the British context is of activists who come up from the grass roots and articulate a particular work generally not established with a political path.

SW: In that sense certainly the workerists were trying to engage with those kinds of people, but they weren't thinking of them through Gramscian terms, because rightly or wrongly, they thought it wasn't possible to free Gramsci from a national-popular framework.

SC: The other point that has come through from what you've said is the way the Italian workerists tried to go back to Marx and read him again in a different way. What were the particular themes that they saw in the Marx of *Capital* particularly concerning what they called the *mass worker*: the worker who had migrated from the southern, less economically developed area of Italy to the north, entering into the factories there in the sixties and the seventies.

SW: This term the 'mass worker' is one which describes a worker who typically found themselves working on production lines, engaged in work for which they had no great love or attachment. From that encounter the workerists started to develop new categories, arguing that struggling against how work is organized, and trying to reduce the amount of work that you have to do, and having more money and more time to enjoy life, as opposed to working, and to work less intensely, is fundamental to the struggle to make a better society.

In terms of Volume 1 of *Capital*, they were particularly interested in how Marx makes sense of the way in which in the workplace capital tries to subordinate workers to machinery, and how workers' creativity – particularly in an assembly line context – is pushed to the side and subordinated to the way work itself is organized, so that people literally become either cogs or buffers within a system.

Someone with an enormous influence upon the workerists, with whom they worked in the late fifties and early sixties, was another Italian called Raniero Panzieri. Panzieri draws out the notion in Marx that science and technology are not as mainstream Marxism had treated them, just neutral tools that anybody can use. He argued that they were stamped by the society in which they developed, and so in a capitalist society that they had to be seen to be infused with capitalist values and capitalist practices.

For example, you couldn't just take over an assembly line and use it in a new kind of anti-capitalist way. Technology itself had to be considered a social product, and you had to think through the implications of that. The other thing that Panzieri developed, and that influenced the workerists greatly, was to challenge the assumption (which was then also part of the Italian Left's common sense) that planning – the planning of production or the planning of economic development by the government – was inherently anti-capitalist. Because for much of the twentieth century, particularly once the Soviet Union had been established, a planned economy was traditionally contrasted to a market economy – the first as a form of socialism, and the second as a form of capitalism.

What Panzieri argued, going back to Marx as well in Volume 1 of *Capital*, was that in the workplace the boss can't even get production started unless he or she plans it. Planning the way in which work is done, so that workers do what they are told and that everything works smoothly towards the aim of producing profit, is inherent to the nature of capitalism. It's far too simplistic to simply contrast planning and the market in the way that (mainstream) Marxists had done. Marx himself once made a throwaway line about how in the capitalism of his time, there was planning in the workplace and anarchy in the market, while Panzieri argued that capitalism had changed in this respect since Marx's time.

SC: This reading of Marx again brings out the question of workers' actual subjectivities, rather than idealizing the worker on the production line. You're looking at how does this person actually feel about being on this production line, where there is this hugely repetitive and physically draining, exhausting kind of work.

The same period also spawned some very significant feminist currents, which took those points about the significance of work and the oppressive nature of the working day and the working hours to make an analysis of domestic labour. One of the most significant examples of this was the book by Mariarosa Dalla Costa and Selma James "*The Power of Women and the Subversion of the Community*' (1975). Dalla Costa was a figure who came out of one of the main workerist organizations (Potere Operaio – Workers Power), and formed an organization called Lotta Femminista (Feminist Struggle). Could you say something about the relationship between those feminists' analyses of domestic labour and its relationship with the working day and the autonomous analyses of those things?

SW: Workers Power was formed at the end of the sixties, and very much focussed upon the mass worker: most commonly a male worker in a large factory on a production line, who hates his work, doesn't think the union understands what his problems are, can see no reason why there is this intricate hierarchy of pay in the workplace, who with his workmates demands that everybody get automatic promotions, that pay increases be the same amount for everybody rather than everybody goes up 3 per cent so that hierarchies and differentials are maintained.

Some of the women in this organization were more and more interested in what was happening in the United States and in other places, where new women's groups were emerging, and thinking through the implications of this for the whole working day. They found that they weren't being taken at all seriously within the workerist organization they belonged to, to the point where they decided to leave. The analyses they developed focussed very much upon the role of women in reproducing workers' capacity to work, to reproduce labour power. They saw that as a fundamental moment that was unrecognized in maintaining and sustaining capitalism.

I won't try and explain the argument in detail here, but the essential part of Marx's argument about what happens in the paid work place is that workers there produce unpaid labour, and that it's masked by the particular form that working for wages takes. The workerist feminists argued that just as there was significant unpaid labour in the paid workplace, there was also a significant amount of unpaid labour that was being done in the home – above all by women – to reproduce workers, to prepare kids to go off to school and to train to become workers eventually as well.

They argued that just as workers were demanding more pay and less work in the factory or the office, women should be demanding more pay and less work and access to control their own pay, rather than all the money going to their husband if they were doing just unpaid work – so having access to money as a form of power as well. And that became a current that had a certain amount of influence in the English-speaking world too. There are other important feminist currents in Italy, but that was certainly the first to become well known outside Italy: probably more so than many of the male workerists, ironically enough.

They also influenced male workerists in the English-speaking world, with number of journals such as *Zerowork* in America in the mid seventies and then *Midnight Notes*, which has been going since the eighties and is still continuing. These were mostly produced by men who had been influenced by Italian autonomist politics, but also took much more seriously than most of their Italian counterparts the arguments of Mariarosa Dalla Costa and Leopoldina Fortunati and a number of others.

SC: There's an interview with Mariarosa Dalla Costa in the book *Utopian Pedagogy* that is worth reading. It's striking how many of those arguments have retuned, for example, in the work of American socialist feminists Barbara Ehrenreich and Arlene Hochschild – particularly Hochschild's work, '*The Second Shift*' (2003). This book looks at the allocation of domestic labour among couples where both are working. What she observes is first that with women now over 50 per cent of the US workforce and children sent to paid carers at younger and younger ages, the responsibility of the household still remains with the woman. It's notable how prescient this part of the workerist feminist current was in terms of issues that are very much still with us.

SW: Does that more recent work explicitly refer back to the likes of Dalla Costa? Someone like Barbara Ehrenreich obviously would be aware of those debates, as she took part in them.

SC: I think what's missing is that more recent material is the critique of work, the critique of the working day, the demand to reduce the working day. This shows the way these issues have been delinked with the collapse of the Left, the weakness of trade unionism, the weakened position of workers, and particularly women, in the workplace as a result of neoliberalism.

Moving to a conclusion: one of the points you made earlier was about the workerist critique of planning as inherently an anti-capitalist activity, and of the planned economy as being in the interest of workers. We are now moving into a period where the collapse of so many of the banks and financial institutions has radically changed the way capitalism is being defended. The figure who has made a major return in the mid of all of this is John Maynard Keynes, the economist who argued that the state should be actively involved in the economy to stimulate demand, or to dampen it down as the case may be. My understanding was that the workerists were very critical of demands, in the face of the emergence of globalization, to bring Keynes back in from the cold. With a rise of Thatcherism and Reagan and the emergence of a neoliberal economic orthodoxy, Keynes was expelled. He's now making a curious return with the collapse of the banking and financial systems. Do you have anything to say, in the light of the insights of workerism, about this return of Keynes, and the dangers this might have as an alternative counter-hegemonic strategy.

SW: It's worth stating from the beginning that in the sixties the workerists were fascinated with Keynes. One of the threads that makes workerism distinctive from other parts of the far Left of the time is the argument that we can't dismiss all sorts of insights that come from our enemies. Enemies here means people who explicitly see their role as doing everything they can to ensure that capitalism continues to exist, but we can't just assume that all of them are simply apologists and have nothing to say that is of interest. There was a great admiration therefore for Keynes' ability to grasp some of the fundamentals about what made capitalism work – and not work – in his own time.

In fact one of the workerists, Mario Tronti, in his usual style of trying to say something as provocative as possible, suggested that Keynes's idea of the downward rigidity of wages was the greatest discovery of western Marxism. Which is a kind of smart, eloquent way of saying that Keynes realized that it was absurd from a capitalist point of view to say that, if the economy was contracting, the best thing to do, as happened again and again in the past, was to cut workers' wages. This would be a way of bringing costs under control, but as Keynes pointed out, this in part would dampen demand in the economic cycle. What Keynes argued instead was that you could give workers more pay as long as their productivity grew even faster than their pay. This could actually make the cake grow – and as far as the workerists were concerned it was still a capitalist cake, which was still locked in the logic of capitalism. But they also thought that this was quite a profound insight, so they focussed upon this and argued, with the notion of the struggle against work, that workers needed to break the link between wages and productivity and be demanding more pay and to be working less.

In terms of the return of Keynesianism, is a Keynesian strategy viable today? Certainly in Australia, the current Labour government is talking quite seriously about embarking on a fairly traditional Keynesian plan of increasing government expenditure to stimulate the economy.

SC: Barack Obama has at times spoken in similar terms.

SW: The danger to remember is that such a strategy – even if it may still be about maintaining the level of wages – is that it's going to be premised upon making people work harder, that someone has to pay for it all. But I think we live in a fascinating period, and certainly things in the last couple of months have been moving at a pace that I wouldn't have expected. I read a useful analysis recently of the current financial crisis where the author quoted what he called an old Marxist proverb: '*there are times when years seem to go by as if they were days and sometimes there were days that seemed to go by like years*'. We've had things happen in the last 6–8 weeks where, as you said, if it hasn't already been discredited, then neoliberalism really has been publicly humiliated to such a point that I'm not sure that its advocates would be able to make the same sort of arguments that they have any time soon. I'm not sure how much its advocates are starting to re-invent themselves, and now we have this return to Keynes who I certainly thought had been banished forever – it's quite fascinating.

In terms of concluding on the note that you raised at the beginning, about the relationship between learning and thinking, and about how you can actually change things. All of us are at a point in time where we really need to understand these processes and I'm not sure, at the moment at least, that I've come across any one particular approach that helps us to understand the politics of money that seem to be making such a difference – and usually a bad kind of difference – to the lives of so many people, whether it's in Britain or North America or Australia, or in the so-called developing parts of the world, where the cost of food for example has been rising dramatically in the last couple of years. We're all facing a steep learning curve, and what's going to be fascinating is whether we can come up with ways of understanding these processes, or whether it's something that will just be left to the experts to tell us about. Because unless we can make sense of what money means and its relationship to class, then we're all going to be in a lot of trouble.

References

In addition to Steve Wright's book (2002) *Storming Heaven: Class Composition and Struggle in Italian Autonomist Marxism*. Pluto Press, London, there are now a number of introductory texts to Italian workerism and related movements available in English:

Edwards, P. (2009) *'More Work! Less Pay! Rebellion and Repression in Italy, 1972–7*. Manchester University Press, Manchester.

Murphy, M. (2012) *Antonio Negri*. Polity Press, Cambridge.

Patrick Cuninghame (2002) *Autonomia: A Movement of Refusal: Social Movements and Social Conflict in Italy in the 1970s*. PhD thesis, Middlesex University. http://eprints.mdx.ac.uk/6688/.

There is also Hardt, M and Negri, T (2001) *Empire*. Harvard University Press.

There are also translations of a range of texts by Sergio Bologna, Mariarosa Dalla Costa, Fortunati, Mario Tronti and other Italian workerists on the libcom.org website. The interview also refers to the book *Power of Women and the Subversion of the Community* by Mariarosa Dalla Costa and Selma James (1975) Falling Wall Press, London, and Hochshild, A and Machnung, A. (2003). *The Second Shift*. Penguin, London and New York

One of the other books mentioned in the interview is edited by Mark Cote, Richard Day and Greig de Peuter (eds) (2007). *Utopian Pedagogy*. University of Toronto Press, Toronto & London. This book contains the article by Borio, Pozzi and Roggero '*Conricera* as Political Action' as well as an interview with Mariarosa Dalla Costa, 'The Diffused Intellectual: Women's Autonomy and the Labour of Reproduction'.

INDEX

Page numbers in **bold** refer to illustrations.